D1557043

The Governance of Corporate Groups

Starting from a discussion of theoretical underpinnings of the place companies occupy in society, this book explores the consequences of the adherence to free market contractualist theory, including the lack of regulatory control of a sufficiently robust nature. The absence of a concept of governance of groups is commented on from a comparative perspective and the consequences of this absence for the conflict of laws considered. The tragic consequences of globalisation by transnationals, including polarisation of income and environmental damage, are highlighted and a possible legal framework to prevent future damage is suggested.

JANET DINE, Professor of Law, University of Essex, and Senior Visiting Fellow, Institute of Advanced Legal Studies, London

Cambridge Studies in Corporate Law

General Editor
Professor Barry Rider
Director of The Institute of Advanced Legal Studies
University of London

Corporate or Company Law encompasses the law relating to the creation, operation and management of corporations and their relationships with other legal persons. Cambridge Studies in Corporate Law is a major new initiative in offering an academic platform for discussion of these issues. Under the general editorship of Professor Barry Rider of the University of London, the series will be international in its choice of both authors and subjects, and aims to publish the best original scholarship in the field.

The Governance of
Corporate Groups

Janet Dine

CAMBRIDGE
UNIVERSITY PRESS

PUBLISHED BY THE PRESS SYNDICATE OF THE UNIVERSITY OF CAMBRIDGE
The Pitt Building, Trumpington Street, Cambridge, United Kingdom

CAMBRIDGE UNIVERSITY PRESS
The Edinburgh Building, Cambridge CB2 2RU, UK   www.cup.cam.ac.uk
40 West 20th Street, New York, NY 10011–4211, USA   www.cup.org
10 Stamford Road, Oakleigh, Melbourne 3166, Australia
Ruiz de Alarcón 13, 28014 Madrid, Spain

© Cambridge University Press 2000

First published 2000

Printed in the United Kingdom at the University Press, Cambridge

Typeset in 10/12pt Plantin   [CE]

A catalogue record for this book is available from the British Library

Library of Congress Cataloguing in Publication data
Dine, Janet.
The governance of corporate groups / Janet Dine.
      p.   cm. – (Cambridge studies in corporate law)
Includes index.
ISBN 0 521 66070 X (hb)
1. Corporate governance – Law and legislation – Great Britain.
2. Corporate governance – Great Britain.
3. Corporation law – Great Britain.
I. Title.   II. Series.
KD2088.D56   2000   346.41'0664–dc21   99–053682

ISBN 0 521 66070 X hardback

Contents

Table of cases

Table of statutes

Preface

My colleagues have commentated frequently on my propensity to see a company law illustration for (nearly) any issue under discussion, accusing me of expecting company law to 'take over the world'. This is the book where I discover that not company law but companies have all but done so and confront us with the frightening reality of polarisation of incomes and the globalisation of poverty. The 'heart' of the book lies in the discussion of groups of companies operating on a global basis and out of regulatory control. However, in order to understand the legal mechanisms that have helped to create this situation I have investigated first the philosophical foundations of single companies, the choice of which informs regulatory mechanisms that are applied both at internal, nation-state level and internationally, shown how impoverished is the concept of shareholder control, investigated regulatory theories, shown how choice of certain underpinning theories militates against a legal concept of a group and its governance and explored the application of conflict of laws as a mechanism for regulating interconnected companies. Finally, after what I hope is a rather frightening analysis of the power and regulatory immunity of global corporations, I have suggested a way of handing some legal tools to pressure groups which could strengthen their ability to mobilise consumer resistance to products produced in a way damaging to the world or its disadvantaged populations.

In completing the book I have to thank all my colleagues at Essex University Law department. I think everyone has felt the force of my obsession at some time over the past two years. Special thanks to Steve Anderman, Nick Bernard, Jim Gobert, Gerry McCormack, David Ong, Peter Stone and Bob Watt. Thanks, too, to Sheldon Leader, especially for the communitaire analysis. As always love and thanks to my family, Keith, Rob, Helen and Liz. Much patience was necessary.

1 Theoretical underpinnings of companies and their governance

Corporations are a product and a part of society. Thus understanding corporations involves insights into the way in which the corporation is viewed as a social phenomenon. This may be discovered by investigating historical and theoretical foundations and forming a conception of the functioning of the corporation as a dynamic entity. The models of companies that have been adopted in various jurisdictions are shaped by the theories concerning the place of companies within society. Different theories concerning the origin and purpose of corporations influence the model of company adopted and thus shape the relationship that companies have with all the participants in their economic activity and with their regulators. Formulating a regulatory structure without such an enquiry invites incoherence. Thus Bottomley:

> The broad and basic purpose of examining corporate theory is to develop a framework within which we can assess the values and assumptions that either unite or divide the plethora of cases, reform proposals, legislative amendments, and practices that constitute modern corporation law. This law has not sprung up overnight. We need some way of disentangling the different philosophical and political perspectives from which it has been constructed.[1]

Or, more pithily, 'one cannot intelligently discuss whether a corporation is acting responsibly when it shuts down a factory without taking a position on the role of corporations in society'.[2]

It should be noted that some theories seek to provide explanations of corporations by studying their origins. Others look at the way in which corporations operate. Some theories have both aspects. Thus, corporations may be seen as the product of a contract between founding members (legal contractualism). This is a foundational theory. But when this is used to justify the pre-eminence of shareholders as 'owners' of the company it becomes an operational theory. Some of the difficult-

---

[1] S. Bottomley, 'Taking Corporations Seriously: Some Considerations for Corporate Regulation' [1990] 19 *Federal Law Review* 203 at 204.

[2] K. Greenfield, 'From Rights to Regulation' in F. Patfield (ed.), *Perspectives on Company Law: 2* (Kluwer, London, 1997), 1.

ies encountered by contractualism in seeking to explain the operation of companies have arisen because foundational theories have been applied to the operation of companies without an understanding of the difference between a foundation contract and the dynamics involved in the operation of a company. The key point in the difference is the way in which the company's constitution operates, not merely as a contract but as an arbiter of the rights and duties of those concerned with the ongoing nature of the concern. One purely operational theory is the organic conception of companies as used in the criminal law to justify conviction of a company as the 'alter ego' of its controlling mind and will.[3] Although this arose primarily to explain how a company could form a will if it was the fictional product of a state concession of power, it could apply to any functioning company whatever its theoretical foundations are seen to be.

A key element in determining what model of company particular societies have adopted and therefore the relationship with participants and regulators is the way in which the 'corporate veil' is viewed. The strength and purpose of the corporate veil is directly derived from the theories that shape the model adopted in any jurisdiction. The status of the corporate veil contains the essence of the model of company adopted and also contains important lessons for those seeking to regulate companies. Corporate personality and the corporate veil may be seen as a shorthand expression to encompass the theoretical and sociological underpinnings of the existence of a company.

It is therefore vital to understand the derivation of companies if progress is to be made in steering them in a desired direction. Such an understanding is also essential for the proper characterisation of contentious issues which will arise. For example: is a dispute between two shareholders about an alteration of the constitution of the company to be classified as a contractual dispute or as a constitutional one that requires the imposition of public law principles? The proper classification may well depend on whether the company is seen as a creature of the state or as a contractual arrangement between a group of people.

This chapter seeks to examine the way in which disparate theories give rise to different models of companies. The analysis has the eventual purpose of determining the optimum basis for regulating companies and continuing the analysis into situations involving groups of related companies.

---

[3] *Tesco Supermarkets v Natrass* [1972] AC 153; *H.L. Bolton (Engineering) Co Ltd v T. J. Graham & Sons Ltd* [1957] 1 QB 159; *DPP v Kent and Sussex Contractors Ltd* [1944] KB 146.

The existence of companies: theories

Theories of company existence are all important in the understanding of the appropriate corporate governance model. Critically, they affect the degree of state interference that is deemed appropriate in the conduct of company affairs, as well as the range of interests that compose the 'interests of the company'. Although theories overlap and interweave, it is suggested that a convenient structure can be imposed by taking as a starting point three theories that have been influential in shaping models of companies. These are the contractual, the communitaire, and the concessionary theories. The contractual and communitaire theories represent two extremes since they reflect notions of the company as a product of laissez-faire individualism and as an instrument of the state, respectively. The concession theory may provide a less extreme 'middle way'.

Contractual theories

Legal contractualism

According to legal contractual theory,[4] two or more parties come together[5] to make a pact to carry on commercial activity and it is from this pact that the company is born.[6] Bottomley labels this the 'aggregate' theory,[7] explaining various versions thus:

Contract supplies the explanatory framework for both the judicial and the political status of the corporation. Internally the corporation is regarded as an association or aggregation of individuals; it comprises contractual relations between members *inter se*, and between members and management.[8]

The logical outcome of the theoretical contractual base is to limit the social responsibility of the company and create an entity remote from regulatory interference because any denial of the right to use the free enterprise tool which is available tends to interfere with this concept of

---

[4] This differs from the economic nexus of contracts theory. See J. Parkinson, *Corporate Power and Responsibility* (Clarendon, Oxford, 1995), 75–76. See also discussion of economic theories below.

[5] It is unclear exactly how this theory adapts to one-person companies.

[6] Bottomley, 'Taking Corporations Seriously'.

[7] Ibid., 208. He attributes the label to J. C. Coates, 'State Takeover Statutes and Corporate Theory: the Revival of an Old Debate' (1989) 64 *New York University Law Review* 806.

[8] See D. Sullivan and D. Conlon, 'Crisis and Transition in Corporate Governance Paradigms: The Role of the Chancery Court of Delaware' (1997) *Law and Society Review* 713.

the company.[9] The theory has the effect of putting the corporation into the sphere of private law, of viewing the legitimation of the power it wields as coming from the entrepreneurial activities of the members and lessening the state's justification for regulatory interference.[10]

In the UK this doctrine is reflected in section 14 of the Companies Act 1985,[11] which reads:

Subject to the provisions of this Act, the memorandum and articles, when registered, bind the company and its members to the same extent as if they respectively had been signed and sealed by each member, and contained covenants on the part of each member to observe all the provisions of the memorandum and articles.

Although this expresses the contractual view well,[12] the difficulties that the courts have had in its interpretation also flag the limits of the doctrine.[13] For example, the 'contract' is unenforceable if the plaintiff is suing in a capacity other than shareholder,[14] and the courts have categorised those given a 'special' right by the articles as 'outsiders' in order to exclude them from the right to enforce the section 14 contract.[15] *Eley v Positive Government Life Assurance*[16] is a case that illustrates the court's dilemma well. In that case, Article 118 of the company's articles provided for Eley's indefinite employment by the company. The article provided that he could be removed only for misconduct. Eley had drafted the articles. Despite the fact that Eley was a shareholder the court refused to allow him to enforce the article.

Although the court often uses contractual language, a better explanation of these cases may be that the vision of the articles as a contract is

---

[9] D. Sugarman and G. Rubin (eds.), *Law, Economy and Society, 1750–1914* (Professional Books, Abingdon, 1984) note (at 12–13): 'The ideology of freedom of contract was an important element in the liberalisation of English company law in the 19th century . . . However, as in other areas of private law, the power of freedom of contract, the rise of legal formalism and perhaps, on occasions, a sympathy for these agencies of economic growth, encouraged the courts frequently to adopt the mantle of legal abstentionism rather than the watchdog.'

[10] Ibid., 209.

[11] And its equivalent, section 180(1) Corporations Law in Australia. See S. Bottomley, 'From Contractualism to Constitutionalism: A Framework for Corporate Governance' (1997) *Sydney Law Review* 281.

[12] See also *Automatic Self-Cleansing Filter Syndicate Co v Cunninghame* [1906] 2 Ch 34.

[13] Bottomley, 'Contractualism'.

[14] *Eley v Positive Government Security Life Assurance Co Ltd* (1876) 1 ExD 88 (Court of Appeal).

[15] See also *Hickman v Kent or Romney Marsh Sheepbreeders Association* [1915] 1 Ch 881; *Beattie v Beattie Ltd* [1938] Ch 708. But management rights appear to have been enforced in *Quin & Axtens v Salmon* [1909] AC 442, *Pulbrook v Richmond Consolidated Mining Co* (1878) 9 ChD 610, and *Imperial Hydropathic Hotel Co, Blackpool v Hampson* (1882) 23 ChD 1.

[16] (1876) 1 ExD 88.

false and they are in fact a constitutional document which requires some public law principles to be applied for its proper interpretation.[17] These might well include preventing a solicitor from entrenching his employment position by using his privileged position as drafter of the constitution. However, as explained below, this vision would require the adoption of a concession notion of the company.

Because legal contractual notions are 'strained' in explaining the effects of this 'contract', Bottomley suggests two explanations.[18] First, he sees the historical development of unincorporated joint stock companies as emerging from an amalgam of partnership and trust concepts, and secondly 'it allows us to define the boundaries of the company by circumscribing the rights of membership'.[19] The first explanation he dismisses as conservative, requiring us to accept that time has stood still since the mid nineteenth century. Although this is a valid criticism, there is more. It can be seen that the climate for companies changed radically between the time when the state conceded both trading and political powers to trading organisations[20] and the later situation where several persons could come together and, provided that the formalities were in order, could form their own company.

It is therefore unsurprising that the emphasis changed from notions such as *ultra vires* to ideas of bargains and contracts between individuals. But the picture is not complete until we accept that the state still plays a significant role in the new companies, the essence of which is their limited liability.[21] Trading with limited liability removes our modern companies a momentous distance from unincorporated joint stock companies. There are therefore two strands to the difference: the advent of incorporation by registration in 1844,[22] and the grant of limited liability in 1855.[23] Despite the possibility that some form of limited liability could have been achieved by private law devices,[24] 'it is clear

---

[17] Contra, K. Wedderburn, 'Shareholder's Rights and the Rule in *Foss v Harbottle*' [1957] *Cambridge Law Journal* 194, arguing that a shareholder may enforce *any* right even if by chance they stand to gain in an 'outsider' capacity. But see G. Goldberg, 'The Enforcement of Outsider Rights under s26(i) of the Companies Act 1948' (1972) 35 *Modern Law Review* 362 and G. Prentice, 'The Enforcement of Outsider Rights' [1980] 1 *Company Lawyer* 179, arguing along constitutional lines.

[18] Bottomley, 'Contractualism', 282.

[19] Ibid., 283.

[20] See below under discussion of concession theory.

[21] For a discussion of some public law issues relating to the control of directors, see R. Nolan, 'The Proper Purpose Doctrine and Company Directors' in B. Rider (ed.), *The Realm of Company Law* (Kluwer, London, 1998).

[22] Joint Stock Companies Act 1844.

[23] Limited Liability Act 1855.

[24] F. Maitland, *Selected Essays* (ed. H. D. Hazeltine, G. Lapsley, P. Winfield) (Cambridge University Press, Cambridge, 1936).

that without the legislative intervention, limited liability could never have been achieved in a satisfactory and clear cut fashion, and it was this intervention which finally established companies as the major instrument in economic development. Of this the immediate and startling increase in promotions is sufficient proof.'[25]

The second criticism rests on the way in which the courts have sought to use the contract to designate insiders and outsiders in order to determine whether or not a right under the articles can be enforced.[26] As we have seen above, the court's treatment of this issue gives powerful force to the argument that the company has a constitution rather than a contract at the heart of its organisational structure. However, a further consequence is that the focus on the contract between *members* and the company has the inevitable effect of excluding other participants in the economic enterprise, thereby giving us a limited model serving the shareholders alone. Thus, this foundational theory has a significant tendency to limit the 'interests of the company' to the interests of those contractors.[27] It also emphasises the free enterprise rights of the contractors.[28] Stokes argues that the contractual model legitimises the power of the board of directors because they are the appointees of the owners: 'Thus, by invoking the idea of the freedom of a property owner to make any contract with respect to his property the power accorded to corporate managers appears legitimate, being the outcome of ordinary principles of freedom of contract.'[29] This in turn leads to 'ends-

---

[25] L. Gower, *Gower's Principles of Modern Company Law* (6th edn, ed. Paul Davies, Sweet & Maxwell, London, 1997) at 46, citing Shannon (1931–2) *Economic History*, vol II, p. 290. Figures given by Shannon indicate 956 companies registered between 1844 and 1856. In the following six years, 2,479 were registered. In 1864 their paid-up capital was £31 million.

[26] *Quin & Axtens Ltd v Salmon* [1909] 1 Ch 311, [1909] AC 442; *Eley v Positive Government Security Life Assurance Co Ltd* (1876) 1 ExD 88 (Court of Appeal).

[27] Bottomley 'Contractualism', at 287: '[Economic] contractualism promises a framework that either eschews or plays down consideration of the company as an analytical construct, focusing instead on the roles of managers and shareholders.'

[28] And the ownership of the founders. It is criticised by M. Wolff, 'On the Nature of Legal Persons' (1938) *Law Quarterly Review* 494 at 497, citing the transference of the property of five promoters to a company. 'If we are to assume . . . that the five members still remain owners of the estate, we are obliged to add the proviso: "But they are treated in every respect as if they were no longer owners and as if a new, a sixth, person had become the owner."' He accepts that it has some justification where 'economic' ownership is the issue rather than 'juristic' ownership but feels that even here it is 'not completely sound; not all the members of a corporation are (from the economic standpoint) masters of the undertaking and owners of the corporation's property. If one member has 95 per cent of all the shares, he alone determines the fate of the enterprise.'

[29] M. Stokes, 'Company Law and Legal Theory' in W. Twining (ed.), *Legal Theory and Common Law* (Blackwell, Oxford, 1986), 155, 162.

orientated'[30] behaviour whereby: 'Provided that corporate actions and decisions comply with the terms of the contract they can be judged primarily in terms of whether they achieve some desired goal, rather than by reference to their impact on the rights or interests of the persons involved.'[31]

As explained above, a key reason for the strain experienced in applying the notion of legal contractualism to the operation of companies is the different considerations that apply to the balancing of rights and duties of the participants when the company is up and running. The foundational theory becomes less convincing at this point.

A reflection of the contractual theory can also be seen in rules such as the UK rule in *Foss v Harbottle*, which accepts that in most cases the majority decision of the contractors, taken according to the constitutional (contractual) rights of the shareholders, represents the will of the corporation. Thus, according to Friedman,[32] a corporation is owned by its shareholders, who should be able to rely on their agents (the directors) to make as much money for them as possible. Taking account of other social concerns would amount to imposing a tax on shareholders to which they had not consented.

This approach has roots in realist[33] theory 'according to which groups have natural moral and legal personality'.[34] The theory sees companies as made up of natural persons, the majority of members representing the will of the corporation. The corporation is thus entitled to autonomy from the state as being the natural expression of the desires of the corporators.

Consequently, corporations obtained their political and thus legal status independently from the state.[35] As Greenfield persuasively argues, the debate about the purpose of corporations becomes bogged down in 'rights' based notions relying on the legal metaphors of ownership and contract.[36]

---

[30] Bottomley, 'Contractualism', at 289.
[31] Ibid.
[32] Milton Friedman, 'The Social Responsibility of Business Is to Increase Its Profits', *New York Times Magazine*, 13 September 1970.
[33] See in particular P. Ewick, 'In the Belly of the Beast: Rethinking Rights, Persons and Organisations' (1988) 13 *Law and Social Inquiry* 175 at 179: 'Individuals can no more be separated or detached from their organisational affiliations than the organisation can be abstracted from its membership.' See also Bottomley, 'Contractualism', 288. For a study of the way in which association means sacrificing selfish 'ends', see S. Leader, *Freedom of Association* (Yale University Press, New Haven, CT, 1992), especially ch. 7; and see below on methods of regulation for a fuller treatment of these issues.
[34] Leader, *Freedom of Association*, 41.
[35] G. Mark, 'The Personification of the Business Corporation in American Law' (1987) 45 *University of Chicago Law Review* 1441 at 1470.
[36] Greenfield, 'From Rights to Regulation', 15.

Legal contractualism differs substantially from economic contractualism because it has a greater flexibility, allowing notions of reasonableness and equity to be considered as integral in a contract. However, both are arguing from a similar foundation in that the essence of the company is seen as residing in the contractual relationships between the actors.

Economic contractualism

The economic analysis starts from the perspective that 'the company has traditionally been thought of more as a voluntary association between shareholders than as a creation of the state'.[37] Cheffins argues that 'companies legislation has had in and of itself only a modest impact on the bargaining dynamics which account for the nature and form of business enterprises. Thus, analytically an incorporated company is, like other types of firms, fundamentally, a nexus of contracts.' For the purposes of economic analysis individuals rather than the state are the legitimation for the operation of the commercial venture. Denial of a separate personality to the entity formed by the human group of actors[38] is a necessary foundation[39] for the application of market theories, since the underlying assumption is the creation of maximum efficiency by individual market players bargaining with full information.[40] Taking the view that free markets are the most effective wealth creation system,[41] neo-classical economists including Coase have analysed companies[42] as a method of reducing the costs of a complex market consisting of a series of bargains among parties.[43] Transaction costs are reduced by the organisational design of the company.[44] 'Corporate law establishes a set of off-the-rack legal rules that mimic what investors and their agents would typically contract to do. Most shareholders, it is assumed, would

[37] B. Cheffins, *Company Law: Theory, Structure and Operation* (Clarendon, Oxford, 1997), 41. Gower, *Principles of Company Law*, disagrees (see above).
[38] S. J. Stoljar, *Groups and Entities: An Enquiry into Corporate Theory* (ANU Press, Canberra, 1973), 40; and G. Teubner, 'Enterprise Corporatism: New Industrial Policy and the "Essence of the Legal Person"' (1988) 36 *American Journal of Comparative Law* 130.
[39] But Bottomley, 'Taking Corporations Seriously', at 211, sees it as a way to 'submerge the tension that exists in making choices between individual and group values'.
[40] Cheffins, *Company Law*, 6.
[41] After A. Smith, *The Wealth of Nations* (J. M. Dent & Sons, London, 1910).
[42] And firms that are not always companies.
[43] Alice Belcher, 'The Boundaries of the Firm: the Theories of Coase, Knight and Weitzman' (1997) 17 *Legal Studies* 22.
[44] O. E. Williamson, 'Contract Analysis: The Transaction Cost Approach' in P. Burrows and C. G. Velanovski (eds.), *The Economic Approach to Law* (Butterworth, London, 1981); Williamson, 'Transaction-Cost Economics: The Governance of Contractual Relations' 21 *Journal of Law and Society* 168.

contract with the business managers to ensure that the managers seek to maximise profit.'[45]

The theories rest on notions of rationality, efficiency and information. The economists posit that a person acting rationally will enter into a bargain which will be to his or her benefit. In a sale transaction, both parties acting rationally will benefit both themselves and therefore society.[46] However, notions of the measurement of efficiency vary. Pareto efficiency requires that someone gains and no one loses. In contrast, the Kaldor–Hicks test accepts as efficient 'a policy which results in sufficient benefits for those who gain such that *potentially* they can compensate fully all the losers and still remain better off'.[47]

The explanation of what is 'rational' also varies widely, from simple wealth maximisation to complex motives including altruism, leading to the somewhat exasperated criticism that '[f]rom the point of view of understanding motivation in terms of rational self-interest . . . if we expand backward with self-interest as an explanation until it absorbs everything, including altruism, then it signifies nothing – it lacks explanatory specificity or power.'[48]

The third pillar for the economic analysis is information flows. The rational actor is seen as making rational choices with full and perfect information at his or her command.

Rational actors utilising perfect information will produce maximum allocative efficiency by making choices that exploit competition in the market. However, allocative efficiency will not occur unless all the costs incurred in the transaction are internalised. Thus, if a company pollutes a river, causing damage to other river users but incurring no penalty, the goods produced by that company will be underpriced. That this type of behaviour causes real problems for those who would impose minimal regulation and rely instead on market behaviour and private law instruments is evident.

Applying market economics to company law involves seeing the company not as a free standing institution but as a network of bargains

---

[45] Greenfield, 'From Rights to Regulation', 10.

[46] Ogus gives the following example: 'Bill agrees to sell a car to Ben for £5,000. In normal circumstances it is appropriate to infer that Bill values the car at less than £5,000 (say £4,500) and Ben values it at more than £5,000 (say £5,500). If the contract is performed, both parties will gain £500 and therefore there is a gain to society – the car has moved to a more valuable use in the hands of Ben . . . this is said to be an allocatively "efficient" consequence.' A. Ogus, *Regulation: Legal Form and Economic Theory* (Clarendon Press, Oxford, 1994).

[47] Explanation given by Ogus, *Regulation*, 24, who immediately points out that there is no requirement for the gainers to compensate the losers. See below in criticism section.

[48] I. Ayres and J. Braithwaite, *Responsive Regulation* (Oxford University Press, Oxford, 1992), 23.

between all involved, all acting rationally with perfect information. The utility of company law is to prevent the high costs of reaching individual bargains with every involved person. Company law thus reduces transaction costs.

This approach has a number of consequences. State interventions, such as the decisions of the courts on constitutional issues, are seen as imposing implied terms in the contract between shareholders, and the duties of directors are imposed because their interests and that of the shareholders are imperfectly aligned. Posner[49] explains that because the interests of management and shareholders are not perfectly aligned the potential of management to divert resources to their own use would lead shareholders in a free bargaining position to insist on 'protective features' in the corporate charter. In this respect the corporate governance aspects of company law reduce transaction costs by 'implying in every corporation charter the normal rights that shareholders could be expected to insist upon,[50] of which the most important right is the right to cast votes. This is a variation of the implied terms approach but it comes close to recognising the constitutional nature of the venture.'[51] As noted above, company law itself is seen as an off-the-shelf set of implied terms that can be adopted to reduce the expense of inventing individual bargains. Regulation is required only as a means of redressing imperfections in the market. Starting from the premise that free, perfect, markets produce optimum wealth implies that only where there is 'market failure' should the state intervene to attempt to redress the failure and permit the market to function again.[52]

One interesting facet of many of the neo-classical economic models is the lowly place occupied by the doctrine of limited liability. It is seen as an incentive to investment[53] but the role of the state in providing this

---

[49] R. Posner, *Economic Analysis of Law* (4th edn, Little Brown, Boston, 1992).

[50] F. Easterbrook and D. Fischel, *The Economic Structure of Corporate Law* (Harvard University Press, Cambridge, MA, 1991) have provided a recent restatement of the contractual theory in the context of public companies raising money from the public. Governance structures are seen as necessary to ensure that promises made on the raising of capital are kept and to prevent the exploitation by managers and others.

[51] Posner, *Economic Analysis*, 411.

[52] It should be noted that this wealth maximisation approach is not without critics. See C. E. Baker, 'The Ideology of the Economic Analysis of Law' (1975) 5 *Philosophy and Public Affairs* 3; R. M. Dworkin, 'Is Wealth a Value?' (1980) 9 *Journal of Legal Studies* 191; D. Campbell, 'Ayres *versus* Coase: An Attempt to Recover the Issue of Equality in Law and Economics' (1994) 21 *Journal of Law and Society* 434, arguing that underlying social relations in transactions have been overlooked; D. Campbell and S. Picciotto, 'Exploring the Interaction between Law and Economics: the Limits of Formalism' (1998) 18 *Legal Studies* 249; and R. Cooter, 'Law and Unified Social Theory' (1995) 22 *Journal of Law and Society* 50.

[53] Posner, *Economic Analysis*, 392.

potentially 'market rigging' mechanism is generally played down,[54] and the argument is made that, if limited liability were not provided by the state as an available attribute of a company, participants would incorporate it into individual bargaining arrangements.[55] However, this belittles a mechanism that fundamentally altered the structure of the market by representing it merely as a mechanism for removing transaction costs and re-creating a more perfect market.[56]

The reluctance to accept a significant state role is thus a product of the contract/group realist theories which reject state power as a source of legitimation for organisations. Linked with the conception that the state's role is solely an 'enabling' one rather than as a controlling power, it is anathema to suggest that the corporation should be used in any way as a form of social engineering. The enabling viewpoint was well put by Professor Ballantine, who drafted new legislation for California in the 1930s. He wrote:

The primary purpose of corporation law is not regulatory. They are enabling Acts, to authorise businessmen to organise and operate their business, large or small, with the advantage of the corporate mechanism. They are drawn with a view to facilitate efficient management of business and adjustment to the needs of change.[57]

It is, however, naive to view any system as wholly enabling. Any structure inevitably limits as well as empowers, so that pure enablement is always a fiction. This is well put by Greenfield who argues:

One would not suggest . . . that Eastern European nations recently freed from communism would succeed as economic powers simply by having the government completely disentangle itself from the economic decisions of its citizens. On the contrary, one would start with putting in place a set of basic rules of economic interaction, supplemented with a system of contract and property entitlements that individuals could negotiate around. One would also seek to guarantee that disputes could be resolved fairly.[58]

---

[54] See F. Easterbrook and D. Fischel, 'Limited Liability and the Corporation' (1985) 52 *University of Chicago Law Review* 89, sidestepping the argument by A. Manne in 'Our Two Corporation Systems: Law and Economics' (1967) 53 *Vanderbilt Law Review* 259 that the modern public corporation with many small investors could not exist without limited liability by arguing that limited liability shifts responsibility to creditors. This may be true but does not explain away the need to raise capital from shareholders.

[55] See Cheffins, *Company Law*, 41 and 502, but contra 250 pointing out the importance of the nineteenth century enabling legislation. See also Gower, *Company Law*, chs. 2 and 3.

[56] For a contrary argument see Maitland, *Selected Essays*, 392, arguing that limited liability would have come about by contract if not introduced by law; and J. Farrah, *Company Law* (4th edn, Butterworth, London, 1998), 21, citing Posner and Williamson.

[57] J. Ballantine, *Equity, Efficiency and the US Corporation Income Tax* (American Institute for Public Policy Research, Washington, DC, 1980), 42.

[58] Greenfield, 'From Rights to Regulation', 19.

The concept of regulation being of use only as a corrective for 'market failure' is a troubling one capable of encompassing almost any situation that is seen as an imbalance in the perfect market, where actors 'act rationally, are numerous, have full information about the products on offer, can contract at little cost, have sufficient financial resources to transact, can enter and leave the markets with little difficulty, and will carry out the obligations which they agree to perform'.[59] The justifications for and shaping of regulations in the context of this approach are addressed below.[60]

Criticism of contractual theories

Economic contractualism tends to be the more extreme of the contractualist theories. Many of the criticisms examined below are aimed at the proponents of those theories, although some also relate to legal contractualism.

The economic contractualist attracts criticism both at the level of the conception of companies and company law and on the basis of the perceived political results of the analysis.[61] The former criticisms go to the utility and accuracy of the analysis itself. The latter include the rejection of state regulation and the consequences of the resulting 'free market', which have been particularly recognised and documented in the context of transnational and global corporations[62] and will be considered in more detail in later chapters.[63]

On the first level we have seen that the conception of rationality is variously perceived and that the further the theorists move away from pure wealth maximisation as motivation the less valuable economic contractualism is as an analytical tool. Further, rationality is bound up with the amount of information possessed by the rational actor. Accepting that 'perfect information' is a myth, most economists accept the notion of 'bounded rationality' or 'satisficing'. Bounded rationality accepts that the capacity of individuals to 'receive, store and process information is limited'.[64] Satisficing is 'searching until the most satisfactory solution is found from among the limited perceived alternatives'.[65] Thus, the 'pure' concept of rationality suffers from the twin problems of simplistic motivation and a defect in the theory of perfect information.

---

[59] Cheffins, *Company Law*, 6.   [60] See ch. 4.

[61] Including feminist theory; see T. O'Neill, 'The Patriarchal Meaning of Contract: Feminist Reflections on the Corporate Governance Debate' in Patfield (ed.), *Perspectives on Company Law: 2*.

[62] D. Korten, *When Corporations Rule the World* (Kumarian Press, Connecticut, 1995); but for an analysis of US effects see Greenfield, 'From Rights to Regulation', 6–12.

[63] And this is true of both legal and economic contractualism.

[64] Ogus, *Regulation*, 41.   [65] Ibid.

The above criticisms are aimed at the conceptual structure of the theories. It must be noted that any identified defect in the underlying assumptions tends to have a cumulative effect, each building block contributing to a picture that emphasises the necessity for a market free of regulatory interference. The basis of the theories on a pseudo-scientific notion of efficiency and the claim that creating wealth is beneficial for society as a whole means that the end result is a picture where interference with the freedom of markets needs to be justified by anyone who argues for any regulation of corporate behaviour.

Take first the Kaldor–Hicks notion of efficiency. The concept that net gains and losses need to be calculated and any net gain to any party is equivalent to efficiency is open to 'several powerful objections, at least as a conclusive criterion of social welfare'.[66] Ogus points to the coercive imposition of losses on individuals, the assumption that one unit of money is of equal value whoever owns it and its hostility to the notion of distributive justice. Ogus gives the following example:[67]

Suppose that the policymaker had to choose between (A) a policy that increased society's wealth by $1 million and benefited the poor more than the rich, and (B) a policy that increased its wealth by $2 million, the bulk of which devolved on the rich? Many would argue for (A) on the grounds of fairness[68] but (B) would be considered to be superior in Kaldor–Hicks terms.[69]

Secondly, the concept of fiduciary duties and implied terms as methods of controlling corporate decision-making has appeal, but economic contractualism rejects the concept of such controls as being the imposition of public interest goals such as equity and fairness. Coupled with the Kaldor–Hicks notion of efficiency, the concept of implied term is a weaker control on the exploitation of minorities by majorities than the public interest concepts that the courts do seem ready to apply. A wonderful example of the convergence of economic theory and the concept of imposition of public interest norms can be seen in Lindley MR's statement in *Allen v Gold Reefs of West Africa Ltd*:[70]

Wide, however, as the language of s50 is, the power conferred by it must, like all other powers, be subject to those general principles of law and equity which are applicable to all powers conferred on majorities and enabling them to bind minorities . . . These conditions are always implied, and are seldom, if ever, expressed.

The contractualist implied term analysis gains support from the latter

---

[66] Ibid., 25.   [67] Ibid., 25.
[68] Ogus, *Regulation*; and see J. Rawls, *A Theory of Justice* (Oxford University Press, Oxford, 1972).
[69] This argument has powerful resonance when the operation of transnational and global corporations is under scrutiny; see ch. 5.
[70] [1900] 1 Ch 656.

phrase, but the passage could equally be read as the imposition of public interest general principles. The emphasis laid by the economists on the freedom of the *parties* to contract diverts attention from the fact that general principles of justice are being imposed by the courts. If the implied term analysis is to hold water it must be expanded to include the legitimate expectations of parties living in a state that imposes principles other than market forces to govern relationships even in the market-place, and this brings back into play public interest justifications for regulation, which run counter to the view that regulation can be justified only as a correction for market imperfections.

A further legitimate criticism of the economic view of companies in action is that it may foster a short-term view of the company's best course of action. It relies on the rationality of the actors involved in the company at any one time. The logical result of this is to exclude considerations of 'future generations'. This point is well made by Ogus in an environmental context,[71] but the same point may be made in relation to all aspects of corporate governance. In effect, this is one facet of the acknowledged problem of 'negative externalities'. This is the term used to indicate transaction costs that may be unfairly allocated by a private bargaining system. This may be because small losses incurred by individual right holders will not be corrected because to incur the expense of court proceedings for a small amount will not be worth while. Ogus describes this as 'market failure' accompanied by 'private law failure'[72] and as a justification for public interest regulation.

Thus it can be seen that the economist's insights are valuable but limited and must be treated with caution, in particular in spheres where overemphasising the role of the individual actors could lead to ignoring public interest goals and lending undue weight to wealth maximisation, particularly for the few, as the ultimate good for society.

Bottomley criticises both economic and legal contractualism on three grounds: first, 'the organisational life of a company is more than the sum of the actions of individual corporate insiders',[73] secondly, contractu-alism favours an 'economic' approach over a 'political' approach; and, thirdly the legitimation of managerial power is predicated on the voluntary consent given by the 'owners'. All these mean that the private law nature of the company is seen as regulation unfriendly.[74]

In both legal and economic contractualism we have seen that there is a struggle to move from the foundational theory into the operational

---

[71] Ogus, *Regulation*, 37.   [72] Ibid., 28.
[73] Bottomley, 'Contractualism', 288.
[74] While not doubting that these ideas have a role in corporate governance, Bottomley believes them to be overstated and thus dangerous.

sphere. One key difficulty with both approaches is the explanation of the rights and duties that arise when the constitution of the company is up and running. We have seen that legal contractualism struggles to explain the failure to enforce the contract in the articles and the regulation of the power of majorities over minorities. Economic contractualism has an exactly similar problem. It relies on an explanation of incomplete contracts. 'Only in a world where some contracts contingent on future observable variables are costly (or impossible) to write ex-ante, is there room for governance ex-post.'[75] Neither accepts the legitimacy of state regulation of power: 'The political approach to corporate governance accords with . . . values about how major institutions in our society should be governed.'[76]

In fact the implied term or incomplete contracts theory could benefit from the insights of Cooter, who argues that all involved in the company internalise not only the organisational norms of the company but also society's norms. Any person involved in the company has therefore an expectation (call it an implied contractual term if you will) that society's norms of fair dealing and freedom from expropriation will be applied to them. Cooter puts his argument in terms of absorption of institutional norms.[77] Cooter[78] posits the idea of thin and thick self-interest in that he believes that the internalisation of moral norms will affect decision-making by the development of a different form of self-interest he calls 'thick self-interest'. This accords with Teubner's belief that 'Franz Wieacker [came close by stating] "the socio-empirical reality of the social group [including corporations] . . . lies in the group consciousness of the members and their partners and in the specific nature of the group's behaviour."'[79] Thus 'the social substratum of the legal person . . . is conceived properly as a "collectivity"'.[80]

---

[75] L. Zingales in *The New Palgrave Dictionary of Economics and the Law* (Macmillan, London, 1998).

[76] J. Pound, 'The Rise of the Political Model of Corporate Governance and Corporate Control' (1993) 68 *New York University Law Review* 1003 at 1009.

[77] Teubner diverges from these analyses. Founding the legitimation of the autonomy of the corporation in its 'overall social function and performance', he nevertheless pays great attention to the group dynamics that occur within the company, seeing the decision-making founded not in separate individual contracts or in the will of policy makers but in 'a "pulsating" sequence of meaningfully interrelated communicative events, that constantly reproduce themselves'. While denying that the group forms the legitimation base for corporate power, Teubner nevertheless makes a contribution to the understanding of the dynamics that underlie the 'actions of the corporation', and his views may be seen as a development of the organic theories. Teubner, 'Enterprise Corporatism', 130.

[78] Cooter, 'Law and Unified Social Theory'; discussed in ch. 4.

[79] Teubner, 'Enterprise Corporatism', 138.

[80] Ibid.

So, within the conception that the company owes its existence to individuals, we have a clear distinction between those who accept that the formation of people into a group activity changes the nature of their relationships and those who do not.[81]

In relating the theories to wider concerns, Bottomley emphasises the relationship between individualism and 'liberal' thought,[82] and Campbell sees the link between laissez-faire economics and the economic theories of the firm. Thus, at the political level, economic theory is anti-regulatory, relying on the mechanisms of the marketplace and allowing regulation only to 'correct market failures'.[83] Where economic analysis is used as an ideology rather than as a tool for analysis the danger is that,

by maintaining that the only obligation of the individual is to honor contracts and the property rights of others, the 'moral' philosophy of market liberalism effectively releases those who have property from an obligation to those who do not. It ignores the reality that contracts between the weak and the powerful are seldom equal, and that the institution of the contract, like the institution of property, tends to reinforce and even increase inequality in unequal societies. It legitimates and strengthens systems that institutionalise poverty, even while maintaining that poverty is a consequence of indolence and inherent character defects of the poor.[84]

Further, the rejection of regulation by the cry of 'free' markets permits this effect to take place in the absence of wealth redistribution programmes imposed by regulation.

The corporation as a nexus of contracts is 'incapable of having social or moral obligations much in the same way that inanimate objects are capable of having these obligations',[85] a view convincingly shown by O'Neill to contain a conceptual error[86] in that 'Jensen and Meckling have evidently confused the idea of having social *responsibilities* with having a social *conscience*.[87] It is true that individuals have consciences (that is the capacity to feel such emotions as guilt and remorse) whereas

---

[81] See Bottomley, 'Taking Corporations Seriously', 211, adopting the suggestion of J. Coates, 'State Takeover Statutes and Corporate Theory: The Revival of an Old Debate' (1989) 64 *New York University Law Review* 806, that the organic theory, in particular, was prompted by the concern that if the company were merely a nexus of contracts it was difficult to justify the incidence of limited liability etc. which did not attach to other contracts.

[82] Bottomley, 'Taking Corporations Seriously', 205–6.

[83] See discussion of models of regulation, ch. 4.

[84] Korten, *When Corporations Rule the World*, 83; and see Dworkin, 'Is Wealth a Value?'.

[85] D. Fischel, 'The Corporate Governance Movement' (1982) 35 *Vanderbilt Law Review* 1259; and M. Jensen and W. Meckling, 'Theory of the Firm: Managerial Behaviour, Agency Costs and Ownership Structure' (1976) 3 *Journal of Financial Economics* 305.

[86] O'Neill, 'The Patriarchal Meaning of Contract', 27.

[87] Italics in original.

organisations can incur responsibilities, and they can incur social responsibilities or contractual responsibilities.'

Economic contractualism, by excluding the social responsibility of corporations, rejecting regulation and weakening control mechanisms within the corporation, has created global monsters.[88]

The communitaire theories

The second group of theories to consider are the communitaire theories, which see the grant of company status not only as a concession by the state but as creating an instrument for the state to utilise. These theories start from a position diametrically opposed to the individualist contractual theories. Companies modelled on these theories were familiar in the former communist countries and in fascist Italy.[89] 'The standard of a corporation's usefulness is not whether it creates individual wealth but whether it helps society gain a greater sense of the meaning of community by honouring individual dignity and promoting overall welfare.'[90] It has two consequences. The company has no strong commercial identity because it has become a political tool with diffused goals. Although diffused goals will give it considerable social responsibility[91] a further consequence is to remove its commercial focus. The state merely uses the corporate tool to further its ends. The emphasis is on identification of the aims of the company with those of society. This contrasts with the concession approach (see below), which emphasises the right of the state to ensure that a corporation is properly run according to its standards of fairness and democracy.

Those who argue that a company should have a social conscience[92] are thus running the risk warned against by Friedman that, once profit maximisation by stockholders has ceased to be the narrow focus of the company, businesspeople would not know what interests to serve.[93] The issue was discussed at length by Berle and Dodd following the insights

---

[88] See Korten, *When Corporations Rule the World*; P. Harrison, *Inside the Third World* (Penguin, Harmondsworth, 1990); J. Karliner, *The Corporate Planet* (Sierra, San Francisco, 1997).

[89] P. J. Williamson, *Corporatism in Perspective: An Introductory Guide to Corporatist Theory* (Sage, London, 1989).

[90] Sullivan and Conlon, 'Crisis and Transition', 713; and see N. Jackson and P. Carter, 'Organizational Chiaroscuro: Throwing Light on the Concept of Corporate Governance' (1995) 48 *Human Relations* 87.

[91] As K. Wedderburn notes in 'The Social Responsibility of Companies' (1985) 15 *Melbourne University Law Review* 4, at 16: 'It may well spell the end of the capitalist pursuit of profit.'

[92] Teubner, 'Enterprise Corporatism', 131.

[93] Friedman, 'The Social Responsibility of Business Is to Increase Its Profits'.

of Berle and Means that the structure of the modern corporation means that ownership and control have been irreversibly separated.[94] Essentially the fear expressed by Berle was that any departure from the view that the board should use its powers solely for the maximisation of profits was to abdicate responsibility over the board.[95] The interests of the company must therefore be seen as coextensive with the interests of the shareholders, or measurement of the directors' performance becomes impossible.[96]

Of course, as Wedderburn notes, a limited 'social' expenditure may be justified by profit maximisation:[97] 'The "social" expenditure so explained becomes no more than "seed corn", sown in the surrounding ground with a long-term view of profit, scattered because: "The best place to do business is in a happy, healthy community."'[98] Wedderburn dismisses this view as giving support only to a very narrow range of corporate social activity. So narrow a view, he believes, cannot explain the full picture but a way to conceptualise the ambit of social responsibility is not readily forthcoming.

In seeking to rediscover the 'social dimension of the legal person' Teubner seeks its legitimation 'primarily not in the consent of those involved, but in its overall social function and performance'.[99] This means that the interests of the 'corporate actor' must be strengthened as against its internal interest groups. 'This turns the current logic of legitimation entirely on its head. It is not pluralism within the firm that justifies the actions of the corporate actor, but the contrary: internal pluralism is legitimate only in so far as it is orientated towards the corporate actor's goals, which in turn must be legitimised by the firm's function and performance in society.' Teubner adheres to a fiction theory in that the legal person is a 'self-supporting construction'. Thus:

Collectivisation means a shift in the attribution of an action from one social construct to another, from a 'natural' to a 'legal' person. A self-description of the system as a whole is produced and to this construct actions are attributed as

---

[94] A. Berle and G. Means, *Modern Corporation and Private Property* (New York, Macmillan, 1962).

[95] E. Dodd, 'For Whom Are Corporate Managers Trustees?' (1931) *Harvard Law Review* 1049; A. Berle, 'For Whom Are Corporate Managers Trustees?' (1932) *Harvard Law Review* 1365.

[96] And see below, the discussion in the concluding section of this chapter.

[97] Wedderburn, 'Social Responsibility', 14–15.

[98] And see Greenfield, 'From Rights to Regulation', 3–4: 'It is tempting to explain away the apparent tension between shareholders and other stakeholders by focusing on the long run. In the long run . . . corporations maximise the return to shareholders by being good citizens. Concern for employees, for example, engenders loyalty, which will induce employees to accept lower wages and care more about product quality and company profitability.'

[99] Teubner, 'Enterprise Corporatism', 131.

actions of the system. This is a self-supporting construction: collective actions are the product of the corporate actor, and the corporate actor is nothing but the product of these actions.[100]

Teubner's adherence to a communitaire viewpoint is qualified because he sees corporations as having a degree of autonomy He believes that the development of the collectivity means that the corporation becomes separate both from internal actors and from the external market environment. Although admitting that this gives the corporation some autonomy, he believes that the change of emphasis from the human actors to the legal person also transfers the obligation to be socially responsible to the organisation itself, so that 'it opens up far-reaching perspectives of economic and political control'. The unexplained issue here is the source of the obligation to be socially responsible. The profit maximisers would dispute its presence either in the individual or in collectivities. Perhaps it lies in the Cooter notion of absorption of moral norms.[101] At any event, Teubner sees its transference to the legal person as a *possible* justification for whatever regulation the state sees fit. His views would thus fit comfortably with the communitaire theorists.[102]

However, Teubner sees the political consequence of his view of corporations to be a legal policy of 'enterprise corporatism' which accepts that the autonomy of the corporation is ultimately beneficial provided that a corporation is seen as a network of decision makers at a lower level than the organic theorists would admit:

flexibility can be brought about not only through contractual arrangements but also through decentralization of organisation, and that a policy based on organisation can additionally use the productivity advantages of a 'producers' coalition' (capital, management, labor, state), which in the conditions of the new industrial divide are becoming increasingly necessary.[103]

Thus, although Teubner's theory would justify state intervention, its communitaire base lies more in the identification of the state and the corporation working together to attain socially acceptable goals. It therefore at once resembles the profit maximisation viewpoint in its emphasis on a producer's coalition and diverges from it by the adherence to the concept of the social conscience of the corporation.[104]

Another version of this theory, known as 'liberal corporatism', may

[100] Ibid., 139.   [101] See ch. 4 below.
[102] From different standpoints, Cooter, Teubner and the organic theorists are attempting to explain group decision-making and their insights will be valuable in attempting to construct a model corporation.
[103] Teubner, 'Enterprise Corporatism', 154.
[104] Although even Teubner seems to doubt the efficacy of this conscience: '[producers' coalitions] may arrive at their agreements at the expense of third parties and even of the public interest.'

also have value in understanding governance structures. The basis of this theory is still a blurring of the line between public and private domains, but emphasis is placed on the role of groups within society to represent various interests (for example, labour represented by trade unions). Although the emphasis on the blurring of lines between public and private concerns may have unfortunate consequences (see below), some theorists lay emphasis on collective goals. Thus Stokes views the company through corporatist lenses as 'an organic body which unifies the interests of the participants into a harmonious and common purpose under the direction of its leaders'.[105] The theory seems to point in two directions simultaneously,[106] both putting forward a public role for companies and emphasising the importance of good balancing between interest groups as the secret of internal regulation. The apparent conflict may only be one of emphasis. Once it has been accepted that any role is played by the state in creating or permitting the company to operate with concessions such as limited liability, the right to regulate on social grounds is conceded and the degree of regulation is then the concern. The attachment of this theory to authoritarian economies makes one wary about accepting the 'public' emphasis too readily.

The efficacy of the company as a commercial tool may well depend on legal recognition of it as an entity separate both from its members and from state interests. A diffusion of goals is widely regarded as ineffi-cient.[107] The issue has gained much prominence in the context of the 'stakeholder' debate,[108] but Deakin and Hughes argue that:

A major difficulty with stakeholder theory, at least as it has been applied in Britain, is that the term 'stakeholding' has been used to refer to a very wide range of interests which are loosely related at best . . . If the category of stakeholding interests is widened to include those of all potential consumers of the company's products, for example, or to refer to the *general* interest of society in the sustainability of the environment, there is a danger that the idea of stakeholding will cease to be relevant.[109]

Thus the move to communitaire theory risks losing sight of the commer-cial goal of the company. On the other hand, the contrasting contrac-tualism viewpoint would narrowly focus the goals of the corporation,

---

[105] Stokes, 'Company Law and Legal Theory', 177.
[106] Though Bottomley sees no conflict – 'Taking Corporations Seriously', 220–2.
[107] M. Howard, 'Corporate Law in the 80s – An Overview' (1985) *Law Society of Canada Lectures*. See also American Law Institute's Principles of Corporate Governance (tentative Draft No. 2), 13 April 1984.
[108] See, for example, the Royal Society of Arts, *Tomorrow's Company* (Royal Society of Arts, London, 1995)and M. McIntosh, D. Leipziger, K. Jones and G. Coleman (eds.), *Corporate Citizenship* (Pitman Publishing, London, 1998).
[109] S. Deakin and A. Hughes (eds.), *Enterprise and Community: New Directions in Corporate Governance* (Blackwell, Oxford, 1997), 4.

aligning them with the interests of a small sector of those involved in any commercial enterprise, the shareholders. This gives a distorted picture of the reality of the commercial endeavour, which involves at least the investment of the capital of the owners, the lives and endeavours of the workforce and the risks taken by the creditors.

Concession theories

Concession theory[110] in its simplest form views the existence and operation of the company as a concession by the state, which grants the ability to trade using the corporate tool,[111] particularly where it operates with limited liability.[112] The contrast between this theory and communitarian notions is that concession theorists accept only that the state has a role to play in ensuring that corporate governance structures are fair and democratic; they would oppose the notion that the company should realign its aims to reflect social aspirations of the state. Hobbes classified as 'bodies politic' those organisations that have been granted corporate personality by 'writ or letters from the sovereign'.[113] Private bodies are 'those which are constituted by subjects among themselves'. In discussing contractualist theories we were examining the company's claim to figure among private bodies. What is to be said for the contrary claim that they are bodies politic? And what follows such a classification? Clearly the historic charter companies fell squarely into the category of companies that owed their powers and privileges to delegation by the Crown. Thus the Charter of the Newfoundland Company:[114]

thinking it a matter and action well becoming a Christian King to make true use of that which God from the beginning created for mankind . . . therefore do of our special grace certain knowledge and mere motion . . . give grant and confirm by these presents unto [various persons] their heirs and assigns, and to such and so many as they do or shall hereafter admit to be joined with them in form hereafter . . . That they shall be one body or communalty perpetual, and shall have perpetual succession, and one common seal to serve for the said body . . . And that they and their successors shall be likewise enabled . . . to plead

---

110 For a good analysis see Bottomley, 'Taking Corporations Seriously', 207 et seq.

111 See G. Mark, 'The Personification of the Business Corporation in American Law' [1987] *University of Chicago Law Review* 1441, examining the *Dartmouth College* decision (*Dartmouth College v Woodward* (1819) 17 US 518).

112 Bratton identifies '[a] strong version [which] attributes the corporation's very existence to state sponsorship. A weaker version sets up state permission as a regulatory prerequisite to doing business.' W. Bratton Jr, 'The New Economic Theory of the Firm: Critical Perspectives from History' (1989) 41 *Stanford Law Review* 1471 at 1475.

113 Thomas Hobbes, *Leviathan* (Oxford, Blackwell, 1960), ch. 22, 146.

114 Taken from H. Rajak, *Sourcebook of Company Law* (2nd edn, Jordans, Bristol, 1995), 20. See also S. Leader 'Three Faces of Justice and the Management of Change' [2000] *Modern Law Review* 55.

and be impleaded before any of our Judges or Justices in any of our Courts and in any actions or suits whatsoever.

This Charter was signed by King James and is not only a clear delegation of state right but delegation by virtue of divine right.[115] The idea of a state concession is closely linked to the concept of the company as a legal fiction. The attributes granted to the Newfoundland Charter Company, particularly perpetual succession and the ability to be sued as a body, flow from state-delegated powers.[116] The personality of the company is a fiction.[117] State regulation to interfere with the company is clearly easily legitimised[118] and the *ultra vires* doctrine is necessary because the body that has delegated powers may not go beyond those powers. Some of the immense confusion that has arisen concerning the *ultra vires* doctrine may thus be seen as flowing from a confusion of its original concession basis and the later justification that it served as a protection for shareholders and creditors as contractually concerned with the company.

The issues were well expressed in *Re Rolus Properties Ltd & Another*:[119]

The privilege of limited liability is a valuable incentive to encourage entrepreneurs to take on risky ventures without inevitable personal total financial disaster. It is, however, a privilege which must be accorded upon terms and some of the most important terms that Parliament has imposed are that accounts be kept and returns made so that the world can, by referring to those, see what is happening. Thus, a total failure to keep statutory books and to make statutory returns is significant for the public at large and a matter which amounts to misconduct if not complied with and is a matter of which the court should take account in considering whether a man can properly be allowed to continue to operate as a director[120] of companies, or whether the public at large is to be protected against him on the grounds that he is unfit, not because he is fraudulent but because he is incompetent and unable to comply with the statutory obligations attached to limited liability. In my view that is a correct approach and the jurisdiction does extend and should be exercised in cases where a man has by his conduct revealed that he is wholly unable to comply with the obligations that go with the privilege of limited liability.

The above analysis accords well with the 'dual concession' approach explained below.

---

[115] Clearly the very strongest version of the concessionary theory.

[116] Wolff, 'Nature of Legal Persons'.

[117] The theory relied on the idea that only human beings can be persons and thus naturally the subjects of rights. Wolff, 'Nature of Legal Persons', 496.

[118] Wolff points out that it was used to confiscate Church property during the French revolution. Wolff, 'Nature of Legal Persons', 508.

[119] (1988) 4 BCC 446.

[120] The case concerned disqualification under the Company Directors (Disqualification) Act 1986.

'Constitutionalism'[121] may be seen as flowing from the acceptance that the state has a legitimate role to play in regulating corporate governance. Bottomley calls for a 'reconceptualisation of the corporate legal structure in political terms',[122] arguing for the importation of values and ideas in public political life which 'should be considered in the legal regulation of corporate governance'.[123] Thus corporate constitutionalism has 'three key features: the idea of *dual decision-making*, which recognises the different roles of the board of directors and the general meeting of shareholders in corporate life; the idea of *deliberative decision-making*, which seeks to ensure that corporate decisions are made on the basis of an open and genuine consideration of all relevant issues; and the idea of a *separation of powers*, which aims to make corporate decision-making power diffuse and accountable.'[124]

The applicability of 'public law' concepts clearly flows from an understanding of corporations as having public law elements and responsibilities. Bottomley calls for governance of corporations using public law concepts 'such as natural justice, procedural fairness or equality of opportunity'. Thus

Companies are political institutions not simply because they are players in social power relations, but also because they themselves are systems in which power and authority, rights and obligations, duties and expectations, benefits and disadvantages, are allocated and exercised, whether actively or passively, collectively or individually. Each company is a body politic, a governance system.[125]

Thus, the concession theory lends itself more easily than the contractual theory to the contentions that the company ought to have a social conscience. If it is a creation of the state, it is a political animal owing duties to the public.[126] The corporation as a body politic might be required to subordinate economic success for social values.[127] Wedderburn has said that 'the crucial question for our company law' is 'the conditions on which private capital in a mixed economy can be allowed the privilege of incorporation with limited liability'.[128] It is easy to build arguments for the social responsibility of companies on the concession

---

[121] Bottomley, 'Contractualism', 277.
[122] Ibid., 278.   [123] Ibid.   [124] Ibid., 278–9.
[125] Bottomley, 'Contractualism', 291. However, Bottomley makes the telling point that adopting only one framework to the exclusion of all others is less than helpful and that the political perspective should be considered as complementary to rather than a substitute for legal and political analysis, 292.
[126] See on this D. Campbell, 'Why Regulate the Modern Corporation? The Failure of "Market Failure"' in J. McCahery, S. Picciotto and C. Scott (eds.), *Corporate Control and Accountability* (Clarendon, Oxford, 1993), 103.
[127] A. Fraser, 'The Corporation as a Body Politic' (1983) *Telos* no. 57, 5–40.
[128] Wedderburn, 'The Social Responsibility of Companies', 4.

theory, but one danger is that such justifications will not stop short of turning companies into an arm of the state and thus becoming indistinguishable from communitaire theories discussed above. It is possible to reach the conclusion that companies should behave in a socially responsible way by an economic, realist route. However, this requires the recognition that the fundamental assumption underlying the neo-classicist economic models that a free market will increase the good of all has limitations[129] and, further, that the economic model can absorb the problem of externalities. If this is accepted,[130] then the group forming the corporation may legitimately wield power but they need not necessarily wield power so as to override legitimate concerns of or to the exclusion of all other members of that society.

One problem encountered by the concession theory is that it may be argued that, if the company exists merely because the state has said it may exist, it can be seen as a mere fiction. This leads to the difficulty in explaining the way in which the corporation functions when it becomes operational. Again, difficulties arise in translating a foundational theory into the operational sphere. Some have argued that this can be done by coupling the concession theory of foundational legitimacy with an organic operational theory whereby the company acts and makes decisions via the policy makers in the company.[131] The organic theory is a description of corporate organisation that identifies the persons capable of forming the corporate will as those with policy-making powers.[132] It identifies the corporate will either by seeing the majority as embodying it or by seeing it as lying with powerful managerial policy makers.[133] It is subject to the criticism that it is a romantic conception: 'the most typical quality of romanticism being perhaps the tendency to endow inanimate things with life.' Wolff argues that the doctrine leads to fallacious legal arguments because of its assumption that the corporation involves a real life of its own or a legal will. He finds particular difficulty with one-man companies because, although he accepts them as legally distinct from their founder, he cannot see that they have a 'will' of their own.[134]

---

[129] See Campbell, 'Ayres *versus* Coase', 434.

[130] Some views on this are discussed in ch. 4.

[131] *Tesco Supermarkets v Natrass* [1972] AC 153; *H.L. Bolton (Engineering) Co Ltd v T.J. Graham & Sons Ltd* [1957] 1 QB 159; *DPP v Kent and Sussex Contractors Ltd* [1944] KB 146.

[132] See judgment of Lord Denning in *H.L. Bolton (Engineering) Co v T.J. Graham & Sons* [1957] 1 QB 159.

[133] The organic view has been taken to extremes. Wolff, 'Nature of Legal Persons', 499, cites John Caspar Bluntschli who 'found something corresponding in the life of the State not only to every part of the human body but even to every human emotion, and designated e.g. the foreign relations of a State as its sexual impulses!'

[134] On this point see the discussion of UK law's move away from the contractual basis by

Wolff sees the one major advantage of the organic theory over the fiction theory as supplying the possibility of the corporation carrying out its own acts rather than having to act through agents. However, his own analysis contains the seeds of the riposte that, if the fiction theory merely regards the acquisition of corporate personality as governed by state law, there is no reason the conceded personality cannot act.[135] The difficulty is not in whether or not it can act but in determining how its decision to act is to be ascertained. It is this element that is supplied by the organic theory.[136] The same debate may be had regarding the ascertainment of the interests of the company. The issue should be not whether or not the company has interests but how to discover them. In both cases the realist and concession theories need to be synthesised in order to achieve a balanced view.

It is clear from the multiple appearances of Teubner's theories in a number of sections of this discussion that his views have complex origins. He contributes to the debate about where the will of the company lies and therefore where the legitimation of its ability to act can be found and in this sense is close to the realist theorists. Another 'realist' element is the wholehearted acceptance of the way in which the collectivity produces a separate legal entity that then 'pressures' the state into granting personality. Nevertheless, he claims fiction/concession theories as the basis for his viewpoint on corporations, sees the source of their personality in the positive law notion that the law can bestow personality on anything it desires and would see those theories legitimating the imposition of social norms. Yet he sees the optimal corporate governance structure as a producer's coalition situated not amongst the 'policy makers' but including decision makers at other levels within the corporation in association. This would include capital, management, workers and the 'state'.[137] This complex vision takes inspiration from a variety of underlying theories and is particularly useful in breaking the mould that sets one school of theorists against another as implacable opponents. To build a corporate model, different foundations may be valuable. It is not necessary to adhere to a single foundation. However, it is necessary to understand the tendencies towards which different foundational theories lean, and the strong concession/communitaire foundation undoubtedly brings the danger of diffused goals and unlimited state control.

J. Dine, 'Private Property and Corporate Governance Part II: Content of Directors' Duties and Remedies' in F. Patfield (ed.), *Perspectives on Company Law I* (Kluwer, London, 1995), 115; and Wolff, 'Nature of Legal Persons', 498–505.

[135] Wolff has adopted the 'weak' version of the fiction/concession theory.

[136] And by Teubner's analysis; see Teubner 'Enterprise Corporatism', 130.

[137] Ibid., 154.

The dual concession theory

I would like us to consider a possible compromise position that would add to the state concession theory a different view, which may be described as the 'bottom up' concessionary theory.[138] This sees the company as something distinct from the contracting partners' original compact but seeks to show that, in coming together and using the corporate tool, the contractors have created an instrument that has a real identity separate from and quite distinct from the original contracting partners. The company, if you like, 'floats free' from its founders and becomes a separate person with its own interests. Inherent in this approach is a distinction between the notion of the *origins* of a company and its dynamic existence after foundation. We have seen that one of the difficulties experienced by the contractual theories is the strain that occurs when foundational theories are applied to the operation of the company. Here it should be accepted that there is a difference and after foundation, as an operational structure, the company should be viewed with fresh eyes. This perception is undoubtedly a factor in the long-running debate as to the nature of the separate personality of the company. Based both on realist theories and on the understanding that to join together to further a particular cause means some curbing of selfish interests,[139] the company is not wholly free of the influence of its owners, but the important factor is that it is its own entity and will no longer bow to the will of the owners, whether voting by majority or otherwise. Thus the concept of the free entity involves an understanding that no longer can the owner's wishes be paramount.[140]

Further, if we accept Cooter's[141] reasoning and understand that those who have formed the company have absorbed society's norms, it is clear that the entity that becomes the operational company should operate only within the restrictions imposed by those norms. It is not a free entity; both its founders and the state have devolved power to it on certain conditions. This reasoning may be a path towards reclaiming some input for local communities who feel the impact of the activities and decisions of large corporations.

---

[138] My theory, but inspired *inter alia* by discussion with my colleague Professor Sheldon Leader.

[139] See Cooter, 'Law and Unified Social Theory', 50, and S. Leader, 'Private Property and Corporate Governance: Defining the Issues' in Patfield (ed.), *Perspectives on Company Law I*, for an understanding of the mechanisms that bring this about, as well as further discussion in ch. 4.

[140] They may be overridden by the 'benefit of the company' idea, for example. See *Dafen Tinplate Co v Llanelly Steel Co (1907) Ltd* [1920] 2 Ch 124; *Allen v Gold Reefs of West Africa* [1900] 1 Ch 671.

[141] See Cooter, 'Law and Unified Social Theory', 50, and ch. 6.

An example of this foundational principle in action can be given by drawing a parallel with international law and the development of the European Communities (EC). The network of treaties that binds states gives rise to treaty obligations and rights, but it was only when the 'new community legal order' was invented[142] that the EC truly became a separate legal personality. There is a similarity between this process and the contracts entered into by shareholders in forming a company. On formation of the company a separate legal order is formed which has rights and duties independent from the rights and duties of the shareholders. After foundation the company gains realist legitimation not only from the founders but from the whole of the community interested in the commercial adventure. Its powers are therefore a concession not from the owners alone but from the wider group involved in attaining its corporate goals. In formulating this approach the narrow notion of concession as a grant of limited powers must be set aside in favour of a more dynamic notion of granting of legitimacy to the changing membership of the company by the whole of any groups of individuals involved. Thus we move away from considerations of the possibility of overturning corporate decisions on the grounds that they are *ultra vires* the interests of the founders, or indeed any other interest group, and move to a notion where the identity and purpose of the corporation are determined by those most closely concerned with the corporate adventure.

As we shall see,[143] this reasoning coincides with the changing perceptions of the basis for judicial review in the public law field. The perception has changed from basing the legitimacy of judicial review decisions on a narrow state concession *ultra vires* view to a foundation more concerned with the concept of participatory justice.[144]

The understanding of the corporation as no longer bound to its founders has the virtue of moving away from the concept of a determination of the 'interests of the company' as an abstract notion,[145] but poses the question raised by Deakin and Hughes[146] about the identification of the interests concerned and the weight to be given to their particular concerns. It is suggested, however, that this viewpoint combines many of the most useful foundational principles that have been discussed so far. There is an awareness that the company needs to justify the power

---

[142] Case 26/62, *NV Algemene Transport-en Expeditie Onderneming van Gend en Loos v Nederlandse Administratie der Belastingen* [1963] ECR 1.

[143] Ch. 4.

[144] G. Richardson and H. Genn, *Administrative Law and Government Action* (Clarendon, Oxford, 1994); P. McAuslan, *The Ideologies of Planning Law* (Pergamon Press, Oxford, 1980).

[145] See ch. 4.

[146] Deakin and Hughes, *Enterprise and Community*.

that it wields by finding a legitimate source for that power. This is seen as coming partly from legitimation by the state in, for example, permitting trading with limited liability and providing the fiction elements of perpetual succession and personality. However, its source is also to be found in the legitimate grouping together of persons to pursue their commercial ends, thus acknowledging the concept that has roots in realist theory 'according to which groups have natural moral and legal personality'.[147] Such a theory may be able to avoid the excesses of the neo-classical economists' reductionist arguments by accepting that the contractual or bargaining base is legitimate and regulation should seek to encourage optimum use of resources, while at the same time acknowledging the role of the state in determining and controlling the social and political power that those involved in companies may wield. It can be argued that the UK has (albeit unconsciously) reached this position (see below). This theory enables us to be open to a constituency model of corporations because the interests of the company are no longer anchored in the interests of the original contracting partners.[148] If we take the analogy of a balloon lifting from the ground, we can now see that it is no longer just the owners who are in the balloon's basket but at least employees and creditors will join them as part of the commercial concern. The difficulty with this theory and model is that it provides constituencies but gives us few clues to how to balance the competing interests and arrive at the interests of the company as a whole.[149] It is not impossible that a fight will break out in the basket of the balloon and someone will be thrown overboard! 'The compelling argument is that stakeholder interests cannot be captured by rights or regulations which, as part of their definition, indicate the *weight* they are to carry over other rights and interests.'[150] Similarly, 'determining what is in the collective interest or what counts as a legitimate individual interest and then mediating between the two is problematic. In large part this is because there is no neat dichotomy between these interests.'[151]

---

[147] Leader, *Freedom of Association*, 41.

[148] See Bottomley, 'Contractualism', 284, pointing out that 'all major aspects of traditional corporate law doctrine begin from the position that the interests of the group have a greater significance than those of individual members'.

[149] Bottomley, 'Contractualism', notes the role of the constitution of the company in directing attention to what it is that unites them as a group: 'a constitution both recognises and reinforces the place of individual *constituents* within the institution, and also *constitutes* them as a group or collective. Constitutionalism therefore directs our attention to what it is that unites these individuals rather than just what separates them.'

[150] C. Riley, 'Understanding and Regulating the Corporation' (1995) 58 *Modern Law Review* 595.

[151] Bottomley, 'Contractualism', 295. He goes on to say: 'The relationship between the

This theory, however, will give the company a strong commercial focus since it is the corporation's interests that are the focus rather than the state's. It will therefore discourage government interference, at least in the details of corporate management. The search must be for a method of determining the legitimate input of the interest groups and thus arriving at a satisfying and dynamic system of corporate regulation.

The public interest: the right to ensure that a company is properly run

If it can therefore be accepted that a state has the right to impose on companies some regulations reflecting public interest norms, the task is to understand what the aims of these regulations will be. Here it is suggested that the first step in understanding the role of state regulation is to understand the role of shareholders within a company. Leader has shown that a shareholder has two distinct rights as a result of share ownership.[152] The first is a *personal* right,[153] which entitles the shareholder to ensure that the value of the share is preserved so far as possible using the relevant constitutional mechanisms such as the right to vote and the personal action under section 14 to achieve this. The second right is a derivative right which is the right to see that the company is properly run. This right is enforced via the derivative action and its overlap with section 459.[154] Of course derivative rights are derived from the company's own right to be managed in its own interests, so that the shareholders' right to see that the company is properly run is a right to see that the company's interests are served. The enquiry into the ambit of *derivative* rights is a matter of determining what standards of morals and ethics society believes it is right to impose on corporate governance. Note that the warnings concerning diffused goals engendered by communitarian models have less resonance here because the public interest is in ensuring proper governance of a company so that it may best pursue its commercial aims rather than a realignment of those aims to serve state purposes. The focus here is on standards of *constitutional conduct or governance*. Thus the aim is to ensure that the company

group and the individual emerges from a continuous process of negotiating and defining power relations.'
[152] S. Leader, 'Private Property and Corporate Governance Part I' in Patfield (ed.), *Perspectives on Company Law I*, 85.
[153] Law Commission Report, *Shareholder Remedies* (1997, Cm 3769, Law Com No. 246).
[154] It is interesting to note that the nearly complete overlap was confirmed by the 1989 amendment of section 459, which enabled an action to be brought where all the shareholders were unfairly prejudiced; there was no need to show personal or class special damage.

is run in a way that democratically and equitably takes account of those constituencies most nearly connected with its commercial function, not to impose general aims of social engineering as the communitaire approach would seek to do. The approach thus avoids imposing aims that may in any event be contradictory, such as an aim to provide the quickest possible road transport distribution system while at the same time preserving the environment. The company should not be viewed as an instrument of social policy; the separate personality of the company should continue to be afforded recognition and *corporate governance* should remain focused on the interests of the corporation, recognising that these interests diverge from both the interests of society and the interests of shareholders, but that the state has a right to control owing to the concession of power it has made. The corporation retains its legitimacy only if it acts within societal norms, for it was on that condition that its separate identity was conceded by its founders.

Who are the guardians of the public interest?

It is arguable that excessive reliance on the contractual theories has left us with shareholders as the only guardians of the public interest in corporate governance. An example illustrates this: section 309(1) of the Companies Act 1985 provides that 'the matters to which the directors of a company are to have regard in the performance of their functions include the interests of the company's employees in general, as well as the interests of its members'. But the only possible mechanism for enforcing this duty to take account of such interests is the shareholders, whose interests may be diametrically opposed to those of employees in certain circumstances.[155] The logic of the situation appears to be not only that the shareholders have a *right* to see that the company is properly run in its own interests, but that society has delegated a *duty* to them to achieve this.

The danger of adopting a model of company that relies on shareholder control[156] is that in many jurisdictions it has been less than useful in controlling management. The whole purpose of providing a company with separate personality is to enable a separation of ownership and control. This allows the directors to use their energies for the benefit of the company, not act as agents of the ownership pressure group.

---

[155] It is interesting that the Law Society calls for 'clear expression of the purposes behind particular provisions of this type'; Memorandum No. 360, *Modern Company Law for a Competitive Economy*, para. 2.4.

[156] See P. Ireland, 'Company Law and the Myth of Shareholder Ownership' [1999] *Modern Law Review* 32.

However, the separation has become extreme in many cases, so that shareholders are no longer an effective governance mechanism, even where guardianship of their *own* interests is the issue. Effectiveness in guardianship of the *company's interest* is manifestly much more unlikely. Ineffectiveness has occurred for many well-known reasons.[157] In large companies small investors are apathetic, caring only for the return on investment. Institutional investors see their primary duty to their investors as best served by leaving a company where management difficulties are experienced, rather than becoming involved. Further, the supply of information is in the hands of management, as may be a significant quantity of 'active' shares and proxies. To rely on shareholders as a governance mechanism is therefore to allow directors almost complete discretion subject to the unpredictable whims of the market for corporate control. For that reason among others, some jurisdictions have adopted a governance mechanism that relies on a two-tier management structure, allowing a supervisory board a greater or lesser degree of control over the executive directors.

The move to constituency/multifiduciary models

Where, as in the UK and the USA, single boards are still the rule, it may be argued that the task of shareholders is becoming increasingly difficult as courts take on board the argument that there is not absolute congruence between the interests of shareholders and the interests of the company.[158] In attempting to guard the interests of the company the shareholders must thus attempt to second guess the perspectives of other (as yet undefined)[159] constituencies.

The rejection of contractualism and the acceptance of the distinction between the interests of the shareholders and the interests of the company can be traced in both jurisdictions. Sullivan and Conlon[160]

---

[157] For a full analysis see Parkinson, *Corporate Power and Responsibility*.

[158] *Pender v Lushington* (1877) 6 ChD 70, 75: 'In all cases of this kind, where men exercise their rights of property, they exercise their rights from some motive adequate or inadequate, and I have always considered the law to be that those who have rights of property are entitled to exercise them, whatever their motives might be for such exercise.' Clear enough it would seem, but strangely he feels supported in this view 'by the case of *Menier v Hooper's Telegraph Works* (1874) LR 9 Ch 250 where Lord Justice Mellish observes: "I am of the opinion that, although it may be quite true that the shareholders of a company may vote as they please, and for the purpose of their own interests, yet the majority of shareholders cannot sell the assets of the company and keep the consideration."' Why support was to be had for his proposition in a statement that set limitations on the selfish exercise of rights is unclear. For arguments rejecting the congruence see Dine, 'Private Property and Corporate Governance'.

[159] As foreseen by Berle, 'For Whom Are Corporate Managers Trustees?'

[160] Sullivan and Conlon, 'Crisis and Transition', 732 et seq.

note that the high point of contractualism came with the court's endorsement of the takeover market as a corporate governance mechanism: 'the discipline of capital markets pushed executives to maximise shareholder wealth so as not to attract the attention of unsolicited suitors.'[161] The vote of shareholders to accept or reject a takeover bid was seen as the ultimate arbiter not only of the shareholders' personal right to maximise the price of their shares but of the company's interest. However,

the relaxation of the fiduciary strictures inspired a variety of nefarious behaviours. Managers and raiders alike subverted shareholder democracy through such esoteric means as supervoting stock, poison pills, classified boards, lock-ups, leg-ups, creeping takeovers, bear hugs, white knights, white squires, black knights, preclusive defences, selective stock buyouts, stock options, greenmail, crown jewel sales, auctions and self-tenders.[162]

Clearly the shareholders were not very effective in safeguarding even their own interests. However, in the move by the Delaware courts away from contractualism, Sullivan and Conlon detect a move towards a 'multifiduciary' model of company. This is described by reference to the demise of the shareholder as a single fiduciary:

Proponents reason that the notion of a single fiduciary in the form of the shareholder is misleading and anachronistic and often destructive. Rather, the multifiduciary model . . . extends fiduciary duty to constituencies such as lenders, suppliers, employees, managers, consumers, bondholders *and* shareholders. As such, the multifiduciary model holds that the rights of the shareholders no longer supersede those of nonshareholders.[163]

The move towards this model is perceived as pivotal in the decision in *Paramount Communications v Time Inc*[164] where the Delaware Chancery Court held that *Time*'s directors were able to decide to reject a takeover offer by Paramount even though it was an offer at a premium price. Chancellor Allen said:

corporation law does not operate on the theory that directors, in exercising their powers to manage the firm, are obligated to follow the wishes of a majority of shares . . . a board of directors, while always required to act in an informed manner, is not under any per se duty to maximise shareholder value in the short term, even in the context of a takeover.

The directors had successfully argued that their long-term plan for the company was a better strategy than a sale of the company to Paramount. An appeal to the Delaware Supreme Court was refused. '*Time* and its progeny hold that shareholders' rights are important but not supreme when management can enunciate a long term strategy that offers

---

[161] Ibid., 734.   [162] Ibid.   [163] Ibid., 716.
[164] 571.A.2d. 1140 (1989), 571.A.2d. 1145 (Del. 1990).

superior benefits to shareholders and "the community of interests the corporation represents".[165]

A similar move from contractualism to a multifiduciary or constituency model can be detected in the United Kingdom. It is clear that the UK courts are moving away from the narrow contractual view of companies. A number of cases involve the extension of the 'umbrella' of the company to cover interests other than the shareholders' interests.

The courts seem to be increasingly accepting that, once the company is formed, not only is it a creature separate from its members[166] but, in exercising their voting rights, members must take account of interests other than their own selfish concerns. This trend may be seen in four types of case: (i) where increasing weight is given to the interests of creditors, (ii) in cases where ratification of a decision by a majority is nullified by the court, (iii) in cases where alteration of the articles of association by a special majority is declared invalid, and (iv) in decisions that have determined the balance of powers between the organs of the company.

Creditors

In *Lonhro v Shell Petroleum*[167] the interests of the creditors were acknowledged by Lord Diplock, who said 'it is the duty of the board to consider . . . the best interests of the company. These are not exclusively those of its shareholders but may include those of its creditors.'[168] The Court of Appeal confirmed this view in *Liquidator of West Mercia Safetywear Ltd v Dodd and Another*.[169] In that case, however, the interests of the company were said to include the interests of the creditors because the company was insolvent at the time. In *Lonhro* insolvency was not an issue. Nor was insolvency an issue in *Winkworth v Edward Baron*,[170] where Lord Templeman referred to a duty owed directly to creditors. In *Brady v Brady*,[171] Nourse LJ regarded the interests of the company as synonymous with the interests of the creditors where the company was insolvent or 'doubtfully solvent'. In *Standard Chartered Bank v Walker*[172] the wishes of creditors were held to be paramount and overrode the wishes of the majority of shareholders.

---

[165] Sullivan and Conlon, 'Crisis and Transition', 745, quoting from Opinion of Chancellor Allen in *Paramount Communications v Time*.

[166] *Salomon v Salomon* [1897] AC 22; *Lee v Lee's Air Farming* [1961] AC 12; *Macaura v Northern Insurance Co* [1925] AC 619.

[167] [1980] 1 WLR 627.   [168] Ibid., 634.

[169] [1988] BCLC 250.   [170] [1987] BCLC 193.   [171] [1988] BCLC 20.

[172] [1992] 1 WLR 561; and see J. Dine, 'Shareholders Denied Voting Rights' (1992) *Insolvency Law and Practice* 150.

Ratification

Shareholders are not permitted to use their majority voting power in their own selfish interests to permit directors to act contrary to a duty owed to the company.[173] The courts have accepted that the majority of shareholders cannot prevail even when their decision is constitutionally correct. Some decisions of directors cannot be ratified even by 100 per cent of the shareholders.[174]

It may thus be argued that UK company law is moving towards a model of company in which shareholders must take account of more than their own immediate interests when determining policy. There is increasing recognition of the company as an entity quite separate from its owners, which is evident not only from the overt recognition of other interests that must be taken account of when decisions are made by management but also from the inability of majorities to drive the company in whichever direction they wish. The point is reinforced by the attitude of the courts to the question of alteration of the articles of association.

Alteration of articles

The courts have reserved the right to prevent any alteration of the articles of association of a company where the alteration is not 'bona fide for the benefit of the company'. To prevent such an alteration means that the court will upset a resolution that has been passed by at least 75 per cent of the shareholders. While struggling greatly to define 'the interests of the company', the court makes it plain that they cannot be equated with the selfish interests of even a very substantial majority of shareholders.[175]

Division of powers

Further light is thrown on the separation of the identity of shareholder interests and company interests by the way in which the division of powers among company organs has evolved.

Historically it was accepted that the powers of directors derived from authority bestowed on them by the shareholders. This meant that

[173] *Prudential Assurance Co Ltd v Newman Industries (No 2)* [1981] Ch 257; *Alexander v Automatic Telephone Co* [1900] 2 Ch 56; *Estmanco (Kilner House) Ltd v GLC* [1982] 1 WLR 2.
[174] *R v Gomez* [1992] 3 WLR 1067.
[175] See *Allen v Gold Reefs of West Africa* [1900] 1 Ch 656; *Dafen Tinplate v Llanelly Steel Co Ltd* [1920] 2 Ch 124; *Greenhalgh v Arderne Cinemas* [1951] Ch 286.

powers so delegated could be retrieved and exercised by the company's shareholders voting in a general meeting. The modern view is that the directors' powers derive from the company itself. Some of the company's powers are devolved to the shareholders acting in general meeting; other powers are devolved directly to the management. This means that there is a division of powers. No longer can the general meeting interfere in the conduct of management.[176] The circle is complete when it is appreciated that the shareholders may interfere by altering the articles (but only 'in the interests of the company') or by ratification (but the court may invalidate the ratification where there has been what Sealy suggests should properly be called a 'fraud on the company'[177]).

The vision of the company as separate from and involving interests apart from the selfish interests of its shareholders is gaining ground. The United Kingdom is beginning to see the company not as a contract made between owners for their own profit but as a commercial enterprise with purposes of its own, which must be furthered by decisions taken with its interests in mind rather than the immediate and narrow property interests of its shareholders.

Conclusion: the crisis in corporate governance

As Sullivan and Conlon have argued,[178] this move from contract to constituency models has created a crisis in corporate governance. Shareholders, directors and the courts have lost the convenient yardstick of the majority decision of the shareholders. If shareholders are ineffective in safeguarding their own interests, how much less likely is it that they can effectively safeguard the public interest in proper governance. However, both legislation and Codes seem to depend only on them as providing protection against poor or fraudulent management.[179] Some other system of regulation is clearly required.

In this chapter we have considered single companies. The next step is

---

[176] *Automatic Self-Cleansing Filter Syndicate Co Ltd v Cuninghame* [1906] 2 Ch 34; *Quinn & Axtens v Salmon* [1909] AC 442; *Breckland Group Holdings Ltd v London and Suffolk Properties Ltd* [1989] BCLC 100.

[177] L. Sealy, *Cases and Materials in Company Law* (5th edn, Butterworth, London, 1995), 476.

[178] Sullivan and Conlon, 'Crisis and Transition'. Note that the full title is 'Crisis and Transition in Corporate Governance Paradigms: The Role of the Chancery Court of Delaware'.

[179] *Report of the Cadbury Committee on the Financial Aspects of Corporate Governance* (Gee, London, 1992). See the Cadbury emphasis on institutional shareholders as a control mechanism and the legislative penchant for demanding ever-increasing disclosure, presumably with a view to the power of shareholders to remove directors, although there may also be an eye to public reaction, particularly where disclosure of salaries is required.

to consider the phenomenon of related companies and their relationships with each other, with their human participants and with the state, remembering that, just as with single companies, groups will be structured and behave in accordance with the underlying philosophy of the societies that produce them.

2   The governance of groups: some comparative perspectives

Perhaps the most astonishing thing about this topic is the lack of an intense debate concerning the corporate governance of groups of companies. The topic is absent from or briefly treated in many of the company law textbooks and treatises on corporate governance[1] and discussion of the problems posed by groups of companies often focuses narrowly on insolvency issues rather than a concern with the governance of groups of companies. Scott traces the lack of debate to classic economic analysis: 'Economic analysis was predicated on the role played by the individual entrepreneur in organising production. Classical economists assumed that "entrepreneurs" headed firms which they personally owned; and they could see no obvious reason to modify this view when analysing the behaviour of the modern, large scale business corporation.'[2] Blumberg identifies two other reasons in the context of US law:[3] the fact that not until 1888–93[4] was it possible for one corporation to become a shareholder in another corporation,[5] and that, when the issue of the liability of parent corporations first came before the courts, not only had the limited liability of shareholders been accepted for decades but that at the time 'American law was experiencing the high tide of formalism, or conceptualism, as the only legitimate form of legal analysis. Shareholders were not liable for the obligations of the corporations of which they were shareholders. A parent company

---

[1] J. Parkinson, *Corporate Power and Responsibility* (Clarendon Press, Oxford, 1993); N. Maw, *Maw on Corporate Governance* (Dartmouth, Aldershot, 1994); L. Gower, *Gower's Principles of Modern Company Law* (6th edn, ed. P. Davies, Sweet & Maxwell, London, 1997); J. Farrar and B. Hannigan (eds.), *Farrar's Company Law* (4th edn, Butterworth, London, 1998); B. Cheffins, *Company Law* (Clarendon, Oxford, 1997), D. Milman 'Groups of Companies, The Path Towards Discrete Regulation' in *Regulating Enterprise*, Hart Publishing 1999.

[2] J. Scott, 'Corporate Groups and Network Structure' in J. McCahery, S. Picciotto and C. Scott (eds.), *Corporate Control and Accountability* (Clarendon, Oxford, 1993), 292.

[3] P. Blumberg, 'The American Law of Corporate Groups' in McCahery, Picciotto and Scott (eds.), *Corporate Control and Accountability*.

[4] First in New Jersey: New Jersey Act, 4 April 1888, ch 269 s1 (1888 N.J. Laws 385).

[5] See also T. Hadden, 'Regulating Corporate Groups: An International Perspective' in McCahery, Picciotto and Scott (eds.), *Corporate Control and Accountability*, 345.

was a shareholder. Ergo, a parent corporation was not liable for the obligations of its subsidiary corporations of which it was a shareholder.'[6]

Despite the 'dramatic change in the underlying relationship',[7] this analysis prevailed and is still evident today in both US and UK[8] jurisprudence. Just as the nexus of the contracts approach to single corporations deconstructs the institution, denying its public role and the status of its constitution, so groups of companies are deconstructed so that they are seen as related to each other only as majority or minority shareholders. The effects of the aggregation of power have been missed and are taken account of only in extreme cases[9] or where the state has intervened following financial scandals.[10] Prentice regards the fragmentation of laws relating to group issues consequent on the contractual approach as beneficial on the ground that, once rules relating to particular issues such as 'consolidation of accounts, disclosure, taxation, directors' dealings within the context of groups, minority shareholder oppression, and insolvency' have been formulated, 'there will be little left to be mopped up by a law which specifically addresses the problem of groups'.[11] He believes that the concept of the group as a single enterprise should be used with caution (see n. 1).

This chapter examines some different legal approaches to corporate group regulation by UK and European laws as a basis for evaluating different methods of regulation. The German model exhibits a wider understanding of the effect of the power relationships within the group. The communitaire theory is perhaps most closely reflected by the single corporate unit approach adopted by EU competition law, although interestingly a justification for anti-trust intervention is often that it is perfecting market failure, namely monopolistic and cartel tendencies.

The simplistic analysis reflecting the contractual viewpoint misses the point that limited liability, which was designed to protect investors not engaged in the conduct of the enterprise, was being extended to parent corporations 'although they manifestly constituted an important part of the enterprise'.[12] This dramatically increased the power of those managing the group structure, since movement of assets was between the limited liability members of the group and was under the control of the

[6] Blumberg, 'American Law of Corporate Groups', 308.
[7] Ibid.
[8] Despite the fact that there never was a ban on companies holding shares in other companies.
[9] *Adams v Cape Industries plc* [1990] Ch 433.
[10] See discussion of protection of creditors, below.
[11] D. Prentice, 'Some Comments on the Law of Groups' in McCahery, Picciotto and Scott (eds.), *Corporate Control and Accountability*.
[12] Blumberg, 'American Law of Corporate Groups', 308.

limited liability parent. Hadden emphasises the institutional dimension of group structures and the potential for avoidance of governmental regulation as well as the difficult policy issues to be addressed in seeking to regulate groups while rejecting the contractualist viewpoint:

It is . . . unrealistic to adopt the view that the relationships between the constituent parts of the group are entirely a matter for contractual agreement . . . [T]here is a need for both national and international regulation to protect the legitimate interests of the principal parties involved in group transactions, notably those of external investors, employees, voluntary and involuntary creditors or consumers and the host and home state of the enterprise involved.[13]

As Scott points out, control and rule should not be confused: control is dependent on the rights conferred by share ownership, whereas 'rulers of an enterprise are those who actually decide upon its corporate strategy and set the framework within which its operations will take place'.[14] However, by permitting the control and rule over subsidiaries to be vested in those managing the parent, the law sanctioned an unprecedented aggregation of power in a central body. Piecemeal attempts to prevent the centralisation of that power[15] have been largely ineffectual, and increased centralisation of decision-making coupled with globalisation has had tragic consequences. The paucity of controls over groups of companies spawned by the free market is beginning to become evident. The regulatory structures considered here are specific to the legal structural control of groups. Wider issues of control and regulation are considered later in the book.

Groups: what are they?

Companies may have a wide range of interconnected relationships. Thus they may be connected by contract, by share ownership or by interlocking directorships. Eisenberg[16] identifies horizontal groups such as cross-ownership groups, of which the Japanese *traditional keiretsu*[17] is the most famous example. In this type of group there is a complex network of small cross-shareholdings. Coordination is achieved through

---

[13] Hadden, 'Regulating Corporate Groups'.

[14] Scott, 'Corporate Groups and Network Structure', 294.

[15] Such as the requirement that directors must act in the interests of the company on whose board they are actually sitting at the time a decision is made.

[16] T. Eisenberg, 'Corporate Groups' in M. Gillooly (ed.), *The Law Relating to Corporate Groups* (Federation Press, Sydney, 1993), 1.

[17] For a general analysis of the Japanese *keiretsu*, see R. Gilson and M. Roe, 'Understanding the Japanese Keiretsu: Overlaps between Corporate Governance and Industrial Organisation' in S. Wheeler (ed.), *The Law of the Business Enterprise* (Oxford University Press, Oxford, 1994), and (1993) 102 *Yale Law Journal* 871, and P. Muchlinski, *Multinational Enterprises and the Law* (Blackwell, Oxford, 1995).

regular meetings of the chairpeople and by interlocking directorships.[18] *Industrial keiretsu* form a half-way house between this pattern and vertical groups in that there is a clearly defined principal holding company but the principal holding company must carry on its own business and may invest a maximum of only 50 per cent of its assets in subsidiaries. It is therefore unusual for wholly owned subsidiaries to exist. Legally vertical groups[19] consist of a parent and one or more subsidiary. Legally horizontal groups are made up of companies with cross-shareholdings. These distinctions use legal concepts of share ownership. A different perspective is used in commercial analysis, in which a vertical group owns the elements of production from banana plantation to retail outlet, whereas a horizontal group owns different production elements but at the same level, for example several retail outlets. Management viewpoints yield yet further different perspectives.[20] Another division relevant to legal vertical groups is the distinction between groups where the subsidiaries are wholly owned and those where they are partly owned. As Austin points out, where subsidiary companies are partly owned important issues of minority shareholder protection arise.[21] With wholly owned groups the major issue is creditor protection. Even within this latter category there is an important distinction between protection of voluntary and involuntary creditors. Using the language of economic analysis it is possible to argue that contractual creditors may use their bargaining position to receive recompense for the risk that they take in lending money to the company[22] (although the argument looks rather thin when disparity of bargaining power is considered, especially if employees are seen in this category).[23] However, it is equally possible to see that where the creditor is involuntary (i.e. the victim of torts or other civil wrongs committed by the

[18] D. Henderson, *Foreign Enterprise in Japan: Laws and Policies* (University of North Carolina Press, Chapel Hill, NC, 1973); R. Clark, *The Japanese Company* (Yale University Press, New Haven, CT, 1979); Hadden, 'Regulating Corporate Groups'.

[19] The terminology varies. Scott, 'Corporate Groups and Network Structure', uses 'total' groups and 'network' groups. See also G. Teubner, 'The Many Headed Hydra: Networks as Higher Order Collective Actors' in McCahery, Picciotto and Scott (eds.), *Corporate Control and Accountability* and Muchlinski, *Multinational Enterprises*.

[20] See discussion at the end of this chapter.

[21] R. Austin, 'Corporate Groups' in R. Grantham and C. Rickett (eds.), *Corporate Personality in the 20th Century* (Hart Publishing, Oxford, 1998).

[22] R. Grantham and C. Rickett, 'The Bootmaker's Legacy to Company Law Doctrine' in *Corporate Personality*; D. Goddard, 'Corporate Personality – Limited Recourse and Its Limits' in the same volume; F. Easterbrook and D. Fischel, *The Economic Structure of Corporate Law* (Harvard University Press, Cambridge, MA, 1991); B. Cheffins, *Company Law* (Clarendon Press, Oxford, 1997), 69 et seq.

[23] See R. Grantham, 'Commentary on Goddard' in Grantham and Rickett (eds.), *Corporate Personality*, 66.

company[24]) 'risk is shifted to such creditors without their having an opportunity to price for it or to negotiate security or other terms'.[25] The implications of this problem, particularly in the light of restructuring to achieve maximum shifting of risk,[26] are considered below.

Multinational and transnational groups

As Farrah points out,[27] the concept of a company carrying on business in several countries is far from new.[28] However this activity has increased enormously in recent years and current statistics contain a rather frightening message. According to the UN's *World Investment Report 1997*, the world has about 45,000 transnational firms controlling 280,000 foreign affiliates. Worldwide sales of these affiliates amounted to about $7 trillion. The largest 100 companies own about $1.7 trillion of foreign assets – a fifth of the estimated global total. Multinational companies account for fifty-one of the world's largest economic entities (the other forty-nine are nation states).[29] It is possible to juggle with definitions and discern a difference between national multinationals, international multinationals and transnational groups of companies.[30] National multinationals have a single parent company of a particular nationality, international multinationals have two or more controlling parents of different nationalities, but as Holt points out this description relates only to the legal structure and does not describe either the commercial activity of a group or the underlying decision-making structures:[31]

Observers often indiscriminately apply the term *multinational corporation* to refer to any company with international interests. Such an all-inclusive meaning fails to distinguish among various types of international organisations. Later discussions will describe companies that merely export domestically made goods, others that only import supplies . . . and many that act in agency role (traders, brokers and expediters). These firms participate in international activities, but they qualify as true multinationals only if they invest directly in foreign facilities and hold management accountable for foreign activities.[32]

It is perhaps in that last phrase that the true importance of the

---

[24] Ibid.   [25] Ibid.   [26] As in *Adams v Cape Industries plc.*
[27] Farrah and Hannigan, *Farrah's Company Law*, ch. 44.
[28] Citing the East India Company and the Hudson's Bay Company.
[29] The rapid growth of multinationals in Europe is attributed to the recovery of the European economy with US assistance following the Second World War; see J. Spero and J. Hart, *The Politics of International Economic Relations* (5th edn, Allen & Unwin, London, 1997). For further statistics see ch. 5.
[30] Farrah and Hannigan, *Farrah's Company Law*.
[31] D. Holt, *International Management* (Harcourt Brace, New York, 1998).
[32] Ibid., 6.

multinational may be seen. What is happening is that management is increasingly responsible for activities on an *international basis*. Its horizons are no longer limited by national or local considerations. The move from this to transnational corporations is generally acknowledged to be unclear,[33] and for some purposes the UN has adopted a catch-all definition of transnationals: 'Enterprises which own or control production or service facilities outside the country in which they are based.'[34] Probably a more useful definition is that put forward by the Commission of Transnational Corporations in its draft code of conduct for transnational corporations. The emphasis is on 'a system of decision making, permitting coherent policies and a common strategy through one or more decision-making centres'.[35] As Holt points out, the difference appears to be in the degree of integration of decision-making structures.[36] If anything, the management is even further removed from local concerns. The whole decision-making structure has the world as its focus. Now, not all nation states have democratic control over their leaders, but democratic deficit does not begin to describe the lack of controls over those involved in exercising the enormous power such wealth gives. Further, where the corporate group has its roots in economic free market theories, the exercise of power can be justified only by profit maximisation efficiency theories. This can have devastating effects on the world. In the light of this central issue, the discussion of legal issues surrounding groups has a distinct air of not grasping the nettle.

The main issues

Much of the debate surrounding the legal structure and treatment of groups has fossilised into a contest between the view of a group of companies as separate and autonomous individual entities and the view of such a group as a single economic unit. Neither is satisfactory: 'neither of the two simplest approaches to the legal status of corporate groups – the maintenance of the traditional view that each constituent company in the group must retain an entirely separate legal personality, and the recognition of the group as a legal entity in its own right which

---

[33] Farrah and Hannigan, *Farrah's Company Law*; Holt, *International Management*.

[34] Group of Eminent Persons, *The Impact of Multinational Corporations on Development and on International Relations* (UN pub E74 IIA 5), 25.

[35] United Nations Economic and Social Council, *Work on the Formulation of the United Nations Code of Conduct on Transnational Corporations – Outstanding Issues in the Draft Code of Conduct on Transnational Corporations* (E/C10/1985/5/2, 22 May 1985).

[36] Holt, *International Management*, 5.

submerges that of its constituent companies – is likely to prove either workable or acceptable.'[37] The following problems fuel the debate:

- The fraudulent or immoral use of the corporate veil to shift resources between companies in order to defeat outside interests.[38]
- The advantages and disadvantages of 'group' decision-making, including the capacity for oppression of minority interests.
- The difficulties of definition of a single economic unit in a changing environment.[39]

Using the corporate veil to shift resources between companies

Under the first head, it is useful to analyse the situation in a number of different jurisdictions. When the management of groups is considered, the national approaches tend to reflect the theories underpinning single corporations in that jurisdiction.

Lack of recognition of group interests in UK case law

Perhaps the most extreme example of separate units is the UK. Not only does the contractual approach lead to a characterisation of parents and subsidiaries as merely linked as shareholders – the group reflecting the nexus of contracts – but the economic free enterprise approach tends to be hostile to regulation other than that perceived as perfecting market mechanisms. These attitudes have informed the UK approach and much of the jurisprudence concerning groups has been developed on this basis. We thus see a very strict approach to the separateness of companies within groups and the consequent 'blinkered' approach to advice to corporate managers.[40] The theory is that managers must focus only on the company they are serving at the moment of decision-making. The extent of the legal adaptation to reality is that the interests of the group may be of relevance in determining the interests of the company[41] and 'whether an intelligent and honest man [*sic*] in the position of the director of the company concerned could, in the whole of the existing circumstances, have reasonably believed that the transaction

---

[37] Hadden, 'Regulating Corporate Groups', 343.
[38] This includes entrenchment of management. For a case study illustrating this, see Hadden, 'Regulating Corporate Groups', 359.
[39] This will include issues of misleading accounts; see Hadden, 'Regulating Corporate Groups', 360.
[40] See cases examined in the next section.
[41] *Nicholas v Soundcraft Electronics Ltd* [1993] BCLC 360.

was for the benefit of the company'.[42] Although this approach may be seen as lessening the centralisation of group management, it is so far from the practical reality of the way in which groups are managed that it is of very doubtful utility.[43]

Do companies with a significant shareholding in other companies have a special relationship? Here we return to Prentice's insight that the UK has many laws that affect groups but no law on groups as such.[44] Thus, although for many tax and accounting purposes groups of companies are treated as one unit,[45] the courts are reluctant to admit the reality of interrelated companies acting in any other way than as a number of separate entities tied together by their relationship as significant shareholders in each other. The governance of groups thus depends on the way in which regulations made to deal with general company law issues impact on groups. The most important rules in this category are:

(i)   the capacity of the court to 'lift the veil' in cases of fraud and the failure to develop a 'law of the enterprise';
(ii)   protection of creditors and the issue of interdependent company liability;
(iii) directors' duties and the oppression of minority shareholders;
(iv)   consolidated accounts and taxation.

Lifting the veil

The approach of the UK courts is epitomised by Templeman LJ in *Re Southard & Co Ltd*:

English company law possesses some curious features, which may generate curious results. A parent company may spawn a number of subsidiary companies, all controlled directly or indirectly by the shareholders of the parent company. If one of the subsidiary companies, to change the metaphor, turns out to be the runt of the litter and declines into insolvency to the dismay of its creditors, the parent company and the other subsidiary companies may prosper to the joy of the shareholders without any liability for the debts of the insolvent subsidiary.[46]

The approach is confirmed by the cavalier treatment by the courts of 'letters of comfort'. Thus in *Re Augustus Barnett & Son Ltd*[47] the

---

[42] *Charterbridge Corporation v Lloyd's Bank Ltd* [1970] Ch 62 at 74.
[43] See discussion of management practice below and Holt, *International Management*, esp. ch. 7; M. Czinkota, I. Ronkainen and M. Moffett, *International Business* (4th edn, Harcourt Brace, New York, 1996), esp. ch. 20.
[44] Prentice, 'Some Comments on the Law of Groups', 372.
[45] See, for example, section 258 of the Companies Act 1985.
[46] [1979] 3 All ER 556.
[47] [1986] BCLC 170, and see *Kleinwort Benson Ltd v Malaysia Mining Corp Bhd* [1989] 1

company was a wholly owned subsidiary of a Spanish company. The subsidiary traded at a loss for some time but the parent company repeatedly issued statements that it would continue to support the subsidiary. Some of the statements were made in letters written to the subsidiary's auditors and published in the subsidiary's annual accounts for three successive years. Later the parent company allowed the subsidiary to go into liquidation and failed to provide any financial support to pay off the debts of the subsidiary. In deciding that this did not constitute fraudulent trading on the part of the parent company, Hoffman J accepted that the assurances of the parent were without legal effect.[48] Prentice notes that 'there was no serious argument in the case that the [parent company] might have misled its subsidiary's creditors and that this would constitute a basis for piercing the corporate veil'.[49]

In general the courts have been hostile to developing a notion of 'enterprise law'. Thus in *Kodak Ltd v Clark*[50] it was held that a 98 per cent controlling interest in a company does not *of itself* give rise to an agency relationship so as to treat the parent and subsidiary as one enterprise. In *Smith, Stone & Knight Ltd v Birmingham Corporation*[51] Atkinson J tried to extract the relevant principles. The issue in the case was that land owned by a subsidiary was compulsorily purchased. The land had been used to carry on the business of the parent company. The subsidiary was not itself able to claim compensation.[52] The court held that the parent could recover. According to Atkinson J, the overall question was whether the subsidiary was carrying on the parent's business or its own. This was a matter of fact to be answered by assessing six factors:

I find six points which were deemed relevant for the determination of the question: Who was really carrying on the business? In all the cases, the question was whether the company, an English company here, could be taxed in respect of all the profits made by some other company, being carried on elsewhere. The first point was: Were the profits treated as the profits of the company? – when I say 'the company' I mean the parent company – secondly, were the persons conducting the business appointed by the parent company? Thirdly, was the company the head and brain of the trading venture? Fourthly, did the company

---

WLR 379. For a discussion of *Augustus Barnett* and an assessment that the result would have been the same under section 214 Insolvency Act 1986, see D. Prentice, 'Corporate Personality, Limited Liability, and the Protection of Creditors' in Grantham and Rickett (eds.), *Corporate Personality*.

[48] They were not fraudulent because Hoffman J accepted that they were true when made. The subsequent change of mind did not make them retrospectively fraudulent.

[49] Prentice, 'Corporate Personality', 116.

[50] [1903] 1 KB 505; see also *Delis Wilcox Pty v FCT* (1988) 14 ACLR 156.

[51] [1939] 4 All ER 116.

[52] Because the subsidiary had a short tenancy and the corporation could have given notice under the Lands Clauses Consolidation Act 1845, section 121.

govern the adventure, decide what should be done and what capital should be embarked on the venture? Fifthly, did the company make the profits by its skill and direction? Sixthly, was the company in effectual and constant control?

Farrah notes that questions 4, 5 and 6 cover much the same ground and criticises the approach as 'incoherent',[53] although it was subsequently followed in *Hotel Terrigal Pty Ltd v Latec Investments Ltd (No 2)*[54] by the New South Wales Supreme Court.

Where these questions can be answered in the affirmative it is possible that the group will be treated as a single entity, although, as we shall see, recent cases seem to indicate that 'enterprise doctrine' has lost rather than gained ground recently. Further, the answers to the questions posed in *Smith, Stone & Knight* can provide only guidelines and the court will determine each case according to its own facts and the context in which the case arises. The background to such cases can be very varied. *Unit Construction Co. v Bullock*[55] involved the determination of the residence of a company registered in Kenya but managed by a parent in the UK. The company was held to be resident in the UK. In *Firestone Tyre Co. v Llewellin*[56] an English subsidiary was held to be the means whereby the American parent company traded in the UK. A similar decision was arrived at in *DHN Food Distributors v Tower Hamlets Borough Council*,[57] but this was not followed by the House of Lords in the Scottish appeal of *Woolfson v Strathclyde Regional Council*.[58] In *Lonrho v. Shell Petroleum*[59] it was decided that documents could not be regarded as in the 'power' of a parent company when they were in fact held by a subsidiary. In *National Dock Labour Board Pinn & Wheeler Ltd & others*[60] the court emphasised that it is only in 'special circumstances which indicate that there is a mere facade concealing the true facts that it is appropriate to pierce the corporate veil'. Similarly, the rule was approved and relied on in *J.H. Rayner (Mincing Lane) Ltd v Department of Trade and Industry*.[61] This approach was upheld by the House of Lords in *Maclaine Watson & Co v DTI, Maclaine Watson & Co Ltd, International Tin Council*[62] and applied in *Adams v Cape Industries plc*.[63] The last provides a particularly stark example of the application of the *Salomon* principle of strict separate corporate personality. Several hundred employees of the group headed by Cape Industries had been

---

[53] Farrah and Hannigan, *Farrar's Company Law.*
[54] [1969] 1 NSWLR 676.   [55] [1960] AC 35.
[56] [1957] 1 WLR 464.   [57] [1976] 1 WLR 852.
[58] (1978) 38 P & CR 521; see F. Rixon, 'Lifting the Veil between Holding and Subsidiary Companies' (1986) 102 *Law Quarterly Review* 415.
[59] [1980] QB 358.   [60] [1989] BCLC 647.
[61] Court of Appeal judgment [1988] 3 WLR 1033.
[62] [1990] BCLC 102.   [63] [1990] BCLC 479.

awarded damages for injuries received as a result of exposure to asbestos dust in the course of their employment. The damages had been awarded in a Texan court. The English Court of Appeal held that the awards could not be enforced against Cape even though one of the defendants was a subsidiary of Cape's and there was evidence that the group had been restructured so as to avoid liability. Slade LJ said:

Our law, for better or worse, recognises the creation of subsidiary companies, which, though in one sense the creation of their parent companies, will nevertheless under the general law fall to be treated as separate legal entities with all the rights and liabilities which would normally attach to separate legal entities . . . We do not accept as a matter of law that the court is entitled to lift the corporate veil as against a defendant company which is the member of a corporate group merely because the corporate structure has been used so as to ensure that the legal liability (if any) in respect of particular future activities of the group . . . will fall on another member of the group rather than the defendant company. Whether or not this is desirable, the right to use a corporate structure in this way is inherent in our law.

And

If a company chooses to arrange the affairs of its group in such a way that the business carried on in a particular foreign country is the business of the subsidiary and not its own, it is, in our judgment, entitled to do so. Neither in this class of case nor in any other class of case is it open to this court to disregard the principle of *Salomon v Salomon* [1897] AC 22 merely because it considers it just so to do.[64]

A similar approach was taken in *Re Polly Peck International Plc (in administration)*,[65] where the court held that where companies were insolvent the separate legal existence of each within the group became more, not less, important, and *Adams v Cape Industries* was cited with approval in the cases of *Ringway Roadmarking v Adbruf*[66] and *Yukong Line Ltd v Rendsburg Investments*.[67] The courts seem increasingly to refuse to countenance the 'single economic unit' argument and confine the instances in which they are likely to interfere with the *Salomon* principle to subjective fraud by the controllers. A distinction made by Otto Khan Freund[68] between capitalist control in the sense of ownership of shares and functional control in the senses identified by Atkinson J in *Smith, Stone and Knight v Birmingham Corp* appears to be becoming increasingly irrelevant as the courts refuse to look behind the corporate veil in any circumstances other than actual fraud. Thus in *Yukong*, Toulson J agreed with the Court of Appeal in *Adams* that some parts of

---

[64] Ibid., 513.
[65] [1996] 2 All ER 433.   [66] [1998] 2 BCLC 625.   [67] [1998] 2 BCLC 485.
[68] 'Some Reflections on Company Law Reform' [1944] *Modern Law Review* 54 226.

the judgment in *DHN Food Distributors* had been too widely expressed and further considered that the same applied to *Smith, Stone & Knight*:

I do not accept Mr Gross's submission that as a matter of general approach the court should ask whether the company was carrying on business as its owner's business or its own business, using as guidance the sub-questions posed by Atkinson J, and should determine the question of agency accordingly. On that approach, *Salomon's* case would surely have been decided differently . . . It was nothing to the point that [Salomon's company] acted on the direction of Mr Salomon and for his benefit. Something quite different would need to be established in order to show that the company, in law an entity independent of its owner, was acting in some respect as agent for its owner, the necessary requirement being to show that the relationship of agency was intended to be created. Ordinarily, the intention of someone who conducts trading activities through the vehicle of a one-man company will be quite the opposite.[69]

Similarly, in both *Ringway* and *Yukong* a passage from *Adams* cited with approval is arguably a very restrictive interpretation of the circumstances other than agency when the veil may be lifted in a group situation:

save in cases which turn on the wording of particular statutes or contracts, the court is not free to disregard the principle of *Salomon v Salomon & Co Ltd* merely because it considers that justice so requires. Our law, for better or worse, recognises the creation of subsidiary companies, which though in one sense the creatures of their parent companies, will nevertheless under the general law fall to be treated as separate legal entities with all the rights and liabilities which would normally attach to separate legal entities.[70]

The lower courts seem to be adopting a policy that would eliminate the agency route to lifting the veil and restrict any general doctrine to statute and cases of fraudulent misuse of the veil. Any concept of an 'enterprise doctrine' is losing ground.

Subjective and objective factors

The move away from agency doctrine as a basis for lifting the veil places emphasis on the distinction between objective and subjective factors in these cases. Factors subjective to the minds of managers such as using companies as a 'sham' or for 'fraud' had in the past been mixed with issues of control and financial independence in such a way that it is not clear on what basis decisions were taken. To an extent a line was drawn in *Adams* between subjective factors such as fraudulent use of the corporate veil, which was said to be an issue of 'should the veil be lifted', and issues of control or agency, which went to whether there was a single economic unit. The distinction is between a focus on the motive

[69] Toulson J, in *Yukong Line Ltd v Rendsburg Investments* [1998] 2 BCLC 485 at 496.
[70] *Adams v Cape Industries plc* [1990] BCLC 479 at 513 per Slade LJ.

for establishing a controlled entity and the fact and degree of control. Where the corporate veil has been disturbed by the court, the conclusion reached at the end of the investigation is remarkably similar, although expressed in a variety of terms. Thus, in the subjective cases the subsidiary is said to be a 'fraud' or 'sham',[71] whereas in the objective cases the commercial reality of the situation is said to be that the subsidiary has no significant existence other than as an offshoot of its parent[72] or that the interests of the related companies are so tied together that they should be regarded as one.

The difference of approach is significant because the prevention of fraud approach may be seen as an application of the concession approach, i.e. the state permitting the use of its entrepreneurial tools within certain limits. The 'single unit' approach comes much closer to an application of communitaire theories by recognising the power unit represented by the group as a whole. The rejection of the application of the communitaire approach and thus the development of a law of the enterprise is to be found in *Salomon* itself in the rejection of the contention that the company was not being used for a dishonest (subjective fraud) purpose but that the use of a company in a way authorised by the Act was contrary to the purposes envisaged by the statute. Thus Lopes LJ:

It would be lamentable if a scheme like this could not be defeated. If we were to permit it to succeed, we should be authorising a perversion of the Joint Stock Companies Acts. We should be giving vitality to that which is a myth and a fiction. The transaction is a device to apply the machinery of the Joint Stock Companies Act to a state of things never contemplated by that Act – an ingenious device to obtain the protection of that Act in a way and for objects not authorised by that Act, and in my judgment in a way inconsistent with and opposed to its policy and provisions.[73]

This analysis was roundly rejected by the House of Lords:

[I]t has become fashion to call companies of this class 'one man companies'. That is a taking nickname, but it does not help one much in the way of argument. If it is intended to convey the meaning that a company which is under the absolute control of one person is not a company legally incorporated, although the requirements of the Act of 1862 may have been complied with, it is inaccurate and misleading; if it merely means that there is a predominant partner possessing an overwhelming influence and entitled practically to the whole of the profits, there is nothing in that I can see contrary to the true intention of the Act of 1862, or against public policy, or detrimental to the

---

71 *Jones v Lipman* [1962] 1 All ER 442; *Gilford Motor Co Ltd v Horne* [1933] Ch 925; *Re Bugle Press Ltd* [1961] Ch 270.
72 *DHN Food Distributors Ltd v London Borough of Tower Hamlets* [1976] 3 All ER 462.
73 *Broderip v Salomon* [1895] 2 Ch 323.

interests of creditors. If the shares are fully paid up, it cannot matter whether they are in the hands of one or many.[74]

This may explain the paucity of UK case law treating the group as a whole and in particular imposing liabilities on related companies for the activities of others within the group.

Protection of creditors

The extreme stance taken by the UK courts has led to a patchwork statutory attempt to ameliorate the difficulties. Limited liability attached to a strong culture of separate personality is a temptation for fraudulent businessmen, as the Cork Committee on Insolvency discussed.[75] In the United Kingdom this threat has been met by a piecemeal approach. The introduction of the wrongful trading provision,[76] which enables the court to order a director to make 'such contribution (if any) to the company's assets as the court thinks proper', appears to have been a result of the pre-existing state of the law, described uncompromisingly by Fletcher thus:[77]

In the realm of corporate insolvency . . . the limitations and deficiencies of legal provisions originally devised during the nineteenth century were capable of giving rise to scandalous malpractice and abuses, particularly in relation to the management and operation of the smaller type of company, where quite commonly the same group of persons constitute the company's shareholders and its board of directors.[78]

This 'lax state of affairs'[79] led, amongst other things, to the abuse of the system by 'Phoenix companies'.[80] The Cork Committee proposed

---

[74] Per Lord Macnaughten, *Salomon v Salomon* [1897] AC 22.

[75] *Insolvency Law and Practice Report of the Review Committee* (Cmnd 8558, June 1982), followed by the White Paper, *A Revised Framework for Insolvency Law* (Cmnd 9175, 1983).

[76] Section 214 of the Insolvency Act 1986.

[77] Ian Fletcher, "The Genesis of Modern Insolvency Law – An Odyssey of Law Reform', [1987] *Journal of Business Law* 365 at 367.

[78] In particular Fletcher emphasises the abuses that frequently occurred in a voluntary winding up where the liquidator was likely to be a 'director's friend' who could 'be relied upon at the very least not to search too diligently for evidence of corporate mismanagement or irregularity which might render the directors liable to incur the various penalties and sanctions – including loss of the vital protection conferred by the principle of limited liability – which are in theory supposed to serve as a deterrent against any delinquent tendencies on the part of company directors'.

[79] W. Sellar and R. Yeatman, *1066 and All That* (Methuen, London, 1930), 28.

[80] Creditors are poorly protected by the general law governing directors' duties because directors owe their duties to the company. Except in the case of an imminent insolvency, this body is not defined as including the creditors. For a discussion of this issue see R. Grantham, 'The Judicial Extension of Directors' Duties to Creditors' [1991] *Journal of Business Law* 1, and N. Hawke, 'Creditors' Interests in Solvent and Insolvent Companies' [1989] *Journal of Business Law* 54.

wide-ranging changes, which led to the reform of the law.[81] Amongst them were a number of measures particularly designed to deter the irresponsible use of limited liability.[82] These included a drastic strengthening of the disqualification provisions[83] and the introduction of the new civil remedy of wrongful trading.[84] Prentice[85] points also to the operation in a group context of provisions on transactions at an undervalue, preferences, defective floating charges and directors' duties to creditors.[86] The New Zealand legislature has taken a much more robust approach, with extensive provisions for pooled liquidations.[87]

In practice the temptations are partially removed by the insistence by banks on personal guarantees. In law there is some amelioration by the ability of the courts to order a contribution to the funds of a company by any director who has been involved in wrongful or fraudulent trading,[88] directors are unable to hide behind others simply by failing to have their control officially recognised,[89] and misuse of companies may lead to a director being disqualified under the Company Director Disqualification Act 1986.[90]

Interdependent company liability

Many authors have argued for liability of parents for their subsidiaries.[91] Together with the problems of defining the boundaries of groups and the 'dominant' relationship noted above, this idea brings a whole host of further difficulties. Some of them are listed by Prentice:

(1) How does one deal with exit – that is, a situation where the subsidiary leaves the group but with a liability which existed at the time it was a member of the group? (2) How does one deal with entry – that is, the acquisition of a subsidiary which has certain liabilities at the time it joins the group? (3) Why should the

---

[81] *Insolvency Law and Practice.* [82] Ibid., chs. 18, 43, 44, 45 and 48.
[83] Ibid., ch. 45. [84] Ibid., ch. 44.
[85] D. Prentice, 'Group Indebtedness' in C. Schmittoff and F. Wooldridge (eds.), *Groups of Companies* (Sweet & Maxwell, London, 1991) and 'Corporate Personality'.
[86] Sections 238, 239, 245 of the Insolvency Act 1986.
[87] Sections 271 and 272 of the Companies Act 1993; and see Austin, 'Corporate Groups'. This includes a discussion of the contrasting inability of liquidators to pool assets in Australia. For the liability of directors in New Zealand in a group situation see T. Telfer, 'Risk and Insolvent Trading' in Grantham and Rickett (eds.), *Corporate Personality.*
[88] See sections 213 and 214 of the Insolvency Act 1986.
[89] Under section 741 of the Companies Act 1985 they would be liable as a shadow director.
[90] See A. Mithani and S. Wheeler, *Disqualification of Company Directors* (Butterworth, London, 1996); L. S. Sealy, *Disqualification and Personal Liability of Directors* (4th edn, Sweet & Maxwell, London, 1993); and J. Dine, *Criminal Law in the Company Context* (Dartmouth, Aldershot, 1995).
[91] See, for example, Blumberg, 'American Law of Corporate Groups', and Hadden, 'Regulating Corporate Groups'.

creditors of the subsidiary find that their claims have to be pooled with the claims of the creditors of the parent or of other members in the group, should the group get into financial difficulties?[92]

The exit and entry questions can, of course, be dealt with by formal solutions such as those applied to entry or exit from a partnership or a European Economic Interest Grouping. The third question is a more interesting one and may contain the seeds of a solution to all three questions, providing a less mechanistic answer to the first two as well as a framework for the liability of interrelated companies generally.

What conclusions for directors' duties?

As we have seen above, the extent to which the interests of related companies can be reflected in the decision-making of directors is limited. The classic statement as to the duties owed by nominee directors is to be found in *Scottish Co-operative Society Ltd v Meyer*.[93] In that case the Scottish Co-operative Wholesale Society formed a subsidiary in order to manufacture rayon. In accordance with the articles of association of the subsidiary, the Society nominated three of the five directors to the board of the company. The Society and the respondents Meyer and Lucas were the only shareholders of the company, with the Society holding the majority of the shares. Meyer and Lucas were the managing directors. At the outset the Society needed the expertise of Meyer and Lucas because the manufacture of rayon was subject to a state licensing system and a licence was obtainable only if experienced persons were available to manage its manufacture. Four years after the establishment of the subsidiary, licensing was abolished, so the Society changed its policy and attempted to close down the subsidiary by setting up a competing rayon business and preventing the subsidiary from obtaining the necessary raw materials. The respondents alleged that the affairs of the subsidiary had been conducted in an oppressive manner contrary to section 210 of the Companies Act 1948. This meant, in effect, that the nominee directors had acted in the interests of the Society, which had nominated them, and not in the interests of the subsidiary. Lord Denning said about the nominee directors:

So long as the interests of all concerned were in harmony, there was no difficulty. The nominee directors could do their duty by both companies without embarrassment. But, so soon as the interests of the two companies were in conflict, the nominee directors were placed in an impossible position. It is plain that, in the circumstances, these three gentlemen could not do their duty by both companies and they did not do so. They put their duty to the co-

---

[92] Prentice, 'Some Comments on the Law of Groups', 372.
[93] [1959] AC 324.

operative society above their duty to the textile company in this sense, at least, that they did nothing to defend the interests of the textile company against the conduct of the co-operative society. They probably thought that 'as nominees' of the co-operative society their first duty was to the co-operative society. In this they were wrong. By subordinating the interests of the textile company to those of the co-operative society, they conducted the affairs of the textile company in a manner oppressive to the other shareholders.[94]

Note that this case concerns not only the duty of directors but the issue of oppression of minority shareholders by a parent majority share-holder. However, unlike in the USA, this issue has not received any systematic consideration. In the *Scottish* case, Viscount Simonds spoke of the difficult situation in which the nominee directors found them-selves and went on to say:

It is, then, the more incumbent on the parent company to behave with scrupulous fairness to the minority shareholder and to avoid imposing on their nominees the alternative of disregarding their instructions or betraying the interests of the minority.[95]

In *Lindgren v L and P Estates* the Court of Appeal accepted that the directors of a parent company have no duties to protect the interests of its subsidiaries when the subsidiaries have independent boards.[96] Counsel in that case argued that the property of a holding company consists of the investment in the shares of its subsidiaries and the duty of a holding company is to promote the interests of the subsidiaries representing that investment.[97] This is indeed a cogent argument[98] and would have afforded a new and ingenious argument for piercing the veil. If successful it would arguably prevent the use of subsidiaries in the *Re Southard & Co Ltd* sense as the 'runt of the litter'. However, it was not successful and the question as to whether the majority shareholder owes a duty to a minority shareholder is still one of considerable debate. In *Allen v Gold Reefs of West Africa* Lindley MR, speaking of the statutory power to alter the articles of association, said:

Wide, however, as the language of s50 is, the power conferred by it must, like all other powers, be exercised subject to those general principles of law and equity which are applicable to all powers conferred on majorities and enabling them to bind minorities. It must be exercised, not only in the manner required by law,

---

[94] See also *Boulting v Association of Cinematograph Television and Allied Technicians* [1959] AC 324; and, for a comparative assessment, E. Boros, 'The Duties of Nominee and Multiple Directors' (1989), 10 *Company Lawyer* 211.

[95] For the contrasting situation in Australia and New Zealand, see Boros, 'Duties of Nominee and Multiple Directors', Austin, 'Corporate Groups'.

[96] [1968] Ch 572.

[97] Mr Ralph Instone at 595 and 604, citing *Farrah's Company Law*, 539.

[98] *Farrah's Company Law*, 539.

but also bona fide for the benefit of the company as a whole, and it must not be exceeded.[99]

However, although this doctrine has waveringly been applied to alteration of articles,[100] the more general rule is that shareholders may vote according to their selfish interests unless to do so amounts to a 'fraud on the Minority'.[101] This common law debate has to a large extent been overtaken by 'unfair prejudice' actions under section 459 of the Companies Act 1985.[102] Although the remedy focuses on unfair prejudice to the members' interests *as members*, it has proved valuable in preventing misuse of powers in group situations. In *Re Little Olympian Each-Ways Ltd (No 3)*[103] the directors sold the company's business to another company at an undervalue. The directors gained substantially from the transaction. Similarly in *Re Full Cup International Trading Ltd*,[104] property of the company was sold by the directors at an under-value to a company controlled by the directors. However, section 459 actions are rarely successful in the case of larger private companies and public companies. The court is more prone to reason that the partici-pants in such companies are involved solely on a commercial basis and, particularly in a public company, are able to sell their shares. Where the actions are permitted by the articles, the court will therefore be reluctant to interfere.[105] This attitude seems to reflect an acceptance of the contractual basis for public companies, but a more ready application of concession notions to private companies.

A curious feature of the case law is the apparent discrepancy between the willingness of the courts to permit a parent company to claim for damage done to a subsidiary[106] and the view that directors owe no duty to a subsidiary. In the latter cases the court has traditionally denied the related interests; in the former cases it has accepted them. The view in the first line of cases is driven by a fear that accepting the duty to

---

99   [1900] 1 Ch 656.
100 *Sidebottom v Kershaw Leese & Co Ltd* [1920] 1 Ch 154; *Dafen Tinplate v Llanelly Steel Co* [1920] 2 Ch 124; *Greenhalgh v Arderne Cinemas Ltd* [1951] Ch 286.
101 *Foss v Harbottle* (1843) 2 Hare 461. See Law Commission, *Shareholder Remedies* (1997, Cm 3769, Law Comm No 246).
102 C. Riley, 'Contracting out of Company Law: s459 of the Companies Act and the Role of the Courts' (1992) *Modern Law Review* 782; D. Prentice, 'Protecting Minority Shareholders' Interests' in D. Feldman and F. Meisel (eds.), *Corporate and Commercial Law: Modern Developments* (London, Lloyd's of London Press, 1996).
103 [1995] 1 BCLC 636.
104 [1995] BCC 682 and affirmed by the Court of Appeal as *Antoniades v Wong* [1997] 2 BCLC 419.
105 *Re Blue Arrow plc* [1987] BCLC 585; *Re Tottenham Hotspur plc* [1994] 1 BCLC 655; *Re Saul D Harrison & Sons plc* [1995] 1 BCLC 14.
106 *George Fischer (Great Britain) Ltd v Multi Construction Ltd, Dexion Ltd (third party)* [1995] BCLC 260.

subsidiaries would cause a radical shift away from the doctrine of separate personality and thus separate limited liability. The latter cases do not pose that threat because the issue is between the parent and a third party, rather than relating to the duties owed by directors to a particular company. Thus it is easier for a court to accept that damage done to subsidiaries was recoverable by the parent company and to recognise that the shareholders' interests in the parent are damaged by damage to a subsidiary. No issue of the parent being liable for another company's debts arises. We thus have the curious spectacle of the court lifting the corporate veil when to do so is to the advantage of parent companies but refusing to do so when it would be to their disadvantage, not because of the application of a coherent strategy but on a case-by-case basis.

In *Adams* a better solution might have been reached if the UK adopted the notion of constitutional disability, which appears to have gained ground following the decision of the European Court of Justice (ECJ) in *Cooperateive Rabobank 'Vecht en Plassengebied' BA v Minderhoud (receiver in bankruptcy of Mediasafe BV)* [107] and which is fully explained in chapter 6. The failure to consult employees concerning restructuring might well be considered fatal to the decisions that were taken if the restructuring had occurred in a situation where the relevant companies were obliged to consult employees as represented by works councils. The disregard of the interests of employees should have meant that the decision was not properly taken, so that the manipulation of the corporate veil should have been challengeable from that standpoint rather than by raising the propositions argued. Thus the group should have been considered a single economic entity, not because of the degree of integration of its businesses but because in setting the group up the directors had failed properly to consider the whole of the interests concerned. Failure to address those interests would thus be a reason to challenge the existence of the subsidiaries as separate.

European Communities law, German law and concepts of 'undertaking' or 'enterprise'

EC law and German law have tended to adopt a wider enterprise view of company structures. In the Germany-wide participation in management[108] there is distinct evidence of a communitaire approach, with the company existing to serve wide social purposes as well as its own

---

[107] Case C-104/96 [1998] 2 BCLC 507.
[108] For a good analysis see Jean du Plessis, 'Corporate Governance: Reflections on the German Two-tier System' (1996) *Journal of South African Law* 315.

commercial interests. The role of the corporation in German society can be traced back to a concept of corporate personality as an expression of a collective will. Kay and Silberton trace this viewpoint back to Gierke,[109] but this concept still underpins modern German perspectives on the corporation[110] and on groups of companies.[111] This attitude is reflected in the greater willingness of the courts and legislature to interfere in the management of the company and define the parameters of the entity with which it is dealing. This can be seen both in EC competition law and in the German approach to groups.

EC law and the concept of 'undertaking' or 'enterprise'
The 'economic unit' approach is exemplified by a number of cases concerning Article 85 of the EC Treaty (now Article 81), which seeks to control unfair competition by preventing 'agreements between undertakings, decisions by associations of undertakings' the object or effect of which is distortion of competition. The European Court of Justice will investigate the parameters of the group structure and the reality of the interrelationships within the group. In *Centrafarm v Sterling* the European Court of Justice said:

Article 85, however, is not concerned with agreements or concerted practices between undertakings belonging to the same concern and having the status of parent and subsidiary, if the undertakings form an economic unit within which the subsidiary has no real freedom to determine its course of action on the market, and if the agreements or practices are concerned merely with the internal allocation of tasks as between undertakings.[112]

Similarly in *Hydrotherm* the Court decided that:

In competition law, the term 'undertaking' must be understood as designating an economic unit for the purpose of the subject matter of the agreement in question even if in law that economic unit consists of several persons, natural or legal.[113]

And, in *Viho Europe BV v Commission of the European Communities (supported by Parker Pen Ltd, Intervener)*,[114] the ECJ decided that, where a company and its subsidiaries formed a single economic unit, the parent company's practice of dividing national markets between its subsidiaries did not make Article 85 applicable, even though the practice

---

109 J. Kay and A. Silberton, 'Corporate Governance' in F. Patfield (ed.), *Perspectives on Company Law II* (Kluwer, London, 1997), 49, 56.
110 G. Teubner, 'Enterprise Corporatism: New Industrial Policy and the "Essence of the Legal Person"' (1988) 36 *American Journal of Comparative Law* 130.
111 Teubner, 'The Many Headed Hydra'.
112 Case 15/74, *Centrafarm BV and Adriaan de Peijper v Sterling Drug Inc* [1974] ECR 1147.
113 Case 170/83, *Hydrotherm Geratebau v Andreoli* [1984] ECR 2999.
114 *The Times*, 9 December 1996.

might be capable of affecting the competitive position of third parties. In this instance the subsidiaries enjoyed no real autonomy in determining how they operated in the market; they were obliged to follow instructions from the parent company.

A similar approach has been taken by the court in determining whether or not there has been an infringement of Article 86 (now Article 82). Acquisition of a controlling interest in a subsidiary, even where it remains a distinct legal entity, may put an undertaking into the position where 'any serious chance of competition is practically rendered impossible'. In those circumstances the acquisition may be an abuse of a dominant position.[115] The court did not concern itself with the legal structures of the companies involved; it was concerned solely with the reality of control, speaking of undertakings 'merging into an organic unity'. In that case the Commission relied on the dominant position of Schamalbach-Lubeca-Werke (SLW) on the German market and argued that the abuse had been committed by a joint subsidiary of SLW and Continental Can, Europembellage. The alleged abuse was the acquisition by Europembellage of a controlling interest in a Dutch licensee. That abuse by acquisition was treated as abuse by the parent. The court discounted the argument that competition rules were intended to apply to practices having a direct effect on the market and not to the restructuring of the market.

German law and the proposed EU Ninth Directive

In Germany there is a law of groups that has been placed on a statutory footing. The *Konzernrecht*[116] is applicable only to stock corporations,[117] although a vigorous body of developing law applies it to other companies.

Under this law a distinction is made between contractual and de facto groups of companies. In contractual groups, the creditors of the subsidiary are protected by a legal obligation of the parent towards the subsidiary to make good losses at the end of the year. Shareholders other than the parent company have a right to periodic compensation payments and must be offered the opportunity of selling their shares to

---

[115] Case 6/72, *Europemballage Corporation and Continental Can Co Inc v Commission* [1975] ECR 495, and see Muchlinski, *Multinational Enterprises*, ch. 9.

[116] *Konzernrecht*: para. 291 et seq of the Atiengesetz or Stock Corporation Act of 1965.

[117] In Germany in 1990 there were 2,682 AGs (stock corporations). Between 1974 and 1992 the number of GmbH (private limited) companies increased from 112,063 to 509,949. See R. Birk, 'Germany', in A. Pinto and G. Viscentini (eds.), *The Legal Basis of Corporate Governance in Publicly Held Corporations* (Kluwer, London, 1998); and K. Hopt 'Legal Elements and Policy Decisions in Regulating Groups of Companies' in Schmitthoff and Wooldridge (eds.), *Groups of Companies*.

the parent at a reasonable price. They have a right to an annual dividend, which is calculated according to the value of their shares at the time of the formation of the contractual group and the likelihood of such dividends without the formation of the group. The board of the subsidiary has to give a report on all transactions, measures and omissions during the past year that result from its membership of the group.[118] The conclusion of the contract between members of the group is encouraged by the ability of the parent company to induce the subsidiary to act against its own interests, thus legitimising the concept of the interests of the group as a whole. However, the concept has been little used. Hopt observes that most groups have chosen 'cohabitation without marriage certificates'.[119] Even where the group relationship has not been formalised, the courts may impose a fiduciary duty on the majority shareholders in a group in favour of minority shareholders in the group or in the group's subsidiaries.

The failure of many groups to formalise their relationship and become 'contractual' groups may be partly because of the burdens imposed on such groups and the reluctance of the courts to interfere in the operation of de facto groups. It may also be the case that insufficient incentives for the formalisation of the relationship were offered. German courts have attempted to distinguish between the two types of group by insisting that in a de facto group the controlling enterprise may not use its influence to induce the subsidiary to enter into disadvantageous transactions unless compensation is given within the same fiscal year. If this does not occur, the parent is liable to its subsidiary unless a diligent and prudent management of an independent company would have acted similarly. As Hopt points out, the practical difficulties of establishing this responsibility and quantifying any damage, particularly in the case of long-term decisions, are formidable.[120]

Partial amelioration of the difficulties

The unsatisfactory reach of the Konzernrecht has led to the extension of the some of the consequences of the contractual group to de facto groups even when they include GmbHs rather than stock companies.[121] Following this decision, a controlling enterprise is liable for the debts of a bankrupt GmbH that it controls if it has managed the business of a GmbH over a long term and in a comprehensive way, unless it can prove that a diligent and prudent director of an independent GmbH would

---

[118] Para. 312 of the Stock Corporation Act, mirrored by Article 7 of the proposed EU 9th Directive.
[119] Hopt, 'Legal Elements and Policy Decisions'.   [120] Ibid., 103.
[121] *Autokran Decision* (1985) 95 BGHZ 330.

have acted similarly. The problem with this incursion into the distinction between contractual and de facto groups and the extension of the statute is that it recreates the uncertain position in which all groups stood before the introduction of the Konzernrecht. It leaves the law in a similar position to that in the UK, where the possibility of the court imposing some link between parent and subsidiary is unpredictable. This must defeat one of the clear purposes of separating the two types of groups.

A proposed EU Directive on company law adopted the concept of the shadow or de facto director,[122] extending it specifically to parent companies, but this approach has not found favour in Germany.

Despite problems experienced in the operation of the German law, the draft proposal for the EU Ninth Directive on company law took a similar route. The proposal would have affected groups of companies and public limited companies controlled by any other undertaking (whether or not that undertaking was itself a company). The proposal was that there should be a harmonised structure for the 'unified management' of groups of such companies and undertakings. Rules would be laid down for the conduct of groups that were not managed on a 'unified' basis. Unless an undertaking that exercised a dominant interest over a public limited company formalised its relationship and provided for some prescribed form of 'unified management', it would be liable for any losses suffered by a dependent company, provided the losses could be traced to the exercise of influence or to action that was contrary to the dependent company's interest.

United States approaches

Blumberg identifies 'a surprisingly wide demonstration of the growing application of enterprise principles in American law', listing piercing the veil jurisprudence, unitary business doctrine, judicial procedure, bankruptcy and statutes of general and specific application to corporate groups.[123] Such a list indicates a more wide-ranging approach than that favoured in the UK, and Blumberg identifies 'an increasing recognition by legislatures, administrative agencies and courts alike of the limitations created by entity law impeding social ordering of the activities of corporate groups . . . [T]he increasingly anachronistic principles of entity law are beginning to yield in many areas to application of entity law.'[124] The jurisprudence made up of cases designated 'traditional

---

[122] Article 9 of the proposed Ninth Directive.
[123] Blumberg, 'The American Law of Corporate Groups', 309.
[124] Ibid., 309–10.

lifting the veil jurisprudence' as described by Blumberg certainly has familiar echoes in UK law: 'American lawyers are faced with hundreds of decisions that are irreconcilable and not entirely comprehensible. Few areas of American law have been so sharply criticised by commentators.'[125] However, Blumberg identifies a change in approach represented by 'liberalised piercing the veil jurisprudence' in which the concern is 'with the economic realities: do the separate corporations actually function as integral parts of the group, or do they operate as independent businesses?'[126] Although, as we have seen, the same enquiry is made of groups in UK jurisprudence, the threshold of proof of an 'entity' operation seems inordinately high and is to be contrasted with the US approach, where the parent's exercise of control over day-to-day decision-making of a subsidiary, for example, is widely recognised as one form of unacceptable exercise of control that will lead to the imposition of liability (or other legal consequences) on the parent. Also important are economic integration, financial interdependence, administrative interdependence, overlapping employment structure and a common group persona.

In bankruptcy law, in particular, there is a movement towards the recognition of enterprise liability, with the Supreme Court setting new rules for evaluating intra-group claims according to fiduciary standards.[127] Further, there are provisions for upsetting preferences to insiders (including related companies)[128] and the emergence of a doctrine of substantive consolidation in which the bankruptcy proceedings of interrelated companies are consolidated and administered jointly.[129]

In a number of ways US law also recognises that dominant shareholders have fiduciary duties towards both the company and other shareholders. Thus, dominant shareholders are distinguished from other shareholders. The latter, as in the UK, are permitted to vote their shares according to their own selfish interests. In *Southern Pacific Co v Bogert*[130] the Supreme Court stated:

The rule of corporation law and of equity invoked is well settled and has been often applied. The majority has the right to control; but when it does so, it occupies a fiduciary relation toward the minority, as much so as the corporation itself or its officers or directors.[131]

---

[125] Ibid., 311.   [126] Ibid., 313.

[127] *Pepper v Litton* (1939) 308 US 295; *Consolidated Rock Products v Du Bois* (1941) 312 US 510; *Comstock v Group of Institutional Investors* (1948) 355 US 211.

[128] Section 547 of the Bankruptcy Code.

[129] 11 USC sect 101(2), 101(28)(B), (E) 547 (1988).

[130] 250 US 483 (1919).

[131] There are echoes here of the UK case *Allen v Gold Reefs of West Africa* [1900] 1 Ch

The principle is widely, if not unanimously, accepted by states. However the implications of the doctrine vary widely. Two states have adopted by legislation a general principle that authorises contracts between parent and subsidiary companies, subject to certain conditions of fairness and procedural requirements for adoption or ratification. In other states a voluminous body of case law is evidence of the different and uncertain effects of the doctrine. Part V of the American Law Institute's *Principles of Corporate Governance: Analysis and Recommendations* deals with the duties of dominating shareholders. The ability to control over 25 per cent of the voting equity would give rise to a presumption of control. It is a strange feature of the definition of control that it focuses solely on control of shareholders' votes. In Tentative Draft No. 5 control is defined as:

the power directly or indirectly, either alone or pursuant to an arrangement or understanding with one or more other persons, to exercise a controlling influence over the management or policies of a business organisation through the ownership of equity interests, through one or more intermediary persons, by contract or otherwise.[132]

Transactions between a dominating shareholder and the corporation are valid if:

(i)   the transaction is fair to the corporation when entered into; or
(ii) the transaction is authorised or ratified by disinterested share-holders, following disclosure concerning the conflict of interest and the transaction, and does not constitute a waste of corporate assets at the time of the shareholder transaction.

If the transaction is ratified according to (ii), the burden of proving unfairness is on the challenging party. Otherwise it is for the dominant shareholder to prove the fairness of the transaction. A transaction is 'fair' if it falls 'within a range of reasonableness'.

Conflicting duties of loyalty owed by directors who sit on boards of parents and subsidiaries are also judged on a 'fairness' scale: 'In the absence of total abstention of an independent negotiating structure, common directors must determine what is best for both parent and subsidiary.'[133] The interrelationship between companies thus focuses principally on the companies as significant shareholders, a clear reflec-

---

656, where Lindley MR stated that the power of a majority is 'subject to those general principles of law and equity which are applicable to all powers conferred on majorities and enabling them to bind minorities'.

[132] Section 1.05.
[133] Commentary on *Weinberger v UOP, Inc* [1983] 457 A.2d 701, discussed by Andre Tunc, 'The Fiduciary Duties of a Dominant Shareholder' in Schmittoff and Wooldridge (eds.), *Groups of Companies*, 60.

tion of the deconstructive tendencies of the contractualist underpinnings. However, there is some recognition of the importance of interrelated companies as a power structure. The difficulty in formulating rules to control the power given to dominant companies in a constituency-based system with a strong corporate veil is evident from the differential application of the rules and the considerable volume of case law.

The divergence in implementation of the various systems across the USA may indicate difficulty in formulating a clear concept of the dominant shareholder's duty; the 'lifting the veil' jurisprudence is still in some confusion. Blumberg's assessment of the American jurisprudence is that it is in the early stages of responding to the challenge posed by the development of groups of companies, particularly in their international and global manifestations.

The advantages and disadvantages of 'group' decision-making

So far as the concept of the benefit of the group as a whole is concerned there are a number of reasons for not developing and/or relying on such a concept. First, it would work with any degree of success only where the group was arranged as a hierarchy, so that there is an identifiable 'holding' company that is used to make strategic policy for the whole group. Many groups are not structured in this way. Otherwise numerous boards will be purporting to make decisions 'in the interests of the group' with no clear grasp of long-term policy. Further, the composition of the group will change from time to time as controls over companies shift, as will the degree of involvement of any of the constituent companies. The identification of the 'benefit of the group' does not solve either of these problems, although it is sometimes thought to do so at least for some purposes.[134]

Secondly, it destroys the separate identities of the companies within the group. It is to be assumed that the group is operated as a clutch of separate companies for particular reasons. Since there is no limit to the size of a company, the reasons for forming separate entities lie elsewhere and may be for legitimate business reasons such as creating a division with managerial autonomy. Eisenberg[135] finds it difficult to identify economic reasons for forming groups but identifies *regulatory*

---

[134] Hadden, 'Corporate Control and Accountability'; Hadden, 'Liabilities in Corporate Groups: A Framework for Effective Regulation' 12 *Il Gruppi Di Societa* (1996).
[135] Eisenberg, 'Corporate Groups', 1.

reasons, including managerial autonomy and national company law requirements.[136]

In these circumstances, to destroy the barriers between entities may remove real business convenience. It is also likely to increase further the distance between management and local issues. Where the focus is still on the interests of the particular company for which the director works and the entities remain separate but linked in the way originally intended, an international or global viewpoint is limited to the global decision makers.[137]

That this perspective is increasingly being lost is evident from analyses of different types of groups for managerial purposes. Hadden notes the increasing internationalisation of management: 'to the currently fashionable divisional structures in which different product lines are operated on a world wide or regional basis which are treated as distinct profit centres.'[138] Teubner and Sugarman have classified different structures as: H-form, typically a holding company monitoring the investments held in wholly or partly owned subsidiaries; U-form, a pyramid of wholly owned and controlled subsidiaries managed in a centralised and integrated way; and M-form, consisting of subsidiaries run semi-autonomously.[139] Pointing out that these complexities are poorly reflected in legal distinctions, Hadden suggests a classification based on the degree of autonomy of parts of the group, but admits that a huge range of categories would result from his classification.[140] The tendency is also evident from works designed to inform the managers or potential managers of international businesses. 'Increasingly, plans call for international experience as a prerequisite for advancement; for example, at Ford, the goal is to have 100 per cent of the top managers with international work experience with the company.'[141] And 'in global corporations, there is no such thing as a universal global manager, but a network of global specialists in four general groups of managers has to work together. Global business (product) managers have the task to further the company's global-scale efficiency and competitiveness.'[142] Further, in a chapter entitled 'Borderless Management', the importance of global decision-making balanced with respon-

---

[136] See also Prentice, 'Some Comments on the Law Relating to Corporate Groups'.
[137] See Holt, *International Management*, ch. 7.
[138] Hadden, 'Regulating Corporate Groups', 356.
[139] G. Teubner and D. Sugarman, 'Unitas Multiplex: Corporate Governance in Group Enterprises' in G. Teubner and D. Sugarman (eds.), *Regulating Corporate Groups in Europe* (Nomos, Baden Baden, 1990).
[140] Hadden, 'An International Perspective on Groups', 358.
[141] Czinkota, Ronkainen and Moffett, *International Business*, 683.
[142] Ibid.

siveness to area markets is plain. The message is that world-wide strategy must be centralised to counter global threats, but that subsidiaries should be left with strategic decisions relating to area markets:

Many multinationals faced with global competitive threats have adopted global strategy formulation, which by definition requires a higher degree of centralisation. What has emerged as a result can be called **coordinated decentralisation**. This means that overall corporate strategy is provided from headquarters, while subsidiaries are free to implement it within the range agreed on in consultation with headquarters.[143]

Holt explains the difference between vertically coordinated hierarchical structures suitable for a domestic market and '[m]anagers of . . . global activities [who] engage in multiple networks of cross-cultural communications, and . . . can only do so within a system of coordinated *interdependent* activities. More specifically, specialisation and vertical coordination imply *dis-integration*, while global coordination implies a move towards "integration".'[144] It will be remembered that the use of integrated decision-making structures formed an important part of the focus of the definition of a global corporation by the Commission of Transnational Corporations. The dangers of this structure in an atmosphere of profit maximisation and a free market approach to regulation are explored in subsequent chapters.

The difficulties of defining a single economic unit

The possible solution to the control of groups offered by the enterprise approach adopted by EU law has to overcome the difficulty of definition of the boundaries of the enterprise. Much tax legislation seeks to consolidate enterprises,[145] but the provisions are complex and lengthy and still remain uncertain of application, even following European attempts to harmonise.[146]

Hadden points to a number of ways in which the difficulty in determining the boundaries of a single economic unit may lead to evasion of regulation.[147] Intra-group transfer may be used to 'massage' individual balance sheets, particularly where constituent companies operate with different accounting periods. Associated companies not technically regarded as subsidiaries for the purposes of consolidation may be used as 'off balance sheet' vehicles to conceal significant transac-

---

[143] Ibid., 724.   [144] Holt, *International Management*, 310.
[145] In the European Union, the Seventh Company Law Directive (OJ 1983 L378/47) and the Eleventh Company Law Directive (branches) (OJ 1989 L395/36) seek to achieve this.
[146] For a brief description see *Farrar's Company Law*, 282.
[147] Hadden, 'Regulating Corporate Groups', 360.

tions. The art of avoidance, however, probably becomes an art form in the 'arcane technical specialism'[148] of transfer pricing. Transnational corporations 'have developed legal structures for transnational corporate capital which take advantage of the ambiguities, disjunctures and loopholes in the international tax system'.[149] An example is that, by 'channelling payments from foreign operating subsidiaries through intermediary conduit companies formed in countries with appropriate tax treaties and accumulating them in offshore holding companies ready for reinvestment, TNCs could minimise their liability to home country taxation on investment returns'.[150] Transfer pricing is an attempt to overcome the impossibility of consolidation taxation of international groups: 'consolidation requires the elimination of all inter-affiliate transactions and the inclusion of the proceeds of sales only once made outside the group; hence it was impossible to consolidate affiliates which were subject to a different tax regime.'[151] The alternative is to devise principles for allocating profits and costs within the group. As can be imagined, the consequent rules fully justify the description 'arcane technical specialism'. Just one example is the attempt to allocate profit on an 'arm's length' principle, i.e. reallocating profit that would have accrued to one constituent company in a group but for the fact that it was not an independent unit. Not only is this extremely difficult in practice but 'the integrated nature of the TNC means that it can economise by sharing many fixed and overhead costs',[152] thus further complicating the allocation of the 'correct' profit. Other methods of allocation such as 'rate of return', 'fractional apportionment' and 'advanced pricing agreements' all have similar failings, leaving considerable freedom for TNCs to minimise their regulatory exposure.

Conclusion

We have thus seen a range of approaches that target the tendency of groups of companies to utilise their legal structure to avoid state regulation. The issue of governance of groups has tended to take second place to individual issues raised by particular concerns. In this way the contractualist approach of the USA has to some extent been overborne by the advance of 'single-issue' legislation, leaving the UK as the starkest example of non-intervention. The concession and communitaire approaches evident in the EU and Germany have taken a different course, with the emphasis much more on the recognition of economic reality.

[148] S. Picciotto, 'Transfer Pricing and the Antinomies of Corporate Regulation' in McCahery, Picciotto and Scott (eds.), *Corporate Control and Accountability*.
[149] Ibid., 387.   [150] Ibid., 394–5.   [151] Ibid., 395.   [152] Ibid., 375

However, the legal responsibilities of those governing transnational groups are largely absent from the agenda and need to be addressed in the light of the legal structures and management structures that have been under consideration in this chapter. That will be done in chapter 6. In the next chapter, the way in which international corporate issues have been addressed by private international law will be examined.

3   Conflict of laws and the governance of groups

This chapter examines a further interface between legal rules, companies and groups of companies. It is particularly important to groups of companies because it attempts to deal with the situation where the facts of a case involve a foreign element, deemed to be 'significant' by a domestic court. Of course, such situations can arise where single companies are concerned but do so more commonly where groups of companies operate across national boundaries. The problems of governance by conflict of laws rule has not been grasped in any systematic way and the rules examined in this chapter resemble a patchwork quilt approach. There is no consistency in the approaches adopted by various different bodies of rule makers, and little consistency in the bodies of rules that have resulted.

The rules of conflicts are informed by two opposing underlying philosophies, which originate in the contractualist, free enterprise approach to corporate law and the concession theory.[1] In this field the opposing theories are the 'place of incorporation' theory, which accords recognition to a company if properly formed according to the rules of the place where it is incorporated regardless of where the company actually operates, and the 'real seat' theory, which will recognise a company only if it has a real connection with the legal system under which it operates. As Drury notes, 'the place of incorporation concept, originated from trading nations, keen to adopt a liberal open approach, with freedom to trade and do business very much in mind. Equally the perceived need for certainty in commercial transactions is capable of having been another mainspring of this approach.'[2] Although the true logic of the concession approach would be to deny recognition to companies outside the jurisdiction that created them on the grounds that a company is 'a creature of the legal system that created it [and] can

---

[1] See ch. 1.
[2] R. Drury, 'The Regulation and Recognition of Foreign Corporations: Responses to the Delaware Syndrome' [1998] *Cambridge Law Journal* 165 at 182.

have no existence outside the ambit of that law',[3] the 'real seat' doctrine retains an element of concession theory by emphasising the right of the state where the company's operations actually occur to regulate and control those activities. As Drury notes, no satisfactory reconciliation of these views has ever been brokered and complications ensue in the field of conflict of laws at several different levels. There is the difficulty of the 'race to the bottom',[4] which expresses the belief that companies will locate in the jurisdiction with the laxest regime,[5] and the countervailing attempts of jurisdictions to enforce local regulations,[6] the difficulties experienced by the European Union in attempting to harmonise company law across the two philosophies[7] and in particular the clash between the two principles of freedom of establishment of companies and non-discrimination on national grounds with the two opposing obstacles of real seat doctrine and national taxation. It is interesting to note that even liberal, free-market-based regimes adopt an element of concession theory where taxation is involved.[8]

What are conflicts rules?

The branch of English law known as the conflict of laws is that part of the law of England which deals with cases having a foreign element.[9]

The main justification for the rules is seen as implementing 'the reasonable and legitimate expectations of the parties to a transaction or occurrence'.[10]

These statements are fundamental to understanding not only why we have conflicts rules but also the methods and tools adopted to solve conflicts problems. At the outset two observations may be made. The

---

[3] Ibid., 176.

[4] B. Cheffins, *Company Law* (Clarendon, Oxford, 1997), esp. ch. 9; F. Easterbrook and D. Fischel, 'Voting in Corporate Law' (1983) 26 *Journal of Law and Economics* 395; D. Fischel, 'The "Race to the Bottom" Revisited: Reflections on Recent Developments in Delaware's Corporations Law' (1982) 76 *New York University Law Review.*

[5] Challenged by some, see previous note; C. Villiers, *European Company Law – Towards Democracy* (Dartmouth, Aldershot, 1998), 17.

[6] In the USA see *Western Airlines v Sobieski* [1968] 191 Cal. App.2d 399, where a Delaware registered corporation that operated mainly in California was required to retain cumulative voting provisions as required by the state of California even though the law of Delaware would have permitted the company to dispense with them. See also Drury, 'Recognition of Corporations', 187.

[7] With the UK and the Netherlands adopting a law of incorporation approach, whereas the real seat theory is adhered to by Belgium, Luxembourg, Greece and Germany.

[8] Case 81/87, *R v HM Treasury, ex p Daily Mail and General Trust plc* [1988] ECR 5483.

[9] A. Dicey and J. Morris, *The Conflict of Laws* (12th edn, London, Stevens, 1993), 3, opening words.

[10] Ibid., 5.

first is that the definitional statement begs a very big question: conflicts rules exist to solve problems only where the foreign element is a *significant* one. What is a significant foreign element? Perhaps one where the reasonable expectations of the parties would lead them to expect a solution other than the straightforward application of domestic law. The tools used to identify these situations and arrive at a legal solution vary widely and, as we will see, some are more effective than others. The tension between certainty of outcome and justice in the individual case is particularly strong in a conflicts situation since the factual situations may vary widely. It is perhaps for this reason that, where the assistance of international instruments is sought, the factual situations covered are defined narrowly so that the situations vary as little as possible.

Conflicts tools

International conventions

International conventions play an increasingly important role in the attempts to find solutions to conflicts problems. The existence of such conventions is complicated by the necessity for statutes to implement the conventions in states that, like the United Kingdom, adhere to a dualist concept; i.e. international treaties do not have the force of law merely by reason of their ratification by the government. Implementing legislation is required.[11] Legislative techniques for giving the force of law to such conventions as well as principles of interpretation of the implementing legislation are all important in determining the effectiveness of the international convention as a conflicts tool.

Two types of convention

Conventions fall into two broad categories: those that seek to lead to the application of uniform conflict of laws rules in the contracting states and those that attempt to harmonise jurisdictional rules without prejudice to the subsequent application of a choice of law rule by the contracting state. In each case the method of implementation and the principles of interpretation of the implementing legislation may prove vital in determining the effectiveness of the convention.

European Union tools

The European Union (EU) may choose to proceed by convention when addressing conflict of laws problems. An example is the European

---

[11] *J.H. Rayner (Mincing Lane) Ltd v Department of Trade and Industry* [1990] 2 AC 418, 477, 500.

Convention on Insolvency Proceedings.[12] However, there is a general consensus that the European Union has become greater than the sum of all its parts and the founding treaties have a different significance compared with other international treaties. A clear difference is the way in which the doctrine of direct effect has been accepted as affecting the rights of individual citizens despite (and indeed because of) the lack of implementing legislation in a particular sphere. Thus, the EU tools of harmonisation and approximation by treaty articles, by regulations and by directives as interpreted by the European Court of Justice and applied by national courts are of significance because they may determine whether or not the law on a particular issue has become the same in all member states, thus eliminating a conflict of laws problem, or may provide insights into the legitimate expectations of the parties by reference to the underlying aims of the EC Treaty.[13]

Direct effect

Article 249 of the EC Treaty (old Article 189) provides that the EU may legislate by using a variety of measures. These are regulations, directives and decisions, as well as recommendations and opinions, which are 'soft law' instruments that do not have directly binding results. In order to ensure that EU law has the widest possible effect within the EU, the European Court of Justice (ECJ) developed twin doctrines of the supremacy of EU law and direct effect. The combined doctrines had the result that any measure held to be directly effective was apt to affect the rights of individual citizens, despite the fact that it was the result of the application of a treaty article in a dualist state,[14] and later despite the fact that it was the application of a directive that by Article 249 was 'addressed' to the member states but where member states were to choose the 'form and method' of implementation. The direct effect of treaty articles has not met with serious challenge. If, therefore, a treaty article is found to be sufficiently clear, precise and unconditional it will be directly applied in a member state and will affect the rights of individuals regardless of the status of the defendant. Regulations are, by Article 249, 'directly applicable' into the laws of the member states, so will equally affect individual rights. The status of directives is more equivocal. Originally they were held to be of direct effect on the same basis as treaty articles. However,

[12] See the Seventh Report of the House of Lords Select Committee on the European Communities; HL paper 59 (1996) – as yet not in force owing to the UK refusal to ratify as a result of petulance concerning the 'beef war'.
[13] Case 294/83, *Parti Ecologiste 'Les Verts' v European Parliament* [1986] ECR 1339, esp. A.-G. Mancini: 'The obligation to observe the law takes precedence over the strict terms of the written law', 1350.
[14] Case 41/74, *Van Duyn v Home Office* [1974] ECR 1337.

the wording of Article 249 does not really sustain this approach and in *Cohn-Bendit v Ministre de l'Intérieure* the French Conseil d'Etat emphasised the role of the member states in determining the form in which obligations imposed by directives would appear in the internal law of those states.[15] It followed that, 'whatever the detail that they contain for the eyes of the member states, directives may not be invoked by the nationals of such States in support of an action brought against an individual administrative act'.[16]

Consequently the ECJ reformulated its explanation of the reasoning behind the direct effect doctrine. It used what is in effect an estoppel base. In *Pubblico Ministero v Ratti*, Advocate-General Reishl formulated the doctrine thus:

Member States which do not comply with their obligations under the directive are unable to rely on provisions of the internal legal order which are illegal from the point of view of Community law, so that individuals become entitled to rely on the directive as against the defaulting state and acquire rights thereunder which the national courts must protect.[17]

From this justification it follows that an individual can rely on a directive only when he or she is asserting a right against a defaulting member state. Directives therefore have only 'vertical' direct effect, i.e. they have effect as between an individual and a member state (or an arm of the state).[18] They do not have 'horizontal' direct effect, i.e. effect between individuals unconnected with the state.[19] This leads to the anomaly that the rights that an individual can assert under this doctrine, for example as an employee, differ according to whether the defendant employer happens to be a public body (part of the state) or a private body. This lacuna was partially cured by the decision in *Francovich v Italian Republic*[20] and subsequent case law. The *Francovich* case was brought against the Italian state by plaintiffs alleging a failure to implement the Employment Protection Directive.[21] According to Article 11 of the directive, member states were bound to establish a guarantee fund that would pay compensation to workers whose firms had gone into liquidation owing them wages. The wages due were to be calculated according to various formulae set out in the directive. Italy had failed to implement the directive by the due date. A compensation claim was

---

[15] [1980] 1 CMLR 543.   [16] Ibid., 563.
[17] [1979] ECR 1629 at 1640.
[18] Case 188/89, *Foster v British Gas plc* [1990] IRLR 353.
[19] Case 152/84, *Marshall v Southampton and South West Hants Area Health Authority* [1986] ECR 723.
[20] Joined Cases C-6 & 9/90, *Francovich and Boniface v Italian Republic* [1993] 2 CMLR 66.
[21] Council Directive 80/987; OJ 1980 L283/23.

brought by the plaintiffs in Italy and referred to the ECJ by way of Article 177. The ECJ held that in these circumstances the plaintiffs were entitled to compensation from the state. Note that the doctrine of direct effect of directives would not have availed the plaintiffs because the employer in question was a private employer.[22]

It is thus arguable that the line of cases stemming from *Francovich* cures some of the anomalies created by the exclusively vertical direct effect of directives. Provided the relevant conditions are fulfilled, individuals will be able to claim compensation from the state even though they are immediately linked only with another private individual. So far as the conflict of laws is concerned, the doctrine of direct effect should ensure a uniform interpretation of EU rules in all member states. This would remove conflicts between member states' rules and is of particular importance so far as directives are concerned because they were originally envisaged as not requiring uniform implementation measures in each member state. The doctrine of direct effect overcomes this possible creation of further conflicts between national laws. It should be noted that direct effect cannot operate until the expiry of the time limit for implementation of the relevant EU provisions.

Interpretative tools (indirect effect)

In *Marleasing SA v La Comerciale Internacional de Alimentacion SA*[23] the ECJ held that the obligations imposed on member states and national courts under Article 5 of the EC Treaty to take all appropriate measures to ensure implementation of directives meant that, 'in applying national law, whether the provisions in question were adopted before or after the directive, the national court called upon to interpret it is required to do so, so far as possible, in the light of the wording and purpose of the directive in order to achieve the result preferred by the latter'.[24]

As a consequence the Spanish court was required to disapply by interpretative means a national provision relating to the nullity of corporations in order to comply with the Second EC Company Law Directive.[25] The obligation to interpret national law in conformity with EU law is independent of any time limit, unlike the operation of the

---

[22] The ECJ held that there were other reasons why the directive would not have been directly effective.

[23] Case 106/89 [1992] 1 CMLR 305.

[24] *Marleasing* is used by way of example because it concerned the interpretation of company law provisions. The duty to interpret in accordance with EC law was first laid down in *Von Colson v Land Nordrhein-Westfalen*, Case 14/83 [1984] ECR 1891, where the court held that implementing legislation must be interpreted by national courts in the light of the wording and purpose of the relevant directives.

[25] EC Council Directive 68/151 of 9 March 1968, OJ 65/8.

doctrine of direct effect.[26] Where such an interpretation is not possible[27] and the *Francovich* conditions are satisfied, the individual may claim against the state for faulty implementation.[28] In such circumstances the member state would be in default of its treaty obligations and should change the laws.

Disapplying national law

Any attempt to apply rules that are in conflict with EU law should be met by refusal by the national courts.[29] A UK example of this was *R v Secretary of State for Transport, ex parte Factortame*.[30] The ECJ determined that:

Community law must be interpreted as meaning that a national court which, in a case before it concerning Community law, considers that the sole obstacle which prevents it from granting interim relief is a rule of national law must set aside that rule.[31]

Article 234 (ex 177) references

By Article 234 of the EC Treaty any doubt as to whether there is a conflict between EU law and national law should be the subject of a reference by the national court to the ECJ for definitive guidance. The clash must, of course, be one that is legally significant in the resolution of the dispute between the parties. The terms of Article 234 oblige a court of last resort to make a reference, but permit a lower court a discretion whether or not to do so, save that the ECJ has ruled that a lower court must refer where it has doubts about the validity of a relevant EU measure.[32] In *CILFIT* the ECJ emphasised the need to ensure uniform interpretation of EC law:

[The] obligation to refer a matter to the Court of Justice is based on co-operation, established with a view to ensuring the proper application and uniform interpretation of Community law in all Member States, between national courts, in their capacity as courts responsible for the application of Community law, and the Court of Justice. More particularly, the third paragraph [the obligation of a court of last resort to refer] of Article 177 seeks to

---

[26] Case 80/86, *Officier van Justitie v Kolpinghuis Nijmegan* [1987] ECR 3969.
[27] For a decision stretching the duty to interpret, see *Litster v Forth Dry Dock & Engineering Co Ltd* [1990] 1 AC 546.
[28] Case 334/92, *T. Wagner Miret v Fondo De Granatia Salarial* [1993] ECR I-6911.
[29] Case 106/777, *Aministrazione delle Finanze dello Stato v Simmenthal* [1978] ECR 629 at 624.
[30] [1989] 2 CMLR 353, (QBD) [1990] 2 AC 85 (HL), Case C-213/89 [1990] ECR 1-2433.
[31] Case C-213/89, *R v Secretary of State for Transport, ex p Factortame* (No 2) [1990] ECR 1-2433 [1990] 3 CMLR 1.
[32] Case 314/85, *Foto-Frost v Hauptzollant Lubeck-Ost* [1987] ECR 4199.

prevent the occurrence within the Community of divergences in judicial decisions on questions of Community law.[33]

In order to ensure this uniformity the ECJ limited the ability of courts of last resort to refuse a reference to situations where (a) the point was irrelevant, or (b) the point had already been decided by the ECJ, or (c) the application of EU law is so obvious that there is no room for reasonable doubt. This doctrine of 'Acte Claire' however was severely restricted by the requirement that:

the correct application of Community law may be so obvious as to leave no scope for any reasonable doubt as to the manner in which the question raised is to be resolved. Before it comes to the conclusion that such is the case, the national court or tribunal must be convinced that the matter is equally obvious to the courts of the other Member States and the Court of Justice.[34]

A national court must consider the particular features of EU law, the EU context and the particular problem of different language versions of the law, all of them equally authentic. In view of these formidable restrictions it may be seen that, in the eyes of the ECJ, the doctrine is a very narrow one indeed in order to prevent conflicts problems concerning the interpretation of EU law arising.

Interpretation of soft law

The duty of national courts to interpret domestic law so as to reflect EU values extends to 'soft law' provisions such as recommendations and opinions. Article 249 provides that these instruments 'shall have no binding force'. However, the ECJ has held that they may give rise to legitimate expectations. If this is the case, which is most likely to arise where the 'soft law' seeks to clarify or explain existing EU measures, the ECJ has held[35] that national courts should take them into account in assisting in the interpretation of EU measures or of national rules that seek to implement EU measures.[36] All these tools tend to reduce conflicts between the national laws of the member states.

---

[33] Case 283/81, *CILFIT v Ministerio della Sanita* [1982] ECR 3415 at 3428. See also *Bulmer v Bollinger* [1974] 2 All ER 1266; *R v International Stock Exchange of the United Kingdom and the Republic of Ireland ex p Elsa* [1993] 1 All ER 420.

[34] Case 283/81, *CILFIT*, 3430.

[35] Case 322/88, *Grimaldi v Fond des Maladies Professionelles* [1989] ECR 4407; and see *Wadman v Farrer Partnership* [1993] IRLR 374, where an Employment Appeal Tribunal referred to the Commission Recommendation and Code of Practice on Sexual Harassment in order to form a view as to whether particular conduct fell within the UK Sex Discrimination Act 1975.

[36] For an analysis of the extent of this duty see J. Dine and B. Watt, 'Hardening the Soft Law' [1994] *European Law Review* 46.

Company law harmonisation
Although there has been an extensive harmonisation programme that
affects company law throughout the European Union,[37] there are many
doubts about its effectiveness. Fundamental differences stemming from
the differences between those member states (especially the UK) that
espouse a contractual-based doctrine of company law, excluding
workers from consideration as part of the company, and jurisdictions
with a wider, inclusive philosophy have led to enormous difficulties in
creating supra-national instruments or even permitting companies to
move across borders within the Union.

Uniform supra-national instruments
The harmonisation programme in its most ambitious phase sought to
introduce a comprehensive company law that would govern all public
companies. The Fifth EC Directive would have applied uniformly to all
public companies in the EU. The failure of this measure has limited the
reach of the harmonisation programme severely.[38] Greater success was
achieved in the introduction of the European Economic Interest
Grouping (EEIG),[39] but this instrument is severely limited by the
restriction that prevents it from pursuing profit as a primary aim. The
Commission still has the aim of introducing a European Company
Statute, which will be an optional instrument for business, although
negotiations on the difficult issue of worker participation are still
continuing. As negotiations have progressed on all these measures it has
become clear that only limited agreement between the member states
can be expected, with the result that each measure has become progres-
sively less comprehensive, relying more and more on references to the
individual domestic laws of the member states to fill gaps where no
agreement is possible.

The EEIG Regulation creates a new instrument for business that may
be formed by persons from at least two member states. It must not have
as its primary purpose the making of profits, and it may employ only 500
employees. When it was a proposal it was envisaged that one of the
purposes for which it would be most used would be joint research and
development, but it is being utilised for a wide variety of purposes.[40]

---

[37] For more detail see J. Dine and P. Hughes, *EC Company Law* (Jordans, Bristol,
looseleaf, 1991), and V. Edwards, *EC Company Law* (OUP, 1998).
[38] See J. Dine and J. J. du Plessis, 'The Fate of the Fifth Directive: Accommodation
instead of Harmonisation?' [1997] *Journal of Business Law* 23.
[39] OJ 1985 L199/1. See M. Anderson, *European Economic Interest Groupings* (Butterworth,
London, 1980); S. Israel, 'The EEIG – A Major Step forward for Community Law'
(1987) 8 *Company Lawyer* 14.
[40] Anderson, *European Economic Interest Groupings*, 9.

The European Company Statute would create a new business organisation, which will be governed partly by the European law contained in the Statute and partly by the law of the member state in which it registers. It will create a new option for businesses – no company need convert into a European company, nor would the proposal require any alteration to current company law, save to add a European company as an extra choice for businesses.

This type of company would also be formed by persons from more than one member state, but there is no restriction on its profit-making capacity, or on the number of employees it may have. All European companies would, however, be obliged to have a system of worker involvement in the important decisions made by the company. This requirement is contained in a draft directive linked to the Regulation which contains the company's structural provisions. The current proposals, based on the report of the Davignon group of experts, bear a close resemblance to the European Works Council Directive, but agreement has still not been reached.

Harmonising directives

The Fourth Directive[41] contains detailed rules regarding the drawing up of the accounts of individual companies. Its importance to groups lies in the extension of similar provisions to consolidated accounts of groups of companies by the Seventh Directive.[42] Both the directives have been implemented in all member states, although there is increasing doubt as to whether the 'true and fair' provisions in particular bear the same meaning in different member states. The ECJ has had an opportunity to set out some general principles in *Tomberger v Gebruder von der Wettern GmbH*.[43]

Also of relevance to companies operating internationally is the Eleventh Directive on the accounting disclosure requirements of branches of certain types of company.[44] This directive deals with disclosures to be made in one member state by branches of companies registered in another member state or a non-EU country (in UK terms, an 'overseas company').[45] The directive recognises that a branch does not have a legal personality of its own, and it would therefore require disclosure of information concerning the company of which the branch is part, including its accounts, drawn up in accordance with the Fourth and

---

[41] OJ 1978 L222/11.   [42] OJ 1983 L193/1.
[43] Case C-234/94 [1996] 2 BCLC 457.
[44] Directive 89/666/EEC; OJ 1989 L124/8.
[45] Seen by Drury as a mechanism for protection against the worst possibilities of the Delaware syndrome; Drury, 'Recognition of Corporations', 191.

Seventh Directives, i.e. in a manner consonant with sections 228 to 230 of the Companies Act 1985, whereby company accounts must give a true and fair view of the state of affairs within that company or group of companies.[46]

The Fifth Directive remains a proposal with a very uncertain future. The proposal has caused a great deal of controversy. If the original proposal had become law, the structure of all public companies in the EU would have had to be changed so that there would be two boards of directors: an executive board and a supervisory board. That proposal has now been modified so that there can be a single board. Further controversy has been caused by the employee participation provisions. Originally, employee participation by appointment to the board was the only model in the proposed directive. This has subsequently been modified, and employee participation can also be by way of informed consultation or by having the power of veto in certain limited circumstances over those appointed to the board.[47]

There is, nevertheless, considerable opposition to this measure, not least from the UK. Adhering to a contractualist viewpoint, the position of the UK delegation is that employee participation provisions are irrelevant to company law. This position is hard for Dutch and German delegations to understand, because the division between company law and labour law is not clear-cut in those countries.

The proposed Tenth Directive[48] concerns cross-border mergers and is progressing no further because fears have been expressed that a cross-border merger could be a way of escaping from worker participation provisions. The draft proposal for a Ninth Directive, which was never formally adopted by the Commission,[49] was suggested in 1984. It was concerned with the conduct of groups of companies. As explained in chapter 2, it was based on a German model that insists on parent companies taking some responsibility for the activities of subsidiaries. There is no immediate prospect of work on this project resuming.

The European Works Council Directive[50] requires the establishment of a European Works Council in EU-scale undertakings for the purpose of informing and consulting employees.[51] As explained in chapter 6, it is a directive that may have a profound effect on the governance of groups of companies.

---

[46] This directive has been implemented in the UK by the Overseas Companies and Credit Financial Institutions (Branch Disclosure) Regulations 1992.
[47] See Villiers, *European Company Law*, 180 et seq.
[48] OJ 1985 C23 28/11.   [49] See also ch. 2.
[50] Directive 94/45/EC (OJ L254/64 of 30 September 1994).
[51] See Dine and Hughes, *EC Company Law*; B. Bercusson, *European Labour Law* (Butterworth, London, 1996); and ch. 6.

One initiative that would have an immediate effect on the way in which companies and groups operate in Europe is the proposal for a Fourteenth European Parliament and Council Directive on the Transfer of the Registered Office or de Facto Head Office of a Company from One Member State to Another with a Change in Applicable Law.[52] This aims to permit companies to transfer their registration or 'de facto head office' from one member state of the European Union to another. The first comment to make is that the major impediment to such a transfer is the taxation that may be incurred,[53] and the proposal does nothing to change that aspect of transfer. At present, non-resident companies from other member states can claim to be treated on an equal footing with domestic companies in all respects.[54]

The proposal seeks to permit the movement of either the registered office or the registered office plus place of central administration to another member state without a change in legal personality but with a change of applicable law. A serious derogation appears in Article 11(2) in that a member state may refuse to register a company if its central administration is not situated in that member state. This may in effect prevent free movement of just the registered office. Several serious and obvious problems arise and are ineffectively dealt with by this draft. The problems are interrelated but also distinct.

The protection of creditors is attempted by the provision that creditors (including public body creditors) may demand 'adequate security'. The exercise of rights so arising is to be governed by the law applicable to the company before its transfer (Art. 8). This does not appear to be workable. First, who is to determine what is adequate? Secondly, security rights are in effect attempts to guarantee priority of payment. If a company moves to another member state and creates other secure creditors, there is nothing to prevent the clash of priorities that will then arise because the new creditors' rights will be governed by the law of the new member state and may (and probably will) destroy the rights of the creditors left behind in the previous jurisdiction. Further, nothing addresses the possibility of a jurisdiction clause inserted into such a 'security' or a clause seeking to prevent a company from creating further securities in its new jurisdiction. What law will govern the validity of such clauses?

---

[52] 1997 XV/6002/97.

[53] See Case 81/87, *R v HM Treasury and Inland Revenue Comrs, ex p Daily Mail and General Trust plc* [1988] ECR 5483.

[54] See Case C33091, *R v IRC ex p Commerzbank* [1993] ECR 1–4017. See also *Centros Ltd v Erhverus – og Selskabsstyrelsen*, ECJ, judgment of 9 March 1999; and see discussion on freedom of establishment below.

Employee rights are minimal. Unless workers have a right to vote in a general meeting, their only right will be to examine the report by the management team (Art. 5), which admittedly will have to contain worker participation proposals, but only where employees are represented on the governing body of the company prior to the proposed transfer (Art. 4(1)(c)). This is unlikely to be an acceptable level of worker participation in the transfer for many member states and also begs the question of the law governing the employment rights of the workers: are their participation rights company law rights that will change with the law of registration of the company? The proposal seems to assume so in Article 4(1), but it could be argued that existing employment contracts do not so change, so that a difficult question might be the extent to which any participation and consultation right is embedded in the contract of employment. It is unlikely that all member states will give the same answer to that question.

Shareholders' rights are dealt with by Article 6, which gives the right to decide on the transfer to the general meeting by a two-thirds vote or, if at least half the company's capital is represented, by a simple majority. This attitude takes a very simplistic view of company structures. The rights of different classes of shareholders may vary widely. There is no provision for class votes. Many member states do not view a company as merely a creature of its shareholders; there is no provision for either creditors or employees to have a say in the actual decision to transfer, save for the ability of creditors to demand adequate security. Article 7 permits member states to enact measures designed to protect minority shareholders, but other constituents have no similar mention.

In previous paragraphs a number of problems of determining the applicable law have arisen. Perhaps the most significant other issue that is ignored by the proposal is the law governing the relationship between parent and subsidiary companies when one or the other changes jurisdiction. A further hole in the proposal is the lack of any method by which a person proposing to lend to a company could tell what liabilities are outstanding in another jurisdiction. There is nothing approaching a European Register of company charges.

Given the lack of protection for employees, creditors and, to a lesser extent, shareholders, either this measure will prompt member states to take 'poison pill' measures in order to prevent companies leaving (such as taxation) or a Delaware effect will be created whereby companies will forum shop to find the least regulated environment. This has had some benefits in the USA where corporate law in Delaware is an industry, but there are many who regard the relocation of companies in this way as 'a

race to the bottom'.[55] It is noteworthy that member states are permitted
to prevent a new registration when company administration and registration are separate, but they cannot prevent the migration of a registered office alone from their own jurisdiction.

The relationship between this proposal and the proposed European
Company (otherwise known as the Societas Europa, or SE) is very
unclear. The whole purpose of the SE is to function across borders, so
that the only additional function fulfilled by the draft Fourteenth
Directive is to permit companies to re-establish in another member state
with no European-tier rules to trouble them or any requirement for a
cross-border operation prior to the change in jurisdiction. The ability of
public companies to change into SEs was deliberately omitted from this
draft of the SE, which seems a curious omission. Further, if the Fourteenth Directive could truly work it seems to throw doubt on the
necessity for an SE, because smooth transition between member states
would be assured and the principle of subsidiarity would make it
unnecessary to have European-level legislation. A strange divergence
between the two documents is the possibility under the draft Fourteenth
Directive that member state public companies would be able to have
head office and registration in different member states, whereas SEs are
required to have their head office and registered office in the same
member state.

The Commission consultation on company law

Further harmonisation awaits the outcome of the consultation process
undertaken by the European Commission. In 1995, Ernst and Young
were asked by the Commission to study the regulations governing public
limited companies in the European Union. The report was published in
December 1995.[56] As a result of the report, the Commission undertook
consultation to try to pinpoint which, if any, of the company law
directives could be simplified and whether other changes could be
made.

The Ernst and Young report observes that regulations based on the
corporate form alone are irrelevant – family or single shareholder public
limited companies (plcs) are not uncommon because of advantageous
tax or social security regimes. It identifies three types of public
company: (i) 'open' plcs that are listed or whose shares are deemed to be
'widely held' – these are almost always large; (ii) 'closed' plcs that are

---

[55] See ch. 5 for a full consideration of the issue of relocation of companies to avoid
regulation.
[56] 'The Simplification of the Operating Regulations for Public Limited Companies in the
European Union' (European Commission, 1995).

large; and (iii) 'closed' plcs that are small. 'Closed' was simply taken to mean that there were a small number of shareholders. The report concludes that regulations devised for closed plcs should be extended to private companies because of their economic similarity.

The report finds that the internationalisation of business has caused a convergence in corporate management structures, although the detailed rules remain very divergent. The authors believe that identified common principles should be embedded in a directive but with some provisions 'transplanted' into the national systems, either under a law or within the framework of a national best practice code. They are less than clear about the balance between directive provisions and the role of national law. It would appear that the report is recognising a role for national law because the provisions of a directive would also need to be implemented. However, the report believes in directive rules where some form of consensus can be found. Consensus is apparent for open companies on:

- proportionality between voting rights and subscribed capital (mysteriously one of the articles removed from the SE provisions in its latest amendment);
- the elimination of multiple voting rights and approval clauses or special majorities in the articles of association.

It is felt that all protection for outsiders that applies to open companies must also apply to large closed companies, but protection for shareholders should be more flexible.

The report finds that the strongest need for simplification is felt by small closed plcs, in particular the wish for a single manager and the avoidance of excessive formalities. The report concludes that simplification can be achieved if there is an increase in the quantity and particularly the quality and accessibility of publicly available information. This could be accomplished by the use of modern communication techniques.

Improvement in tax harmonisation is called for, but on the major issue of freedom of establishment the report takes the line that co-determination issues would affect only 1 per cent of companies in the EU if the directive was restricted to companies with over 500 employees. It suggests that different rules should be drafted to cover such companies and the issue should not be addressed for smaller companies, thus permitting much quicker progress on the integration of rules for smaller companies.

The governance of groups of companies as a separate issue is addressed only marginally, so it is fair to conclude that little progress in creating legislative structures for groups of companies is envisaged by the EU in the foreseeable future.

Freedom of movement of companies

The application by the European Court of Justice of the principles enshrined in Articles 43 and 48 (ex 52 and 58) of the EC Treaty regarding the free movement of companies has been instrumental in preventing discrimination against companies.[57] This has particular repercussions for the connecting factors used to determine company law issues. In particular, it raises the issue of the legality of the residence connecting factor, which is often used for tax purposes. Because of this, the issues are discussed in the context of the residence of a corporation (see below).

UK domestic tools

Characterisation

English rules of conflicts are based on a system in which a factual problem is assigned to a legal category. Each legal category has certain factors that, if foreign, are considered to require the court to consider whether or not a foreign system of law would be more appropriately applied to find a substantive solution. It is the evaluation of the weight and significance of these connecting factors that will lead a court to the determination of the correct 'choice of law' to govern the issue. An example is *Re Bonacina*[58] where, despite the fact that an Italian agreement was entered into without the consideration that would have been necessary to create a binding contract under English law, the correct characterisation was held to be contract, which led to the connecting factor of the place with which the contract was most closely connected. That place was Italy, where the relevant law provided that the agreement was valid and enforceable. In a complex case involving the aftermath of the Maxwell affair, Staughton LJ explained the steps involved in finding a solution:

First it is necessary to characterise the issue that is before the court. Is it for example about the formal validity of a marriage? Or intestate succession to moveable property? Or interpretation of a contract? The second stage is to select the rule of conflict of laws which lays down a connecting factor for the issue in question. Thus the formal validity of a marriage is to be determined, for the most part, by the law of the place where it is celebrated . . . Thirdly, it is

[57] See generally J. Wouters and H. Sneider (eds.), *Current Issues in Cross-Border Establishment of Companies in the European Union* (Kluwer, London, 1995).
[58] [1912] 2 Ch 394.

necessary to identify the system of law which is tied by the connecting factor found in stage two to the issue characterised in stage one.[59]

Citing Dicey, Staughton LJ concluded that the court should proceed by considering the 'rationale of the English conflict rule and the purpose of the substantive law to be characterised'.[60] This seems like an excellent guide but in cases such as the instant one the rationales of the two conflicting characterisations were almost equally balanced. The Court of Appeal was faced with a situation in which a number of share transfers had been effected without the knowledge of the owner, including transactions where the shares had been used as security for loans. The claimants included the original owners and those claiming under the securities apparently created by using the shares as security. The transactions had mostly taken place in New York. At first instance the court held that the issue was one of the priority of competing claims to the shares and held that this should be governed by the law of the place where the transactions took place. There was no reference to this being an issue connected to a company. The Court of Appeal affirmed the decision but on the grounds that the issue was whether or not there was an available defence of *bona fide* purchase. Most importantly, however, it determined that the competing claims related to *shares*, so that the correct characterisation was that this was an issue relating to the *situs* of the shares, which it held to be the law of the place of incorporation. The possible characterisations were: issues of rights to property (*lex situs*), chattels (*lex situs*), negotiable instruments (*forum* law or law of place of negotiation to determine negotiability, *lex situs* to determine ownership), choses in action (law of contract between assignor and assignee generally, but law of right to which assignment relates to determine assignability, or *lex situs*).

The Court of Appeal rejected the House of Lords' finding in *Colonial Bank v Cady and Williams*,[61] where the plaintiffs were the executors of a deceased holder of shares in an American company. The executors signed blank transfers to entitle them to have the shares registered in their names. They handed the certificates to their brokers, who fraudulently deposited them with the defendant banks as security for money due from the brokers. American law would have held that the banks obtained good title. The House of Lords, 'hardly surprisingly',[62] held that the law of England was applicable as the law of the place where the transactions took place. Only the issue of whether or not an effective transfer of shares would constitutionally entitle a shareholder to be

[59] *Macmillan Inc v Bishopsgate Investment Trust Plc and others* [1996] 1 WLR 387.
[60] Ibid., 44.   [61] (1890) 15 App Cas 267.
[62] Per Staughton LJ in the *Macmillan* case, 403.

registered would be referred to the law of the place of incorporation. The case illustrates vividly the difficulty of identifying the relevance of the connection with the company when property transactions are involved. There is no easy answer to identifying a proper connecting factor when the parties to the case have a connection with the company only because of the fortuitous fact that the property in which they are dealing happens to be shares. The lesson of the *Macmillan* case seems to be that the device of characterisation leaves the issue open for the court to arrive at the solution it prefers. However just this may be in the individual case, it means that forecasting a likely result is exceptionally difficult.

Issues in company law conflicts

Traditionally, conflicts questions relating to companies have been classified as relating to the domicile and residence, status, capacity and internal management, and insolvency of companies. These classifications tend to disguise the complexity of the issues involved because they have to some extent (particularly with regard to the domicile and residence of corporations) been 'read across' from the rules applicable to individuals. The time is overdue when the classifications should reflect more accurately the nature of corporate issues that arise. The following categories are suggested.

Recognition

One issue that arises in this context is the recognition of a body formed under a foreign law. This is really a two-part issue since the recognition of the artificial entity as such inevitably leads to a consideration of the legal consequences that attach to that recognition, for example whether or not limited liability will attach to the members of the company.[63]

Free movement

The question here is whether a company can move from one jurisdiction to another and continue to function without a change in its legal form. Although akin to matters of recognition, the problem involves other

---

[63] This was extensively discussed in *J.H. Rayner (Mincing Lane) Ltd v Department of Trade and Industry* [1990] 2 AC 418. See also *Associated Shipping Services v Department of Private Affairs of H.H. Sheikh Zayed Bin Sultan Al-Nahayan, Financial Times*, 31 July 1990 (CA) and *Bumper Development Corpn v Commissioner of Police for the Metropolis* [1991] 1 WLR 1362 (CA), and see Drury, 'Recognition of Corporations', 165.

aspects. In the context of the European Union, it involves issues of a conflict between the general principles of EU law, which provide for the free movement of individuals (including legal individuals) backed by rules against non-discrimination on the grounds of nationality, and domestic rules, which obstruct free movement either by creating corporate law obstacles (such as the doctrine of *siège réel*, whereby the seat of a company is regarded as the place where the company is registered *and* where its head office is situated) or by other non-corporate rules such as taxation restrictions.[64]

Equivalence of treatment of constituencies

With continuing globalisation of business, shareholders, employees and managers may be domiciled, resident and working in different jurisdictions and in places far removed from the place of registration of the company and/or its head office. One issue that has not been sufficiently addressed is to what extent the varying rights of the constituencies that make up corporations are governed by company law and to what extent they are contractual or founded in tort law, so that the existence of the corporation as one party to the contract or perpetrator of the tort pales into insignificance. One of the reasons for this difficulty is the uncertain nature of the rights held by parties who are involved in corporate activities. Shareholder rights are more than merely contractual; they have constitutional implications, and the exercise of the apparent rights can be constrained in a number of ways by equitable doctrines. Similarly, employment rights have contractual elements but may also have constitutional implications, for example where rights of information, consultation and representation of employees are concerned. Problems arising from the very different ways in which corporations are viewed in different jurisdictions have caused immense complications in the attempts by the EU to solve conflicts questions by harmonisation measures.

Insolvency

The issue of rights in insolvencies is perhaps one of the most intractable problems with which the conflicts of law has to deal.[65] Different treatment of creditors in an insolvency in different jurisdictions is one of

---

[64] Case 81/1987, *R v HM Treasury, ex p Daily Mail and General Trust Plc* [1988] ECR 5483.

[65] For conflicts matters relating to insolvency see A. Boyle and R. Sykes (eds.), *Gore-Brown on Companies* (44th edn, Jordans, Bristol, looseleaf), ch. 37.

the most significant barriers to the free movement of companies because creditors will be extremely wary of the desire of a corporation to move to a different jurisdiction if this means that they will lose any security over the assets of that company that they might otherwise hold. The problem is really threefold: creditors will dislike a change of jurisdiction if it means litigation in a foreign court; any change of jurisdiction will mean that a company will have access to different instruments to create secured creditors and a creditor will not necessarily have access to information about the foreign legal instrument; the foreign system of priorities may demote existing secured creditors to a less secure position. The cumulation of problems raised by the above issues may be illustrated by the current attempts to solve them in the EU.

The current English law

Jurisdiction

A company registered under the Companies Act 1985 or any other relevant UK statute is amenable to the jurisdiction of the relevant UK courts.[66] A distinction is now drawn between a company incorporated outside the UK and Gibraltar that has a branch in Great Britain and a foreign corporation that establishes a place of business in Great Britain. The former is required to file with the Registrar of Companies a return containing particulars of the names and addresses of persons resident in Great Britain authorised to accept process on the company's behalf in respect of the business of that branch.[67] The latter type of company, i.e. one that has only a place of business in the UK, is required by section 691(1)(b)(ii) to file with the Registrar of Companies the name and address of a person resident in Great Britain authorised to accept service of process on behalf of the company. By section 695(2), if a company defaults on this obligation or if the person named dies or ceases to reside in Great Britain or refuses to accept service or for any other reason cannot be served, process may be served by leaving it at or sending it to any place of business established by the company in Great Britain.[68]

---

[66] Section 725 of the Companies Act 1985.

[67] SI 1992 No 3179, Companies Act 1985, section 609A and Sched 21A, para. 3(e). But process can be served in respect of business carried on both by the branch and by an overseas eminence of the company: *Saab and Another v Saudi American Bank* [1998] *Times Law Report*, 11 March.

[68] The process must be addressed to the person named and not to the company: *Boocock v Hilton International Co* [1993] 1 WLR 1065, but the irregularity may not be fatal, in that case cured by the CA under RSC Ord 2 r 1.

'Place of business' has a wide definition. The place of business must be fixed and definite,[69] and the activity must have been carried on for sufficient time for it to be characterised as a business, although a stand for nine days at a trade exhibition has in the past been held to be sufficient.[70] Apart from the carrying on of business from a fixed place, 'the corporation must be "here" by a person who carries on business for the corporation in this country. It is not enough to show that the corporation has an agent here; he must be an agent who does the corporation's business for the corporation in this country.'[71] The emphasis put on various aspects varies from case to case. Thus in *South India Shipping Corporation Ltd v The Export-Import Bank of Korea*[72] it was held that a company had established a place of business within the jurisdiction where it leased premises and had a staff within the jurisdiction despite the fact that no banking transactions were carried out with the general public there.[73] The definition of 'branch' for the purposes of SI 1992 No 3179, Companies Act 1985 section 609A and Sched 21A para. 3(e), is said to be the same as that in the Eleventh Company Law Directive,[74] which also contains no further enlightenment on the subject.

The concept of 'branch or agency' was considered by the ECJ in *Establissements Somafer SA v Saar-Ferngas AG*.[75] The court held that the concept of branch or agency implies a place of business that has the appearance of permanency, has a management and is materially equipped to negotiate business with third parties so that the latter, although knowing that there will if necessary be a legal link with the parent body, whose head office is abroad, do not have to deal directly with such parent body but may transact business at the place constituting the extension. This test is close to the 'place of business' test applied by the English courts, although there is perhaps more emphasis on the actual transaction of business than was necessary in the *South India Shipping Corporation* case. In *Schotte v Parfums Rothschild* (Case 218/86 [1987] ECR 4905 the ECJ signalled a more liberal approach.

---

[69] *The Theodohos* [1977] 2 Lloyd's Rep 428.

[70] *Dunlop Pneumatic Tyre Co Ltd v A G Cudell & Co* [1902] 1 KB 342. See also *Okura & Co Ltd v Fosbaka Jernverks Aktiebolag* [1914] 1 KB 715; *Deverall v Grant Advertising incorporated* [1954] 3 All ER 389; *The World Harmony* [1967] P 341; *South India Shipping Corp Ltd v The Export-Import Bank of Korea* [1985] BCLC 163.

[71] Per Buckley LJ in *Okura & Co Ltd v Fosbaka Jernverks Aktiebolag* [1914] 1 KB 715.

[72] [1985] BCLC 163.

[73] See also *Adams v Cape Industries plc* [1990] Ch 433, where the issue was the presence or residence of a corporation for the purpose of enforcing a foreign judgment.

[74] 89/666/EEC, OJ 1989 L124/8.

[75] [1979] 1 CMLR 490, Case 33/78.

Where the company has not fulfilled its statutory obligations, it seems that it will be amenable to the jurisdiction of the English courts if it fulfils the tests laid down in *Adams v Cape Industries*,[76] which determined jurisdiction for the purposes of recognition of a foreign judgment. In that case the Court of Appeal concluded that the presence of a corporation within a jurisdiction was sufficient and that this was to be established by an investigation into the activities of the person who had been carrying on the corporation's business, including all aspects of the relationship between him and the corporation. The following factors were regarded as important:

(a) whether or not the fixed place of business from which the representative operates was originally acquired for the purpose of enabling him to act on behalf of the overseas corporation; (b) whether the overseas corporation has directly reimbursed him for (i) the cost of his accommodation at the fixed place of business; (ii) the cost of his staff; (c) what other contributions (if any) the overseas corporation made to the financing of the business carried on by the representative; (d) whether the representative was remunerated by reference to transactions (e.g. by commission) or by fixed regular payments or in some other way; (e) what degree of control the overseas corporation exercises over the running of the business conducted by the representative; (f) whether the representative reserves (i) part of his accommodation, (ii) part of his staff for conducting business relating to the overseas corporation; (g) whether the representative displays the overseas corporation's name at his premises or on his stationery and, if so, whether he did so in such a way as to indicate that he was a representative of the corporation; (h) what business (if any) the representative transacted as principal exclusively on his own behalf; (i) whether the representative makes contracts with customers or other third parties in the name of the overseas corporation, or otherwise in such a manner as to bind it; (j) if so, whether the representative requires specific authority in advance before binding the overseas corporation to contractual obligations.[77]

According to Slade LJ, the 'list of questions is not exhaustive, and the answer to none of them is necessarily conclusive'.[78] However, the court agreed with Pearson J in *F & K Jabbour v Custodian of Absentee's Property of State of Israel* that the 'principal test' would be 'to ascertain whether the agent has authority to enter into contracts on behalf of the corporation without submitting them to the corporation for approval'.[79]

The jurisdiction of the UK courts is restricted by Article 16(2) of the 1968 and Lugano Conventions on civil jurisdictions and judgments and the Civil Jurisdictions and Judgments Act 1982. Section 43 implements Article 16(2) of the Conventions, which provides for exclusive jurisdiction over proceedings principally concerned with the validity of the

---

[76] [1990] Ch 433.   [77] Slade LJ [1990] ch 443 at 507.
[78] Ibid.   [79] [1954] 1 All ER 145, at 152.

constitution, the nullity or the dissolution of companies or other legal persons, or the decisions of their organs. For these purposes exclusive jurisdiction is in the country of the corporation's seat. When a company has its seat in a contracting state other than the UK, no UK court will have jurisdiction in those matters. For these purposes a company has its seat in the UK only if it satisfies one of the following tests: (a) it was incorporated or formed under the law of a part of the UK or (b) its central management and control are exercised in the UK.[80] In *Grupo Torras SA v Sheikh Mahammed al Sabah*[81] the Court of Appeal held that Article 16(2) had no application to an action for abuse of authority as opposed to actions outside the authority of a company director or organ.

Recognition of corporate entities

English law attributes the grant of legal personality to the legal system governing an entity's creation or dissolution[82] where that law is part of a system of domestic law. The degree of recognition that will be afforded to international law as being capable of conferring legal personality in the absence of a domestic rule implementing the relevant treaty is a matter of some difficulty. In *J.H. Rayner (Mincing Lane) Ltd v Department of Trade and Industry*[83] recognition of an international organisation (the Tin Council) was held to turn not on the interpretation of the international treaty but on the extent to which the treaty had been incorporated into English law. In *Arab Monetary Fund v Hashim (No 3)*[84] a domestic law made in the United Arab Emirates was held by the House of Lords to confer legal personality on the organisation, so that it could be recognised as having capacity to sue before the English courts. The organisation was an international banking organisation established by treaty between twenty Arab states and the Palestine Liberation Organisation. However, in *Westland Helicopters Ltd v Arab Organisation for Industrialisation*,[85] *Arab Monetary Fund v Hashim* was held by the House of Lords to be confined to the narrow issue of capacity to sue. It was not in any way concerned with the interpretation of issues of constitution or

---

[80] For a discussion of central management and control, see the discussion of residence below, and P. Stone, *Conflict of Laws* (Longmans, London, 1995), 134.

[81] [1996] 1 Lloyd's Rep 7.

[82] Dicey and Morris, *Conflict of Laws*, 1103, Rule 154; *Bonanza Creek Gold Mining Co v R* [1916] 1 AC 566 (PC); *Lizard Bros v Midland Bank* [1933] AC 289; Foreign Corporations (Application of Laws) Act 1989, sections 7, 8; *Toprak Enerji Sanayi A.S. v Sale Tilney Technology Plc* [1994] 1 WLR 840; *International Bulk Shipping and Services Ltd v Minerals and Metals Trading Corp of India* [1996] 1 All ER 1017; *The Kommunar* (No 2) [1997] 1 Lloyd's Rep 8.

[83] [1990] 2 AC 418.   [84] [1991] 2 AC 114.   [85] [1995] QB 282.

governance of the fund or of issues concerning the authority of the officers of the fund to represent it in transactions with third parties. These questions of interpretation of the constitution were relevant in *Westland*. The court held that, where an organisation created by international treaty was given personality under the law of Egypt (one of the contracting states), questions as to the meaning, effect and operation of the constitution of the organisation, in so far as they were issues that, according to public international law, could be determined only by reference to the treaty and to the principles of public international law, must be determined by those rules and should not be resolved by the domestic law of Egypt. This gives us the strange result that the personality of such an organisation can be granted only by a domestic rule but, once that has occurred, reference is made to the treaty and rules of international law to determine the way in which the organisation should function. It seems that the House of Lords may regret the strict application of the dualist doctrine in *Rayner* and *Arab Monetary Fund*, but if so it is perhaps unfortunate that they did not reverse *Rayner* on this point and reach the more logical position – in line with the law concerning entities created by domestic laws – that recognition of the personality of the entity should flow from the law by which it is created.

Identification of the law of the place of incorporation

The Foreign Corporations Act 1991, section 1, provides that if at any time any question arises whether a body that purports to have or, as the case may be, appears to have lost corporate status under the laws of a territory that is at that time not a recognised state[86] should or should not be regarded as having legal personality as a body corporate under the law of any part of the UK, and it appears that the laws of that territory are at that time applied by a settled court system in that territory, that question and any other material question relating to the body shall be determined as if that territory were a recognised state. Dicey identifies two problems that this fails to solve[87] but it is suggested that the same approach will be adopted for both. One is where the state is recognised but rebels operate a legal system of some sort, and the second is where rival states claim sovereignty over a territory. Although the question may arise in different ways, the solution should be similar: either one of the states is recognised but there is a different legal system operating, which is analogous to the rebel issue, or neither of the states is recognised, in which case the Act would apply.

[86] I.e. recognised by the UK government (s1(2)(a)).
[87] Dicey and Morris, *Conflict of Laws*, 1110.

It will be for the courts to determine the issue of what law applies as a matter of fact. During the time when the UK government was in the habit of recognising governments, the question of whether or not courts could recognise an act of an unrecognised body exercising effective control was not settled.[88] The option is now clearly open and may be settled with the assistance of the Foreign Office giving evidence as to the factors considered in *Republic of Somalia v Woodhouse Drake and Carey (Suisse) SA*.[89] These factors were: (a) whether it was the constitutional government; (b) the degree, nature and stability of administrative control, if any, that it exercised over the territory of the state; (c) whether the United Kingdom government had any dealings with it and, if so, what was the nature of those dealings; and (d) in marginal cases the extent of international recognition that it had as the government of the state. Dicey suggests that 'it is likely that the courts will continue to adopt a realistic attitude and look not at whether a territory is a recognised state but at what actually happens in the territory and the law that is in fact applied there'.[90]

The Contracts (Applicable Law) Act 1990

This Act implements the Rome Convention on the Law Applicable to Contractual Obligations in the United Kingdom. It will apply to determine the law applicable to a contract entered into after 1 April 1991.[91] However, the Convention does not apply to 'questions governed by the law of companies and other bodies corporate or unincorporated such as the creation by registration or otherwise, legal capacity, internal organisation or winding up of companies and other bodies corporate or unincorporated and the personal liability of officers and members as such for the obligations of the company or body'.[92] These matters were excluded from the Convention because of the work being done on harmonisation of the EC substantive law relating to companies in the EC.[93]

Some guidance on the scope of this exclusion is given by the Giuliano-Lagarde report,[94] which suggests that the scope of the rule is flexible 'in order to take account of the diversity of national laws'. The

[88] *Carl Zeiss Stiftung v Rayner & Keeler Ltd (No 2)* [1967] 1 AC 853, 907, 908; *Hesperides Hotels Ltd v Aegean Turkish Holidays Ltd* [1978] QB 205, 218, affirmed on other grounds by the House of Lords [1979] AC 508.
[89] [1992] 3 WLR 744.
[90] Dicey and Morris, *Conflict of Laws*, 1110.
[91] OJ 1980 L266.   [92] Article 1(2)(e).
[93] See *Gore-Brown on Companies*, ch. 15, and Dine and Hughes, *EC Company Law*.
[94] OJ 1980 C282/12.

report is neither conclusive nor binding but, in determining any question as to the meaning or effect of any provision in the Convention, a court may consider the report.[95] The report suggests that the exclusion 'affects all the complex acts (contractual, administrative, registration) which are necessary to the creation of a company or firm and to the regulation of its internal organisation and winding up i.e. acts which fall within the scope of company law'.[96] Internal organisation is said to include 'the calling of meetings, the right to vote, the necessary quorum and appointment of the officers of the company or firm etc.'.

The law relating to mergers and groups is not specifically mentioned and it is unclear whether or not it will be covered in view of the dismal failure of the EU draft Ninth Directive on groups and draft Tenth Directive on cross-border mergers. The Commission stated in December 1997 that there was a possibility of attempting to revive one or both of these draft directives, which might lead to their being considered as issues within the company law harmonisation programme and thus within the scope of the exclusion in accordance with the reason for the exclusion. 'It is highly likely (and desirable) that the exclusion in Article 1(2)(e) should be given an autonomous interpretation focusing on the principle of an intent to exclude matters of company law from the purview of the Convention and having particular regard to the work of harmonisation of company law being undertaken in the European Community.'[97] The exclusion of legal capacity does not include *ultra vires* acts by organs of the company or firm, which are excluded from the Convention by Article 1(2)(f), which provides for the exclusion from the Convention of the question as to whether an organ may bind a company or body corporate or unincorporated to a third party.

Difficult questions arise as to the scope of the exclusions where issues of pre-incorporation contracts are concerned, particularly whether or not a company may assume the obligations entered into by promoters in pursuance of starting a company.[98] Section 36C of the Companies Act 1985 (as inserted by Companies Act 1898, section 130) now extends to companies incorporated outside Great Britain by SI 1994 No 950, Regs 2 and 3. This extends a purported implementation of the EC First Directive on Company Law[99] to companies incorporated outside the UK. Section 36C provides:

[95] Section 3 of the Contracts (Applicable Law) Act 1990.
[96] OJ 1980 C282/12, 12.
[97] Dicey and Morris, *Conflict of Laws*, 1115.
[98] Or an EEIG. See J. Dine, 'The EEIG: Some Private International Law Problems' (1992) 13 *Company Lawyer* 10, 11–12.
[99] Council Directive 68/151, 9 March 1968, OJ 1968 spec ed.

A contract which purports to be made by or on behalf of a company at a time when the company has not yet been formed, has effect, subject to any agreement to the contrary, as one made with the person purporting to act for the company or as agent for it, and he is personally liable on the contract accordingly.

This extension of English law to foreign companies appears to be in line with one interpretation of the Giuliano-Lagarde report, which provides that 'acts or preliminary contracts whose sole purpose is to create obligations between interested parties (promoters) with a view to forming a company or firm are not covered by the exclusion'.[100] Indeed, the wording of the exclusions does not seem particularly apt to cover all issues relating to pre-incorporation contracts.

In fact three separate issues may arise in respect of pre-incorporation contracts. The first is the contractual obligations between the promoters *inter se*. If the report is followed, these should be covered by the Convention. The second issue is the liability between the promoters and a third party,[101] which is now to be covered by the extended section 36C of the Companies Act 1985. It is suggested that this extension is in accordance with the aim of the exclusions, which is to leave untouched concerns covered by the EU company law harmonisation programme. Section 36C was an attempted implementation of the EC First Directive and so should be excluded from the Convention. The most difficult question is whether or not the exclusion in the Convention covers the third type of case, which concerns the problem of whether or not the company itself will be bound by a pre-incorporation contract. Here, the concern is the implementation of the EC First Directive, Article 9 of which provided that:

If, before a company being formed has acquired legal personality, action has been carried out in its name and the company does not assume the obligations arising from such action, the persons who acted shall, without limit, be jointly and severally liable therefore, unless otherwise agreed.

The Directive clearly envisages a mechanism whereby a company can 'assume' such obligations, and it is arguable that section 36C of the Companies Act 1985 is an incomplete implementation of that article. If such a mechanism were provided and/or if the UK provisions are seen as an incorrect implementation of the First Directive, then the matter should be regarded as a company law issue and be covered by the exclusion. It could also be argued that the issue relates to the capacity of the company and thus is also excluded from the Convention. However,

---

[100] OJ 1980 C282/12, p12.
[101] As in *Rover International Ltd v Cannon Film Sales* [1987] BCLC 540; *Oshkosh B'Gosh v Dan Marbel* (1988) 4 BCC 795; and *Cotronic (UK) Ltd v Dezonie t/a Wenderland Builders Ltd* [1991] BCLC 721.

although in the UK this issue to do with pre-incorporation contracts is often considered in a company law context, ordinary contractual law rules apply,[102] so there is doubt as to whether the exclusion is in fact apt to cover this particular issue.[103]

In any of these disputes that are covered by the Convention the basic principle will be that the contract is to be governed by the law chosen by the parties.[104] The choice must be expressed or demonstrated with reasonable certainty by the terms of the contract. If it is not certain, the contract will be governed by the law with which it is most closely connected.[105]

The domicile and residence of corporations

Domicile

In English law the domicile of a corporation is in the country under whose law it is incorporated.[106] The attribution of a domicile to a corporation is described by Dicey as infelicitous[107] and is by analogy with the domicile of origin of an individual. The attribution of domicile by the Civil Jurisdiction and Judgments Act 1982, section 42, is distinguished from the traditional attribution of domicile because it relates not to the creation of the company but to the location of the seat of the company. The domicile of a corporation is separate from the domicile (and nationality and residence) of the shareholders owing to the recognition by the court of the company as a separate legal entity with corporate personality. However, in *Daimler Co Ltd v Continental Tyre and Rubber Co (Great Britain) Ltd*[108] the House of Lords held by a majority that, although the Continental Tyre Company was incorporated in England, it was capable of acquiring an enemy character so that it could not sue or be sued in an English court. This attribution of enemy status was held to result from the fact that all except one of its shares were held by persons resident in Germany and all the directors resided in Germany. The secretary, who held the remaining share, resided in England and was a British subject. Lord Parker of Waddington made the attribution by speaking of the 'character' of the

---

[102] *Re Northumberland Avenue Hotel* (1886) 33 ChD 16; *Howard v Patent Ivory Manufacture Co* (1888) 38 ChD 156.
[103] On this see Dicey and Morris, *Conflict of Laws*, 1115, suggesting that personal liability of promoters should be subject to the exclusion.
[104] Article 3.   [105] Article 4.
[106] *Gasque v Inland Revenue Commissioners* [1940] KB 80; *The Eskbridge* [1931] P 51; A. Farnsworth, *The Residence and Domicil of Corporations* (Butterworth, London, 1939).
[107] Dicey and Morris, *Conflict of Laws*, 1103.
[108] [1916] 2 AC 307.

company rather than its domicile, residence or nationality, although he used concepts of nationality and domicile to discern the 'character' of the company. Thus:

A natural person, though an English-born subject of His Majesty, may bear an enemy character and be under liability and disability as such by adhering to His Majesty's enemies. If he gives them active aid he is a traitor but he may fall far short of that and still be invested with enemy character. If he has what is known in prize law as a commercial domicil among the King's enemies, his merchandise is good prize at sea, just as if it belonged to a subject of the enemy power. Not only actively, but passively, he may bring himself under the same disability. Voluntary residence among the enemy . . . identifies an English subject with His Majesty's foes.[109]

Taking the view that place of incorporation fixed both the domicile and residence of a corporation and noting that these cannot be changed, Lord Parker stated that another test must therefore be used to determine the character of the corporation. Fixing on the concept of control, he held that a company could assume an enemy character 'if its agents or the persons in de facto control of its affairs, whether authorised or not, are resident in an enemy country, or, wherever resident, are adhering to the enemy or taking instructions from or acting under the control of enemies.'

The inadequacy of determining issues relating to the company by simple references to the place of incorporation appears from Daimler but unfortunately constitutional capacity is governed by the law of incorporation (see below).[110] A company incorporated under the Companies Act 1985 cannot have more than one domicile because re-incorporation in another country entails re-incorporation under the laws of that country and therefore the creation of a new company domiciled in the state of new incorporation.[111]

Residence

Determining the residence of a corporation is fraught with a number of difficulties. In *Daimler* a system of attributing residence to the place of incorporation was criticised as being immovable and therefore falsely representing both the place of control and the character of the corporation. Nevertheless, that is the test adopted for the purposes of UK taxation.[112] However, such a system may be incompatible with EU

[109] Ibid., 338–9.
[110] An example is the Income and Corporation Taxes Act 1988, sections 65(4), 749(1).
[111] But see the discussion on the free movement of companies, below, and the draft Fourteenth Directive above.
[112] Finance Act 1988, section 66 and Sched 7.

rules, which seek to support the free movement of companies by a prohibition on non-discrimination against companies on the basis of nationality. It also tends to emphasise the significant differences between two distinct approaches to determining the 'proper law' to govern company issues and the ability of companies to function in more than one jurisdiction. These two approaches may be described as the 'registration' or 'incorporation' approach, followed in the Netherlands, the UK, Ireland and Denmark, and the '*siège réel*' approach, followed by a majority of the remainder of the member states of the EU. In the former, a company is regarded as fully formed and constituted under the national law if it has its registered office within that state. This equates to the place of incorporation and the UK tax residence rules. In the latter, a company will not be regarded as fully constituted in a state unless it has both its registered office and its central administration in the same jurisdiction. If such a company splits the registered office and the place of central administration, for example by moving the place of the central administration, the followers of the latter doctrine will view the company as losing the nationality of the place of origin, and the new country will not recognise it until it has been reconstituted according to local laws so that it can have a local registered office.

The *siège réel* doctrine has gained some limited recognition in English law, which holds that for most purposes the place of residence of a foreign corporation is the country in which the central management and control of corporate affairs are actually to be found. Determining which factors influence that determination is another difficulty. In *Re Little Olympian Each-Ways Ltd*[113] the central management and control test was adopted to determine the ordinary residence of a corporation for the purposes of the provisions of the Rules of the Supreme Court, Order 23 rule 5.1, which concern security for costs. The court (Chancery Division, Lindsay J) was obliged to determine whether the plaintiff corporation was ordinarily resident out of the jurisdiction for the purposes of considering whether to order it to give security for costs. The test adopted was where central management and control actually abides. Lindsay J was of the opinion that 'ordinarily' was an important addition to the notion of residence, even in the case of a corporation:

It connotes a degree of continuity being required, a reference to the way in which things are usually or habitually ordered . . . Whilst the added word might not have a corresponding effect in the case of an individual, as I see it it is more difficult for a corporation to be ordinarily resident in more than one place than it would be for it merely to be resident in more than one place.[114]

---

[113] [1995] 1 WLR 560.   [114] Ibid., 565.

The justification for reading 'residence' as 'central management and control' was found in the judgment of Lord Radcliffe in *Unit Construction Co Ltd v Bullock*,[115] in turn citing Lord Loreburn in *De Beers Consolidated Mines v Howe*.[116] Despite the fact that the substitution of the phrase 'central management and control' is admittedly a 'judicial formula for the general words of the statute, a form of limitation which one normally seeks to avoid',[117] the utility of its adoption for the purpose of granting security for costs was accepted by Lindsay J:

Given that there is no insuperable difficulty in adopting the meaning of ordinary residence used in tax cases, given the difficulty in formulating any alternative test and given the emphatic endorsement of Lord Loreburn LC's long-established *De Beers* [1906] AC 351 test in the *Unit Construction Co Ltd* case [118] only a short while before Order 23 was introduced.[119]

In adopting the test, Lindsay J rejected two other possibilities that had been argued before him. One was a test based on *Adams v Cape Industries Plc*[120] where the Court of Appeal adopted a passage from Pearson J's judgment in *F & K Jabbour v Custodian of Israeli Absentee Property*,[121] which adopted a residence test based on a 'fixed place of business' within the country. This approach was dismissed on the basis that the issue in both the cases cited was either 'presence' or at most 'residence', which was to be contrasted with ordinary residence 'with its connotation of continuity'.[122] The other reason given for the rejection of this test is more controversial because it indicates that 'residence' might have different meanings for different purposes. Lindsay J preferred the *De Beers* case 'because the *Adams* case was concerned with the question of whether, to English eyes and for the purpose of enforcing in England a foreign court's order, a foreign court could properly have held a corporation to be within that foreign court's jurisdiction for the purpose of making the order against it, a question which would likely to be especially coloured by considerations of comity and reciprocity, issues which so far have played little part in questions of security for costs'.[123] This reason for rejecting the 'fixed place of business' test for residence (a test that clearly would be easier to satisfy than central management and control) is apt for some situations and not for others, quite apart from any qualification as to the 'ordinariness' of the residence. Although it is true that it has long been accepted that for the purpose of recognition of foreign jurisdiction a less stringent test applies

[115] [1960] AC 351 at 366. [116] [1906] AC 455 at 458.
[117] Per Lord Radcliffe in *Bullock* [1960] AC 351 at 366.
[118] [1960] AC 351, 366. [119] [1995] 1 WLR 560 at 567.
[120] [1990] Ch 433.
[121] [1954] 1 WLR 139, 146. [122] [1995] 1 WLR 560 at 567. [123] Ibid.

(see below), the issue in *Jabbour* was an issue of substantive law, i.e. the *situs* of an insurance policy which was at the residence of the insurance company. The company's principal place of business was England, but the court held that it was also resident in Palestine/Israel because its agent there had authority to enter into contracts on its behalf without submitting them to it for approval. The company thus had two residences. It seems, then, that different rules apply for jurisdiction, for determination of the *situs* of property[124] and for tax and other issues including security for costs.

Determination of the place of central management and control

The House of Lords held in *Swedish Central Railway v Thompson*[125] that a corporation may have more than one residence, although in *Paulo (Brazilian) Ry v Carter*[126] it also held that the place of central management and control is of paramount authority. Dicey and Farnsworth[127] regard these as inconsistent statements,[128] although the Court of Appeal sought to reconcile the two positions by suggesting that 'the power of final arbitrament'[129] should not be equated with the place of central management and control. In *The Rewia*,[130] central management and control was equated with the place where ultimate control was exercised. The line between 'power of final arbitrament' and 'place of paramount authority' is difficult to draw but it may be done: the word 'final' denotes the moment of completion of a decision whereas 'paramount authority' may rest in a body of decision makers in different jurisdictions. The place of paramount authority may therefore 'be divided or even, at any rate in theory, peripatetic'.[131] Dicey suggests that, in these exceptional cases, dual residence occurs[132] and the corporation is resident in both countries where 'some portion of controlling power and authority can be identified'.[133] The logical difficulty may be less when the multitude of factors taken into account in order to determine the issue of the place of central management and control is examined. The idea that it is only necessary to search for the pinnacle of power in order to determine the issue falls away somewhat when the

[124] Also mentioned by Lindsay J, citing *Kwok v Commissioner of Estate Duty* [1988] 1 WLR 1035.
[125] [1925] AC 495.   [126] [1896] AC 31.
[127] Farnsworth, *Domicil and Residence of Corporations*.
[128] And Stone regards them as an obsolete concept; Stone, *Conflict of Laws*, 107, n9.
[129] *Union Corporation v IRC* [1952] 1 All ER 646 at 654–63.
[130] [1991] 2 Lloyd's Rep 325.
[131] *Unit Construction Co v Bullock* [1960] AC 351, 366.
[132] Dicey and Morris, *Conflict of Laws*, 1106.
[133] Ibid., citing Lord Radcliffe in *Bullock* at 367.

multitude of factors and the different weight given to them are examined.[134] Thus weight has been given to the provisions of a company's objects clause,[135] to the place of incorporation,[136] to where the real trade and business of the company is carried on,[137] to where the books of the company are kept,[138] to where the administrative work is done,[139] to where the directors with a full power to disapprove of local steps and to require different ones to be taken themselves met or were resident,[140] to where directors to whom the management of the company was confided ordinarily met,[141] to considerations as to the physical presence of the company, as where it 'keeps house',[142] to where the chief office is situate or the company secretary is to be found.[143]

What is, however, clear is that the place where the constitution decrees that central management shall take place is by no means conclusive. The court will conduct an enquiry into the reality.[144] Identification of the place of residence is not considered to be synonymous with an identification of the pinnacles of power. The court will conduct an investigation to determine the jurisdiction where significant power was in fact exercised.[145]

Capacity and internal management

Both the capacity of a company and all other matters concerning the constitution of a company are governed by the law of the place of incorporation,[146] as modified by the Companies Act 1985. The law is now partially on a statutory basis by virtue of sections 36, 36A and 36C of the Companies Act 1985 as extended to companies incorporated outside Great Britain by SI 1994 No 950, as amended by SI 1995 No 1729, in force from 16 May 1994. These regulations provide that a company incorporated outside Great Britain may make a contract in any manner permitted by the laws of the territory in which it is

---

[134] *Re Little Olympian Each-Ways Ltd (No 3)* [1995] 1 BCLC 636, 638.
[135] *Cesena Sulphur Co Ltd v Nicholson* (1876) 1 ExD 428, 454.
[136] Ibid., 444, 453.   [137] Ibid., 452.   [138] Ibid., 455.
[139] Ibid., 455.   [140] Ibid., 456.
[141] *Goerz & Co v Bell* [1904] 2 KB 136, 138, 148; *De Beers Consolidated Mines v Howe* [1906] AC 455, 459; *Swedish Central Railway Co Ltd v Thompson* [1925] AC 495, 503.
[142] *De Beers* [1906] AC 455, 458.
[143] *Jones v Scottish Accident Insurance Co Ltd* (1886) 17 QBD 421, 422–3.
[144] *Bullock* [1960] AC 351.
[145] It may be that the 'pinnacle of power' approach was influenced by the organic theory of companies whereby the 'mind' of the company is seen as situated in the policy makers. See *H L Bolton (Engineering) Co Ltd v T J Graham & Sons* [1956] 3 All ER 624; *Task Supermarkets Ltd v Nattrass* [1972] AC 153.
[146] Dicey and Morris, *Conflict of Laws*, Rule 156, at 1111, and 1997 Supplement.

incorporated[147] by any person who, by that law, is acting under the authority (express or implied) of that company.[148] A document may be exercised in any manner permitted by that law[149] and such a document, if it is expressed to be executed (in whatever form of words) by the company, will have the same effect as one executed by a company incorporated in England and Wales. In favour of a purchaser, a document is deemed to be duly executed by a company incorporated outside Great Britain if it purports to be signed by a person or persons who, in accordance with the laws of the territory in which the company is incorporated, is or are acting under the authority (express or implied) of that company.[150] As Sealy points out in respect of section 36A generally, this appears to be wide enough to cover an outright forgery.[151] These provisions leave it to the law of incorporation to govern the issue of who is regarded as acting under the express or implied authority of the company[152] and the manner of execution of documents, but apparently extend English law to the issue of whether the document is 'expressed to be executed by the company'. The regulation also extends the English rules on pre-incorporation contracts to foreign companies with the effect that a promoter would be personally bound on such a contract. Whether this affects the issue of whether the company would be bound is unclear and may still depend on the law of incorporation, unless the wording of section 36C as extended is found to exclude that possibility in favour of imposing personal liability on the promoters, which is the sole effect of section 36C for companies incorporated under the Companies Act 1985. The statutory provisions leave the issue of the overall capacity of the company to the common law rule referring to the place of incorporation. Thus, in *The Saudi Prince*[153] it was held that a company whose constitution as interpreted by the law of its incorporation had no power to enter into a transaction for the purchase of land cannot purchase land in any country. As Dicey notes, the English courts are reluctant to interfere in any matter concerning the internal management of a company,[154] refusing to interfere with discretionary powers granted by its constitution,[155] but these matters relate to the interpretation of the constitution and therefore no other applicable law would

---

[147] Regs 2, 3 and 4(1)(a).   [148] Regs 2, 3 and 4(1)(b).
[149] Regs 2, 3 and 5(a).
[150] Section 36A(6), as adapted by SI 1994 No 950, regs 2, 3 and 5(b).
[151] L. Sealy, *Cases and Materials in Company Law* (6th edn, Butterworth, London, 1996), 83.
[152] See *Banco de Bilbao v Sancha and Rey* [1938] 2 KB 176; *Presentaciones Musicales SA v Secunda* [1994] Ch 271.
[153] [1982] 2 Lloyd's Rep 255.
[154] Dicey and Morris, *Conflict of Laws*, 1112–13.
[155] *Pergamon Press v Maxwell* [1970] 1 WLR 1167.

make sense. It is clear that the contractual right of a company member is governed by the law of incorporation,[156] the extent of the member's limited liability[157] and the right of succession to assets on amalgamation with another company.[158]

The residence connecting factor and freedom of establishment

As previously mentioned, this issue involves the clash between the desire of member states to control the activities of companies that are active within their jurisdiction, either by the application of the 'real seat' doctrine or by imposition of taxation, and the principles of freedom of establishment of companies and non-discrimination on national grounds. The clash has given rise to a complex body of case law and is still rapidly developing.

Primary establishments

In *R v HM Treasury, ex parte Daily Mail and General Trust plc*[159] the ECJ examined the right of companies to move jurisdictions and the ability of member states to hinder their free movement. The Daily Mail holding company applied to transfer its central management and control to the Netherlands. This transfer would have saved a considerable amount of capital gains tax under more favourable Dutch rules. The UK Treasury therefore withheld consent for the transfer and a preliminary question of the validity of this refusal in the light of Articles 52 and 58 of the EC Treaty[160] was referred to the ECJ. The court held that the tax authorities of the home member state could require settlement of tax liabilities before consenting to the transfer. In the absence of a Convention under Article 220 to permit the transfer of a seat and the inability to agree a directive on the subject,[161] the court held that companies as creatures of national law had only restricted freedom of movement. This disappointing judgment has kept alive many of the difficulties experienced in the EU because of excessive attachment to national models of company law.

---

[156] Although Dicey suggests this may be because of an implied choice of law of the contract. Dicey and Morris, *Conflict of Laws*; *London and South American Investment Trust Ltd v British Tobacco Co* [1927] 1 Ch 107; *Re F H Lloyd Holdings plc* [1985] BCLC 293.

[157] *J H Rayner (Mincing Lane) Ltd v Department of Trade and Industry* [1990] 2 AC 418; *Kutchera v Buckingham International Holdings Ltd* [1988] IR 61.

[158] *National Bank of Greece and Athens SA v Metliss* [1958] AC 509; *Steel Authority of India v Hind Metals Incorporated* [1984] 1 Lloyd's Rep 405.

[159] Case 81/1987 (1988) ECR 5483.   [160] Now Articles 43 and 48.

[161] See now the draft Fourteenth Directive.

Secondary establishments

In *Commission v France*[162] the use of a connecting factor based on the residence of the corporation was rejected by the ECJ. The facts concerned French tax legislation under which insurance companies whose registered office was in France, including subsidiaries set up in France by foreign insurance companies, benefited from a shareholder's tax credit in respect of dividends on shares that they held in French companies. This benefit was denied to branches or agencies established in France but where the registered office was in another member state. The Commission found that the different treatment amounted to discrimination based on nationality, contrary to Article 52(3), and brought an action against the French government. One of the justifications for the rule advanced by the French government was that there was an internationally recognised distinction between residents and non-residents so far as fiscal measures are concerned.[163] The court, however, did not accept that the distinction was based on residence, but regarded the connecting factor of residence as a disguised nationality test:

with regard to companies, it should be noted in this context . . . that it is their registered office . . . that serves as the connecting factor with the legal system of a particular State, like nationality in the case of natural persons. Acceptance of the proposition that the Member State in which a company seeks to establish itself may freely apply to it a different treatment solely by reason of the fact that its registered office is situated in another Member State would thus deprive that provision [Art 58] of all meaning.[164]

However, as Ceroni points out, the court went on to accept that the 'nationality' connecting factor would be acceptable 'in some circumstances' without giving guidance about what factors would influence the decision as to whether the nationality connecting factor was acceptable or not acceptable in any given set of circumstances. The court also rejected arguments that the branches and agencies could have avoided discrimination by becoming subsidiaries: 'Article 52 expressly leaves traders free to choose the appropriate legal forms in which to pursue their activities in another member state and that freedom of choice must not be limited by discriminatory tax provisions.'[165]

---

[162] Case 270/83 1986 ECR 273.
[163] For a discussion of the other justifications and a more general analysis of the topic, see Luca Ceroni, 'The Barriers to the International Mobility of Companies within the European Community: A Re-reading of the Case Law' [1999] *Journal of Business Law* 59.
[164] Ibid., 304.   [165] Ibid., 305.

The ECJ has been criticised for pursuing an aim of preventing discrimination against secondary establishments too vigorously. In *Segers v Bedrijfsvereniging*[166] this led the court to embrace the 'incorporation' theory of connection with a jurisdiction and came to a conclusion at odds with its own decisions concerning the provision of services. Mr Segers was a Dutch national who owned and was a director of a private limited company formed and with its registered office in England. However, the company carried on all its business through a subsidiary set up in the Netherlands. Mr Segers was refused admission to the Dutch sickness insurance scheme on the grounds that it applied only to directors of companies that had a registered office in the Netherlands. The Dutch Insurance Association argued that this discrimination was necessary to prevent fraud since a company incorporated in one state but pursuing all its economic activities through a secondary establishment in another state could circumvent rules in force in the latter country. The ECJ held that, if a company is formed under the law of a member state and has its registered office there, 'the fact that the company pursues its activities through an agency, branch or subsidiary in another member state is entirely material'. Discrimination would therefore be unjustified unless Article 56 could be relied on to show that discrimination was justified on the grounds of public policy, public security or public health. The present case was held not to fall within these exceptions. The 'forum shopping' effect of this finding was accepted by the court, which accepted the view of the Advocate-General that it was a necessary consequence of the rights granted by Articles 52 and 58. However, the court accepted that the company was 'established' in England solely on the basis of the fact that it was incorporated there and had a registered office there. It could have insisted that it also had its main office within the jurisdiction before it qualified as 'established'. Not to do so is an acceptance of the incorporation theory, which is adhered to by only a minority of the member states. A second possibility is that the court should have lifted the corporate veil in order to discover how real the link with England was before finding that the company was established there. Either approach would reduce the forum shopping possibilities. The approach in *Segers* is at odds with other jurisprudence of the court, which gives a higher priority to the avoidance of rules in force in the state where a provider of services operates.[167] However, it seems to be confirmed by the recent case of *Centros Erverhaus – og*

---

[166] Case 79/1985 [1986] ECR 2375.
[167] See *Centre Distributeur Leclerc and Others v Syndicat des Librairies de Loire-Ocean* 229/83 [1985] ECR 1; and *Johannes Henricus Maria van Binsbergen v Bestour van de Bedrijfvereniging Voor de Metalnijverheid*, Case 33/74 [1974] ECR 1299.

Selskabsstyrelsen,[168] where Denmark was held unable to insist on minimum capital requirements that would have prevented a UK company registering in Denmark. The company had been legally formed in the UK but did not carry on any business there and intended to operate solely in Denmark. The argument that this procedure was simply a method of circumventing Denmark's minimum capital requirements cut no ice with the ECJ, which may perhaps be seen to be moving in the direction of adopting the law of incorporation theory.

A case concerned with UK taxation extended the prohibition to indirect discrimination. In *R v Inland Revenue Commissioners, ex parte Commerzbank AG*[169] a public limited company incorporated in Germany granted loans to American companies and paid tax on the interest it received. It then obtained a refund of the tax but was refused a repayment supplement because it was not resident in the UK for tax purposes. If it had been resident it would not have been exempt from tax and therefore the issue of a supplement on this particular payment could not have arisen. However, companies with UK tax residency had a general right to a repayment supplement on overpaid taxes. The ECJ indicated that the use of fiscal residence as a criterion for granting the repayment supplement was likely to work to the disadvantage of companies established in other member states. It was therefore a method of indirectly discriminating against them. The UK argued that the situation was no more than differential treatment of two disparate situations. The ECJ disagreed, taking the view that the true comparison was not between the situation of a resident company paying tax, so that no right to a refund would arise, and a non-resident's exemption from tax, which gave rise to the refund, but between two companies paying legally undue taxes.[170] The question is the extent to which residence-based distinctions are compatible with EU law.[171] Ceroni[172] argues that an analogy ought to be drawn with *Schumacker*,[173] which accepted that for direct taxation the status of residents and non-residents is not comparable since the state of residence normally has all relevant information relating to the personal and family circumstances of its residents and the major part of income is normally concentrated in the state of residence. Consequently the refusal of state benefits to a non-resident is not normally discriminatory. Applied to companies Ceroni argues that this would reverse the rule relating to companies, but the analogy should not

---

[168] Judgment of the ECJ, 9 March 1999, unreported.
[169] Case C-330/91 [1993] ECR 1–4017.
[170] See also Case C-264/96, *ICI Industries Plc v Colmer* [1999] 1 WLR 108.
[171] Raised by J. Wouters, 'Fiscal Barriers to Companies Cross-border Establishment in the Case-Law of the European Court of Justice' (1990) *Yearbook of European Law* 91.
[172] Ceroni, 'Barriers to International Mobility of Companies', 59.
[173] Case C-279/93, *Finanzampt Koeln-Aldstadt v Roland Schumacker* [1995] ECR I-225.

be too strictly applied because the arguments concerning personal and family circumstances are inapplicable and the likelihood that a non-resident obtains a major part of income from the state of fiscal residence 'may become weaker in the case of large multinational companies'.[174]

In the absence of harmonisation measures the use of the general Treaty articles on establishment appears to be a blunt weapon that encounters the difficulty of residence-based tax treatment. On the issue of the choice between incorporation and 'real seat' theories the ECJ seems to have gone a long way to adopting incorporation theories.

Conclusion

The conflicts rules present us with an incoherent set of responses to the inherent tensions between the desire of corporations and free market states to permit trading in any jurisdiction with the minimum of regulations and the wish of some states to adopt the concession view and control the corporations operating within their territory. The conflict between basing taxation on residence and the resulting clash with EU principles of freedom of establishment and non-discrimination on the grounds of nationality perhaps shows the dilemma at its most intractable. It seems unlikely that a coherent system of private international law will be adopted, either within the EU or beyond unless the issue of conflicting philosophies is properly addressed.

We saw at the beginning of the chapter that conflicts rules were developed in order to protect 'legitimate expectations'. In this chapter we have seen that there are a number of conflicting legitimate expectations and the courts have not made a clear choice between them. Later in this work it will be suggested that conflicts tools can be adopted to give some voice to the legitimate expectations of communities affected by the operations of transglobal corporations and that this could be achieved by adopting an amended version of the *siège réel* doctrine not to determine recognition of a company but to judge the validity of its decision-making according to its constitution. Thus validity of decision-making would be reformed not to the law of the place of incorporation (as in UK law) but to the law where central decision-making actually took place or to the law of the place of significant impact of the decision. This would import some of the same mechanisms as is evident in the private international law relating to contracts, which refers to the paper law of the contract being the place with which the contract has its most significant connection. The way in which this rule might work is further discussed in chapter 6.

---

[174] Ceroni, 'Barriers to International Mobility of Companies', 62.

4 Theories and models of the regulation of corporations and groups

Reasons for and structure of regulations

In this chapter we revisit the theories underpinning companies and examine the structures of regulation that result from the espousal of those theories. It is important to distinguish between *justifications* for regulations and *justifications for methods or models* of regulation. Sometimes the one naturally flows from the other but this is not always the case. For example, the concession theories recognise that the state has a right to regulate corporate behaviour but this recognition does not dictate the method the state should use. Thus, several levels of approach may be noted. At the first level there is an evaluation of the degree to which the theories supply a justification for regulation and the strength and reach of that regulation. This can most clearly be seen by the examination of the free market contractualist theories, which are hostile to most state regulatory interventions save where there is 'market failure'. The strength and reach of justified regulation is explored in discussing the *regulatory consequences of the theories*. At the second level, theories of regulation may provide a guide to the method or model of regulation to be adopted. For example, paradoxically, regulation by the criminal law may be linked to adherence to contractualist views as state regulation is pushed to the margin. Only extreme anti-social behaviour may be regulated so that a model of the regulator as outside the company wielding a big stick may be espoused. At the most detailed level, there are differences in the types of rule that should be used. Although this discussion does not intend to address the type of rule issue in any depth, it should be noted that even at this level of detail the underlying theories of corporate structure may be very significant; for example, the contractualist vision would regulate as far as possible by using presumptive rules (may waive)[1] or default rules[2] so as to preserve the bargaining status of participants.

[1] B. Cheffins, *Company Law* (Clarendon, Oxford, 1997), 218.
[2] S. Deakin and A. Hughes, chapter 3 in *Company Directors: Regulating Conflicts of Interest*

Justifications for regulation

Justifications for regulation closely follow the theories underpinning companies. The concept of correction of market failures follows the transaction cost economics theories, which share with legal contractual theories a call for minimum interference with contractual decision-making. Concession and communitaire theories make companies open to state regulation and permit a conceptualisation of the company with a 'social conscience'. Thus both types of theory have significant regulatory consequences. It is noticeable that only the latter theories permit the use of companies as a direct social engineering tool or a method of distributive justice. The absence of such a direct use is replaced in the contractualist theories by the notion that profit maximisation for shareholders involving economic growth will best serve the world; 'To address poverty, economic growth is not an option: it is an imperative.'[3]

Why companies require distinct treatment

Two extreme views about the company would mean that we would not be required to identify regulations that concern corporate matters as opposed to those that concern the community generally. Thus the extreme view of the company as consisting only of a nexus of contracts means that regulation would be necessary in this sphere, as elsewhere, only in order to ensure that markets remain perfect. It must be recalled that the extreme reductionist economic theory relies very heavily on private law instruments and free enterprise theories. To rely on these theories as an exclusive approach to regulation is dangerous for a number of reasons discussed below. Ogus comments: 'no industrialised society has ever relied exclusively on a system of private law general principles.'[4] He finds the reason for this easy to discern:

Rationally, individuals and firms will only seek to enforce rights where the expected benefits exceed the expected costs, which include not only legal expenses but also time and trouble . . . many legitimate claims are for this reason not pursued. Thus externalities which affect large numbers but which impose only a small loss on each individual right-holder will not be 'internalised'

and *Formulating a Statement of Duties*, Law Commission Consultation Paper No. 153 (Law Commission, London, 1999).
[3] Mahbub al Haq, former World Bank Vice President and special adviser to the UN Development Programme's annual *Human Developments Report* in his Barbara Ward Lecture to the 21st World Conference of the Society for International Development, Mexico City, April 1994, cited in D. Korten, *When Corporations Rule the World* (Kumarian Press, Connecticut, 1995).
[4] A. Ogus, *Regulation: Legal Form and Economic Theory* (Clarendon Law Series, Oxford, 1994), 27.

by private law instruments . . . The inhibitory impact of the costs of private enforcement is exacerbated in cases where it is difficult to acquire the information necessary to pursue a successful claim, particularly where high technology is involved, and where complex causation questions arise.[5]

Riley puts the distinction well by speaking of constraints which 'must be satisfied *before* profit-maximising decisions are taken. The goal of the corporation is unchanged by the constraints imposed by society's norms.'[6] The admission by some economists that a company may have to satisfy 'negative externalities' before being free to pursue the goal of profit maximisation lends the notion of the company as an institution some credibility and is an admission that collective goals and company goals diverge. The community is no longer a seamless web of contracts all pursuing maximum profitability. Ogus takes the example of 'Jill' polluting a stream.[7] It is not feasible to deal with the problem on a contractual basis, firstly because of the high transaction costs involved in making the numerous bargains required to compensate those down-stream and secondly because 'the problem of dispersion of third party effects may be exacerbated by time and uncertainty. For example, the harm arising from Jill's pollution, if it is toxic, may adversely affect an indeterminate number of people over an indeterminate time-period. Alternative legal solutions are obviously necessary.' Unfortunately, as we shall see, this view of matters is not universally adopted and the desire of companies to minimise their compliance with rules regarded as negative externalities in order to maximise profits can clearly be seen as a major cause of the globalisation of poverty.[8]

The other view that would marginalise the inside–outside distinction is the extreme communitaire view, whereby the company is merely an instrument of state policy. It has already been argued that this view blurs the essentially commercial role of the company. Therefore, unless the whole world is seen as only a perfect market or the company is seen only as an instrument of social policy there will be circumstances in which the interests of society and the interests of the company diverge. If this is so it is necessary to make a distinction between outside and inside regulation. The correct balance between inside and outside regulation will depend on the model of company each society wishes to operate.

---

[5] Ibid., 27–8; and see Cheffins, *Company Law.*
[6] C. Riley, 'Understanding and Regulating the Corporation' (1995) 58 *Modern Law Review* 595.
[7] Ogus, *Regulation*, 19.
[8] Korten, *When Corporations Rule the World*; J. Dunning (ed.), *Governments, Globalisation and International Business* (Oxford University Press, Oxford, 1996); J. Karliner, *The Corporate Planet* (Sierra, San Francisco, 1997); P. Harrison, *Inside the Third World* (3rd edn, Penguin, Harmondsworth, 1993).

First we must examine the full implications of the two extreme theories, the economic and communitaire theories.

Perfecting the market as a justification for regulation

The neo-classical economics approach is essentially a de-regulatory model. Its wholesale rejection of the concessionary theory leaves the state validly able only to correct market failure. The rejection of regulation to enforce social values on companies is perhaps most stringently put by Milton Friedman,[9] who argues that businessmen subjected to a 'social responsibility other than making maximum profits for stockholders' cannot know what interests to serve.[10] Further, society would not tolerate public functions of taxation and expenditure being exercised by persons chosen by private groups.

This is an extreme free enterprise private law view of companies, rejecting wholly any state interest or justification for intervention. This wholesale rejection of any state role is suspect, particularly in view of the growing power and influence of large corporations in the twentieth century.[11]

As observed in chapter 1 above, the concept of regulation being of use only as a corrective for 'market failure' is a troubling one, at once capable of encompassing almost any situation that is seen as an imbalance in the perfect market (where actors 'act rationally, are numerous, have full information about the products on offer, can contract at little cost, have sufficient financial resources to transact, can enter and leave the markets with little difficulty, and will carry out the obligations which they agree to perform'[12]) and simultaneously acting as a justification for allowing absolute freedom to corporations to move capital around the world and to force freedom of trade to the detriment of many developing societies.[13]

As discussed in chapter 1, criticisms may be levelled at the funda-

---

[9] M. Friedman, 'The Social Responsibility of Business Is to Increase Its Profits', *New York Times Magazine*, 13 September 1970.

[10] It was, of course, the subject of a long debate between Berle and Dodd – E. Dodd, 'For Whom Are Corporate Managers Trustees?' (1931) *Harvard Law Review* 1049; A. Berle, 'For Whom Are Corporate Managers Trustees?' (1932) *Harvard Law Review* 45, 1365 – the fear expressed by Berle being that the 'interests of the company' must be given content if they are to be used as a yardstick; see also ch. 1.

[11] For Wedderburn's strong rejection of it see K. Wedderburn, 'The Social Responsibility of Companies' (1985)15 *Melbourne University Law Review* 4; see also A. Fraser, 'The Corporation as a Body Politic' (1983) *Telos* no. 57, 5–40.

[12] Cheffins, *Company Law*, 6.

[13] M. Chossudovsky, *The Globalisation of Poverty* (Pluto Press, Halifax, Nova Scotia, 1998); Korten, *When Corporations Rule the World*; Harrison, *Inside the Third World*.

mental assumptions underpinning these theories, including the concept of the 'rational actor' and of rational action in the actor's self-interest. In relation to regulatory concerns further criticisms are relevant. One line of thought is highlighted by the thinking of Robert Cooter.[14] His analysis of the economic theory of law and its success explains that economics found a vacant niche in the intellectual ecology and rapidly filled it.[15] It provided a scientific theory to predict the effects of sanctions on behaviour by treating sanctions as equivalent to prices. As Cooter explains, this works well where the behaviour of the players is non-strategic. The difference between strategic and non-strategic behaviour he illustrates thus:

In American football, a player often runs around the right side as a decoy to fool the other team while the player carrying the ball runs around the left side. In contrast, a mountain climber never starts up the south slope as a decoy to fool the mountain while the main party climbs up the north slope.[16]

As Cooter points out, 'When people interact in the shadow of the law, their behaviour often depends upon what each person thinks the other will do.'[17] Thus, says Cooter, the 'economic analysis of law found a technique for analysing strategic behaviour as if it were non-strategic . . . thus the Coase Theorem treats strategic theory as a transaction cost'.[18] However Cooter is critical of this approach: 'In reality, strategic behaviour does not resemble the cost of oranges, haircuts or any other good. Calling strategic behaviour a "cost" postpones analysing it.'[19] Recognising that economic theory has much of value to contribute on evaluating laws with regard to their efficiency and likely effect on the distribution of wealth, Cooter nevertheless believes that '[t]he economic analysis of law has X-Ray vision, not peripheral vision'.[20] Cooter takes the core foundations of economics theories to be the concepts of maximisation, rationality, equilibrium and efficiency. These concepts are valuable, but

the 'meat' of economics lacks some essential nutriments to nourish social science. Specifically, economics 'takes preferences as given' which means that it does not attempt to explain how people acquire their goals . . . Economists typically assume that a person pursues his or her self-interest as he or she perceives it . . . A person acquires values by internalising them. Internalised values are essential to morality and law. Economics offers no account of how internalisation occurs. In other words, economics offers no account of how a person becomes the self in which he or she is interested.[21]

---

[14] R. Cooter, 'Law and Unified Social Theory' (1995) 22 *Journal of Law and Society* 50.
[15] Ibid., 51.   [16] Ibid., 52   [17] Ibid.   [18] Ibid.
[19] Ibid.   [20] Ibid., 54.   [21] Ibid., 59–60.

Cooter proceeds to offer a way forward. He argues that in a large organisation the self-interest of employees is imperfectly aligned with the interest of the organisation.

Eliciting effort and creativity requires aligning the self-interest of agents [employees] with the principal's interest [the organisation]. But the narrow self-interest of agents never aligns perfectly with the principal's interests. The agency problems become manageable in modern economies because people internalise occupational roles, which broadens their self-interest . . . Internalising an occupational role involves accepting the norms of an occupation so intimately that they enter the individual's self-conception. As soon as an individual takes norms into his or her self-conception, he or she distinguishes two kinds of self-interest. The simplest self-interest, which I call 'thin self-interest', looks only to objective payoffs in wealth or power. The more complex self-interest, which I call 'thick self-interest', modifies objective payoffs to encompass the subjective value of morality.[22]

Cooter argues that the concentration of economics on the 'thin' self-interest has created a 'fundamental' tension between economics and law: 'The ideal economic decision maker is ' "perfectly rational" which means utterly instrumental in pursuing explicit ends. The ideal legal decision maker is "completely reasonable" which means that he or she has internalised social morality.'[23] Cooter then explains how the internalisation of norms in a community occurs by cooperation to acquire a 'local public good'. Once this behaviour is seen as valuable it becomes a norm of that society. This vision discards the individualist notion of corporations entirely and points directly at the concept of social norms within the company itself as holding some of the keys to regulating decision-making behaviour. Cooter's work supplies two key factors that regulators ignore at their peril. One is the importance of internal regulation for controlling corporate behaviour, which in terms of regulatory theory and practicality is a constantly recurring theme. The second is the importance of taking account of strategic behaviour. Both these themes have been further developed in the work of Ayres and Braithwaite, which is discussed below in the context of regulatory theory.

Campbell has also argued that underlying social relations which underpin economic transactions are undervalued, particularly in economic contractualist models.[24] Taking a wider perspective, Campbell further argues that basing regulation on an attempt to restore a free market is wholly wrong: 'The inherent absurdity of the goal of this type

---

[22] Ibid., 60–1.   [23] Ibid., 61.
[24] D. Campbell, 'Ayres versus Coase: An Attempt to Recover the Issue of Equality in Law and Economics' (1994) 21 *Journal of Law and Society* 434; and see Cooter, 'Law and Unified Social Theory'.

of regulation prevents its energetic pursuit even within its self-defeat-ingly narrow limits. With a breath-taking leap of abstraction, capitalism is conceived of as *laissez-faire* without internal contradictions, and economic harmony is held to follow from reducing the corporation to the market governance of this wholly mythical capitalism.'[25] Campbell examines the work of Coase:

Coase himself never really examines the market as such; for it is assumed to exist . . . [T]here is a very substantial problem with this which relates to the peculiar abstraction of the perfect market. This market is typically introduced as a purely theoretical assumption; yet it is to function as an aspiration. The difficulty is that when this type of market reasoning needs to be given a concrete form, the form it is given is that of *laissez-faire*. This is never made explicit (at least in academic writings), for the way it takes place is rather surreptitious. Nevertheless in this way the ideological equation of efficiency with a mythical view of *laissez-faire* . . . is found at the heart of the realism of transaction cost economics and, indeed, is given probably its most vulgar academic expression in Posner.[26]

The fundamental issue is the assumption that the laissez-faire market is a good thing. On the contrary, it may well be viewed merely as a method by which there will be overproduction, which will lead to vicious competition, cartelisation and periodic financial crises.[27] The founda-tion stone of the economist's theory that market forces will ultimately benefit all is therefore brought into question:

Economic analysis holds, on its normative side, that social wealth maximisation is a worthy goal so judicial decisions should try to maximise social wealth, for example, by assigning rights to those who would purchase them but for transaction costs. But it is unclear *why* social wealth is a worthy goal. Who would think that a society that has more wealth . . . is either better or better off than a society that has less, except someone who made the mistake of personifying society, and therefore thought that a society is better off with more wealth in just the way an individual is? Why should anyone who has not made this mistake think wealth maximisation a worthy goal?[28]

Dworkin answers this question[29] by considering the relationship between wealth and social value. An important distinction is between

---

[25] D. Campbell, 'Why Regulate the Modern Corporation? The Failure of "Market Failure"', in J. McCahery, S. Picciotto and C. Scott (eds.), *Corporate Control and Accountability* (Clarendon Press, Oxford, 1993), 103 at 105. His analysis concentrates on 'the giant corporations which are the principal institutions of the advanced capitalist economy'.

[26] Campbell, 'Why Regulate the Modern Corporation?', 112.

[27] See also C. Craypo, 'The Impact of Changing Corporate Strategies on Communities, Unions and Workers in the United States of America' in S. Deakin and A. Hughes (eds.), *Enterprise and Community: New Directions in Corporate Governance* (Blackwell, Oxford, 1997), 10.

[28] R. M. Dworkin, 'Is Wealth a Value?' (1980) 9 *Journal of Legal Studies* 191 at 194.

[29] In the negative; see below.

social wealth as a component of social value 'that is, something worth having for its own sake and social wealth as an instrument of social value i.e. valuable because the wealth may be used to promote other values by a distributive process either deliberate or "through an invisible hand process"'.[30] Of social wealth as a component of social value Dworkin identifies a modest and an immodest claim. The former argues that social wealth is one component of social value. 'One society is *pro tanto* better than another if it has more wealth, but it might be worse overall when other components of value, including distributional components, are taken into account.' The immodest version 'holds that social wealth "is the *only* component of social value"'.[31] On social wealth as an instrument of social value Dworkin makes three distinctions: (a) there may be a claim that improvements in social wealth cause other improvements; 'improvements in wealth, for example, improve the position of the worst-off group in society by alleviating poverty through some invisible hand process';[32] or (b) there may be a claim that wealth is valuable because it provides the possibility of engineering such improvements; or (c) 'social wealth is neither a cause nor an ingredient of social value, but a surrogate for it. If society aims directly at some improvements in value, such as trying to increase overall happiness among its members, it will fail to produce as much of that goal than if it instead aimed at improving social wealth.'[33] This he deems the 'false-target approach'.

A further distinction of vital importance to the impact of these theories on the regulation of companies and groups is the 'strong institutional theory', by which Dworkin means the idea that, 'although wealth maximisation is only one among several components of social value, it is nevertheless a component that courts should be asked single-mindedly to pursue, leaving other components to other institutions'.[34] Dworkin is here speaking about court decisions in general, but it can immediately be seen that where companies are concerned this line of thought has considerable resonance.

If we begin from the viewpoint that a company's principal purpose is wealth maximisation, such regulation as there must be must enable this process. Where distributive issues are to be considered, let that be by means other than company law. This is the famous enabling versus regulating debate considered in chapter 1. If our building blocks for regulating companies and groups consist of (i) *any* of Dworkin's identified meanings of wealth as a value, coupled with a belief (ii) that in any event the role of companies as institutions is wealth maximisation, (iii)

[30] Dworkin, 'Is Wealth a Value?', 195.
[31] Ibid., 195.   [32] Ibid.   [33] Ibid.   [34] Ibid.

that there is an obligation to provide enabling mechanisms for wealth maximisation, (iv) that the free market is the best enabling mechanism, (v) that groups of companies, however rich and powerful, are in no different position from individual small entrepreneurs as envisaged by Adam Smith, then the inherent dangers of such an approach may begin to emerge. No one component of this structure has caused the transnationals to run out of control; it is a cumulative effect. If we narrow Dworkin's concerns to focus on companies and groups, two separate but interlinked questions arise. One concerns the role that companies fulfil in society. Are they institutionally merely wealth-creation machines? The second concerns the role of the company *as* a society. How does the value of wealth creation function within the institution itself? If we apply Dworkin's analysis of values to the functioning of the company as a society we find that the analysis has been pre-empted by the deconstruction of companies into the individual relationships between bargain makers. If the company is viewed as a society it could be argued that its increased wealth has social value because it could be used to benefit those worst off; the society *could* be valued as better or worse, taking into account distributional components. Viewing the relationships as individual contracts prevents this by denying the structural reality of the corporation and turning the shareholders into a siphon of wealth rather than an instrument for redistributive justice. An interesting way forward for regulatory theory is to investigate whether the internal and external facets of this question have a significant impact on each other; in other words, if companies *are* considered as institutions and not merely engines for wealth maximisation by shareholders, what effect would internal regulation to ensure social justice within the organisation have on the external operations of companies and groups?

There seems to be growing evidence[35] that the alternative view built on the steps set out above has given rise to 'a crisis of governance born of a convergence of ideological, political and technological forces behind a process of economic globalisation that is shifting power away from governments responsible for the public good and toward a handful of corporations and financial institutions driven by a single imperative – the quest for short-term financial gain'.[36]

Campbell canvasses two solutions 'not limited by the constraints of capitalist ownership'.[37] One is removing profit maximisation as the overwhelming goal of economic effort: 'There can be no doubt that the

---

[35] See ch. 5.
[36] D. Korten, *When Corporations Rule the World*, 12; Chossudovsky, *The Globalisation of Poverty*; Dunning (ed.), *Governments, Globalisation, and International Business*.
[37] Campbell, 'Why Regulate the Modern Corporation?', 127.

limitation placed by production for private profit on the volume of economic activity is a major distortion of potential rational outcomes – such as planned reduction in the amount of necessary labour time – and it is the continuance of capitalist private property in the corporation which produces it.'[38] The other possible solution is an expansion of demand by the political raising of incomes 'by means other than competitive wage struggles in the context of a massively skewed distribution of wealth'.[39] Neither of these is seen as the whole answer but they are put forward for consideration as part of a solution:

> But it is the corporation that excludes them. The regulatory initiatives that follow from the market failure approach are bound to be wrong-headed because they are based on the systematic suppression of the structural problems of the market which the corporation was brought into existence to solve . . . if we want to bring corporate conduct under optimal governance, the formulation of the appropriate governance structure cannot always be biased towards private ownership of the means of production . . . [S]uch 'economic' indicators as now remain relevant to the corporation are the expressions not of productive governance but of our failure properly to bring the corporation under self-conscious and responsible control.[40]

Many authors[41] have argued that appropriate governance structures should be determined by procedures that accept that it is not market failure that is being corrected but real political choices being made. Because of this, the choice should not remain in the hands of a 'small band of elite capitalists' but should occur 'in a proper public fashion'.[42]

A similar argument against de-regulation is put forward by Craypo:

> As labour standards began to decline, various scholars, statesmen, and pundits predicted that lower labour costs would make American industry more efficient and globally competitive. They continue to say so. But little has transpired to support the claim . . . It is reasonable to conclude that corporations have forfeited the historic privilege of unilateral and exclusive decision making and activity in view of the damage they have done and that labour, government and community stakeholders should now be given authority to share this crucial process.[43]

In assuming that the true purpose of regulation is to restore the perfect market, one must proceed cautiously, noting that although some attempts are made to align the neo-classical economics approach with ethical considerations[44] the pure contractual approach, whether viewed from an ownership legal perspective or an economist perspective, would put in place minimal restraints on managerial power and would not

[38] Ibid., 128.   [39] Ibid., 129.   [40] Ibid., 129.
[41] Ibid., and Dworkin, 'Is Wealth a Value?'; Korten, *When Corporations Rule the World*.
[42] Campbell, 'Why Regulate the Modern Corporation?', 130.
[43] Craypo, 'The Impact of Changing Corporate Strategies', 23.
[44] Cheffins, *Company Law*, 158.

restrain the power of a majority of shareholders to expropriate the
property of a minority provided they acted correctly in accordance with
the company's constitution.

Communitaire and corporatist views: the company with a social conscience

Arguing from a stance described as 'institutional', Selznick believes that
the social costs of moral indifference (distorted priorities, defrauded customers,
degraded environments, deformed babies) have created an irrepressible demand
for enhanced accountability, more external regulation and a stronger sense of
social responsibility . . . The enterprise has come to be perceived as infused with
value and thickened by commitment. In recent years there has been a growing
understanding that if moral competence is to be meaningful, it must be built
into the social structure of the enterprise. Thus understood, the corporate
conscience is not elusive or indescribable . . . it consists of specific arrangements
for making accountability an integral part of decision-making.[45]

The essential thrust of this approach is an attempt to align the 'morality'
of the company with the morality of the wider community. This is
pursued despite the admission that the process of 'embedding the
organisation in a social environment . . . is a potential source of distraction and incoherence'.[46] The justification for regulation is clear, as is the
reach of the regulation into the heart of the corporation. What is much
less clear is if or how the interests of the company can emerge from the
'distraction and incoherence' and how managers can be held to account
for decision-making in the interests of the company where those interests are so dispersed. In this instance the arguments of Berle and
Friedman have considerable resonance.[47]

Concession theory

Since the core notion of the concession theory is that the state has the
right to set limits on the operations of companies[48] it may be seen to
provide a free hand for regulation to flourish. However, if this freedom is
pursued relentlessly, the result will become indistinguishable from that
brought about by communitaire doctrine. It does, however, leave the

[45] P. Selznick, 'Self-Regulation and the Theory of Institutions' in G. Teubner, G. Farmer
and E. Murphy (eds.), *Environmental Law and Ecological Responsibility* (Wiley,
Chichester, 1994), 398.
[46] Ibid., 397.
[47] Berle, 'For Whom Are Corporate Managers Trustees?', 1049; Friedman, 'The Social
Responsibility of Business'.
[48] See ch. 1.

freedom to pursue different methods of regulation – the imposition of external norms or the provision of models of internal decision-making structures being just two of the options considered below.

In the context of concession theory it is arguable that the notion of the 'interests of the company' is a mere fig leaf to disguise state interference and to give such interference a free enterprise flavour, whereas in reality the courts are exercising an 'equitable' jurisdiction. Thus in *Peter's American Delicacy Company Limited v Heath* Dixon CJ said:

if no restraint were laid upon the power of altering the articles of association, it would be possible for a shareholder controlling the necessary voting power so to mould the regulations of a company that its operations would be conducted or its property used so that he would profit either in some other capacity other than that of member of the company or, if as a member, in a special and peculiar way inconsistent with conceptions of honesty so widely held or professed that departure from them is described, without further analysis, as fraud. For example, it would be possible to adopt articles requiring that the company should supply him with goods below cost or pay him ninety-nine per cent of its profits for some real or imaginary services.[49]

Now the concept of an unconscionable contract is not impossible to reconcile with the notion of freedom of contract but it certainly takes the gloss off it. However, the justification for the court's intervention as being 'in the interests of the company' does not ring true. The intervention is clearly made in the interests of imposing objective standards of justice and fairness on the parties involved. The notion of the interests of the company represents a flight from the pure contractual/realist approaches because it seeks to impose the fiction of a true identity on the company and use this as a method both of allowing managerial discretion and of imposing state control on that discretion by preventing managers acting in their own interests. It represents a divergence from the simplistic fiction/concession school because, instead of imposing simple external regulations, it goes to the heart of decision-making within the company. It therefore represents a sophisticated concession approach by bowing to the notion of disparate groups within the corporation requiring discrete protection from each other on a balancing of interests basis rather than the mere imposition of substantive state normative intervention. Further, it accepts that the company is a legal fiction, with attributes and personality bestowed by the state, which simultaneously involves the interaction of the state and the company and disparate groups within the company.

---

[49] High Court of Australia 1938 (1939) 61 CLR 457.

Regulatory consequences of the theories

The contractual theories

Primacy of shareholder control

In chapter 1 we explored the important consequence of the contractual theories which elevates the shareholder to the single most important regulator over management power. We turn now to the regulatory consequences of these theories. The first of these is the consequence of the central position of the shareholders.

Posner wrote: 'Separation [of ownership and control] is efficient, and indeed inescapable, given that for most shareholders the opportunity costs of active participation in the management of the firm would be prohibitively high.'[50] Of course, this separation means also that management interests become divorced from those of shareholders. However, the profit maximisation goal means that even a perfect alignment of interests would still result in the effects described by Campbell and Korten above. The discussion of the effectiveness of shareholders as a governance mechanism for corporations thus attains an air of unreality.

It is suggested below that the intervention by the courts in corporate decision-making concerning the alteration of the constitution of the company involves an imposition of a 'fairness' standard. This intervention would be unjustified by the perfecting the market approach if it is accepted that a Pareto standard of efficiency is difficult to achieve and thus a Kaldor–Hicks standard is espoused. It will be remembered that the Pareto test of efficiency is met when at least one individual gains and no one loses. A Kaldor–Hicks improvement occurs where those who benefit do so in a way that outweighs the loss to others. Thus they could *potentially* compensate those who lose. Ogus puts the objections to this test succinctly: 'First, it allows for the coercive imposition of losses on individuals. Secondly, because it balances gains against losses in terms of money, it assumes that one unit of the currency has the same value whoever owns it or may receive it.'[51] Ogus points out that this is a false

---

[50] R. Posner, *Economic Analysis of Law* (2nd edn, Little Brown, Boston, 1977), 411. Admittedly he calls for 'machinery for discouraging management from deflecting too much of the firm's net income from the shareholder to itself', but it is less than clear what this may be in the absence of any effective monitoring class. Reliance on the market for corporate control and incentive schemes is increasingly admitted by some economists not to 'constitute a fully-fledged solution to the divergences of interest which exist between management and other corporate participants' (Cheffins, *Company Law*, 125).

[51] Ogus, *Regulation*, 25.

assumption because the relative value of a unit of currency will vary according to the wealth of the recipient. An efficient decision may benefit western shareholders to the detriment of poor countries.

Jurisdictions adhering to these foundational theories adopt a system where theoretically the general meeting of the body of shareholders has considerable power to make decisions affecting the management of the company. This theoretical power of control is in practice severely limited. If the majority of the shares in a company are held by those controlling that company (and they often are), those controllers can perpetrate all kinds of wrong-doing to the detriment of the minority and then vote that the company should not take legal action to gain compensation. As we have seen, this model has been less than useful in controlling management. Shareholders are no longer an effective governance mechanism.[52]

Purpose of shareholder control

Thus we see not only that shareholders are ineffective in their role of controlling management; but that, even were they effective, it might well be argued that the theories that elevate them to their supreme position of power would contribute to some of the problems identified as flowing from the liberal economist perspective. Thus, if the purpose of shareholder control is seen as aligning the interests of managers with those of shareholders for the purpose of profit maximisation, their control would only prevent managers acting in their own self-interests. It would do nothing at all to further any interests of others who must come in contact with the company's operations. These theories thus present us with a double whammy by elevating shareholders to a role in which they are ineffective, but even were they effective they would have destructive results.

The interests of the company

It follows from the above that the interests of the company and the interests of the shareholders (assumed to be profit maximisation) coincide. It is, of course, the interests of the company that inform and restrict the actions of the controllers. Following this theoretical base means that other interests such as those of employees are excluded from consideration unless they contribute to profit maximisation or are the subject of external regulation, in which case they are a 'negative externality' to be conformed with in as minimalist a way as possible in order to maintain the primary aim of profit maximisation. This is an

---

[52] For a full analysis, see J. Parkinson, *Corporate Power and Responsibility: Issues in the Theory of Company Law* (Clarendon, Oxford, 1993).

extreme vision and there is considerable evidence that practice in companies does not conform to this model. However, the underlying theory means that departure from this mindset needs justification, whether by arguing that happy employees are more productive or that enthusiastic compliance with environmental legislation will give the products of the company a good press.

What other controls over management structure flow from the free enterprise theories?

Market for corporate control

Contractual and in particular free market economic theories are under-pinned by a theoretical control mechanism known as the market for corporate control.[53] 'The contractarian model sees the hostile takeover as a particularly important device for reducing monitoring costs.'[54] If a wealthy company's assets are not being fully utilised by lazy or inefficient managers, then the company presents a tempting target for a predator company, which may make an offer for the shares (which will be under-valued because of the poor performance of management), acquire control of the company, put in an efficient management and restore the efficiency and profitability of the company. 'Executives fear takeover bids since they usually lose their jobs after a successful offer. This anxiety has, however, a beneficial by-product: managers, with their jobs potentially on the line, have an incentive to run their companies in a manner which maximises shareholder wealth.'[55] Further benefits are said to be provided by an efficient reallocation of productive assets away from declining industries.[56]

This theory shows the free market creating its own efficiency police but unfortunately for the credibility of the theory it works in a far from systematic way:[57] 'the selection of takeover targets is not well correlated with levels of managerial performance.'[58]

---

[53] F. Easterbrook and D. Fischel, *The Economic Structure of Corporate Law* (Cambridge, MA, Harvard University Press, 1991).
[54] S. Deakin and G. Slinger, 'Hostile Takeovers, Corporate Law, and the Theory of the Firm' (1997) 24 *Journal of Law and Society* 124 at 126.
[55] Cheffins, *Company Law*, 119; and see J. Macey and G. Miller, 'Corporate Governance and Commercial Banking: A Comparative Examination of Germany, Japan and the United States' (1995) 48 *Stanford Law Review* 73.
[56] M. Jensen, 'Takeovers: Their Causes and Consequences' (1988) 2 *Journal of Economic Perspectives* 21.
[57] See Cheffins, *Company Law*, 1–2.
[58] Deakin and Slinger, 'Hostile Takeovers', 126; and see A. Cosh, A. Hughes, K. Lee and A. Singh, 'Institutional Investment, Mergers and the Market for Corporate Control' (1989) 7 *International Journal of Industrial Organisation* 73.

Evidence concerning post-bid performance also casts doubt on the disciplinary hypothesis. Several studies have identified long-term share-price declines following mergers, whether resulting from a hostile or an agreed bid and the most comprehensive study has found that this negative effect intensifies over time . . . [E]arlier research which, rather than taking share price movement as the benchmark of company performance, was based on accounting data concerning companies' sales, assets and profits . . . found that companies which were acquired by tender offers had slightly below industry-average cash flow and sales performance both before and after takeover, so that 'the hypothesis that takeovers improve performance is not supported'.[59]

Further, the reallocation of production may cause the sudden decline of a geographically disadvantaged region. The Law Society of Scotland challenged the assumption[60] that takeovers were beneficial:

The view that the shareholders are invariably in the best position to determine what is in the best interests of the company, and that therefore the market in companies' capital should be allowed to operate with the least hindrance possible, is not universally adhered to among Scottish commentators. The consequences of a free market in takeovers are seen to be potentially serious not only for the workforce directly involved but also for the wider community, and this may justify a more cumbersome regulatory structure if that is what is required to enable these competing interests to be taken into account.[61]

Again, much-vaunted efficiency considerations may siphon wealth away from poorer areas into wealthier ones.

Communitaire theories

The consequences of embracing communitaire theories vary with the degree to which the state and the enterprise are regarded as assimilated. Soviet law provided a model that could hardly be more different from the economic free enterprise approach. Thus 'when a production entity is created it is allocated basic and circulating assets by the State'.[62] It

---

[59] S. Deakin and Slinger, 'Hostile Takeovers', 144, and see T. Langeteig, 'An Application of a Three-factor Performance Index to Measure Stockholder Gains from Merger (1978) 6 *Journal of Financial Economics* 365; E. Magenheim and D. Mueller, 'Are Acquiring Firm Shareholders Better off after an Acquisition?' in J. Coffee, L. Lowenstein and S. Rose-Ackerman (eds.), *Knights, Raiders and Targets: The Impact of the Hostile Takeover* (New York, Oxford University Press, 1988; A. Agarwal, J. Jaffe and G. Mandelker, 'The Post Performance of Acquiring Firms: A Re-examination of an Anomaly' (1992) 47 *Journal of Finance* 1605; D. Ravenscraft and F. Scherer, 'Life after Takeover' (1987) 36 *Journal of Industrial Economics* 147; F. Scherer, 'Corporate Takeovers: The Efficiency Arguments' (1988) 2 *Journal of Economic Perspectives* 69.

[60] Contained in a DTI consultation document on the EC Thirteenth Directive on Takeovers (1989).

[61] Law Society of Scotland, 'Memorandum on the Thirteenth Directive on Takeovers' (1989).

[62] W. Butler, *Soviet Law* (Butterworth, London, 1988), 245–6.

was perfectly possible for an enterprise to operate at a loss, according to a state plan, and despite the fact that the entity was regarded as having a separate legal personality and could 'conclude those legal transactions which are within the scope of its charter', it was highly confined in its use of resources:

Soviet legislation imposes highly specific requirements upon the disposition of assets by a production entity, and upon the goods and services produced by the entity through plan and planned contracts. All dimensions of enterprise autonomy, consequently, have no independent raison d'etre; they exist conditionally to serve a larger economic function within the planned economy.[63]

The consequent stultification and bureaucracy are legendary.

Concession theories

In chapter 1 it was argued that the concession theory leads to the conclusion that the state's rights extend to a right to ensure that the company is properly run according to notions of equity and fairness, embedded in particular in public law concepts. One consequence of adopting this underlying theory is thus the need to examine more closely the relationship between the public and private notions of companies and the relevance of public law concepts.

As Nolan has noted, 'somewhat strangely, there has been no sustained attempt in England to use relevant elements of public law and writings about those elements to further understandings of how private law, and in particular company law, might control discretionary power vested in a company board or in a director'.[64] The explanation may well be the apparent adherence of English law to contractual foundational theories and the consequent pretence of an absence of public law principles from the court's decision-making. When there was clear acceptance of the doctrine that the power of companies to act was a concession from the Crown and acts beyond the powers that had been granted were void, *ultra vires* applied as much to companies as to state officials. This is precisely in line with the 'orthodox' explanation of the *ultra vires* doctrine defended by Forsyth, who takes the Browne-Wilkinson formulation of the doctrine in *R v Lord President of the Privy Council, ex parte Page*:[65]

The fundamental principle [of judicial review] is that the courts will intervene to ensure that the powers of public decision making bodies are exercised lawfully.

---

[63] Ibid.
[64] R. Nolan, 'The Proper Purpose Doctrine and Company Directors' in B. Rider (ed.), *The Realm of Company Law* (Kluwer, London, 1998).
[65] [1993] AC 682.

In all cases [except error of law on the face of the record] . . . this intervention
. . . is based on the proposition that such powers have been conferred on the
decision-maker on the underlying assumption that the powers are to be
exercised only within the jurisdiction conferred, in accordance with fair
procedures and, in a *Wednesbury* sense, reasonably. If the decision-maker
exercises his powers outside the jurisdiction conferred, in a manner which is
procedurally irregular or is *Wednesbury* unreasonable, he is acting *ultra vires* his
powers and therefore unreasonably.[66]

The rise of both economic and legal contractualism was in direct
opposition to the concession, fiction theorists and meant that the role of
the state was minimalised. Judges backed off. But it is interesting to note
that the *method* by which the judges absented themselves was very close
to the 'ouster' clause mechanism feared by Forsyth. This is the drafting
of legislation to contain a clause preventing review of the decision.
Forsyth quotes from a 1953 South African statute: 'no court shall be
competent to enquire into or to give judgment on the validity of any . . .
proclamation made under s3 of the Act.'[67] Thus the court's jurisdiction
is 'ousted' by cunning draftsmanship. A parallel process can be seen in
the capitulation of the courts to contractual theories, permitting their
inherent jurisdiction to be undermined.

Further, as we shall see, having abandoned any effective doctrine of
corporate *ultra vires*, judges found themselves in a wilderness, unable to
review company decisions on a coherent basis, and instead appealing to
strange contractual contortions[68] and the false concepts of the 'interests
of the company'[69] or a 'wrong done to the company'.[70]

Christopher Forsyth has entered an eloquent plea for the doctrine of
ultra vires remaining the acknowledged foundation for the majority of
the doctrine of judicial review.[71] Company lawyers can only shudder
and agree. The dismantling of the *ultra vires* doctrine has seen a hideous
mess wrought by the judiciary out of the contest for supremacy between
the contractual and concession notions. Thus, judges instinctively
would wish to retain the ability to review discretionary power exercised
by directors since the consequences of those decisions are wide ranging
and could affect many innocent people. However, the contrary argu-

---

[66] C. Forsyth, 'Of Fig Leaves and Fairy Tales: The *Ultra Vires* Doctrine, the Sovereignty
of Parliament and Judicial Review' (1996) *Cambridge Law Journal* 122, at 129–30.
[67] Ibid., 130.
[68] In the interpretation of section 14 of the Companies Act 1985.
[69] In seeking to protect minorities where there is a change of articles of association.
[70] In protecting minorities where there is a 'fraud on the minority or a fraud on the
company'.
[71] Defending it against its realist critics, including Dawn Oliver, 'Is the Ultra Vires Rule
the Basis of Judicial Review?' [1987] *Public Law* 543; P. Craig, *Administrative Law* (3rd
edn, Sweet & Maxwell, London, 1994), esp. 12–17.

ment that all those involved are merely freely exercising their contractual rights resonates through many decisions. Thus we see the initial doctrine that the company cannot act outside its objects, as stated in the memorandum extended to registered companies in *Ashbury Railway Company v Riche*[72] on the basis of protection 'not merely, perhaps I might say not mainly, for the benefit of the shareholders for the time being in the company, but were enactments intended also to provide for the interests of two other very important bodies; in the first place, those who might become shareholders in succession to the persons who were shareholders for the time being; and secondly the outside public, and more particularly those who might be creditors of companies of this kind.'[73]

Here we may see the interplay between three competing theories. Traditional and bottom–up concessionary theories vie with contractualist notions, causing inevitable confusion. State concession theory dictates that the ambit of the delegation of state power to a corporation should not be exceeded, but the protection of both future shareholders and 'the outside public' may be seen as based in a different concession approach. Here, it is submitted, it is a question not of the state restricting the operation of the company for state purposes, but of an imposition of social justice norms. It may thus be seen to be a product of a 'bottom–up' concessionary approach, which feeds into corporate behaviour expectations of the general public since it is from the general public that the individuals forming the corporation have gained the legitimacy for its operations.

Now, future shareholders and the general public do not figure in contractualist doctrine and, clearly, creditors would be expected to make their own bargains and not rely on state protection. There is thus clear evidence of a concession approach here.

Starting from the traditional delegation approach, it is significant[74] that the doctrine had been applied earlier to statutory companies incorporated by special Act of Parliament. This was necessary because such companies often had compulsory purchase powers over land required for the construction of railways and canals.

Craig[75] and Forsyth[76] both point out that monopolies were subject to the doctrine of *ultra vires* even when that power existed de facto. Corporations were even more subject to that doctrine, particularly

---

[72] (1875) LR 7 HL 653.   [73] Per Lord Cairns LC.
[74] L. Sealy, *Cases and Materials in Company Law* (6th edn, Butterworth, London, 1996), 126.
[75] Craig, *Administrative Law*, 222–5.
[76] Forsyth, 'Of Fig Leaves and Fairy Tales', 124.

where the only type of known corporation was formed by a direct grant from the Crown. Clearly the historic charter companies fell squarely into the category of companies that owed their powers and privileges to delegation by the Crown. The courts had also decided in *Re Crown Bank*[77] that a proper statement of objects had not been made where the objects of the company were expressed in terms (in the words of North J) '[s]o wide that it might be said to warrant the company in giving up banking business and embarking in a business with the object of establishing a line of balloons between the earth and the moon'.

The move to a contractualist approach later began to influence the courts significantly, in particular when it was determined that it was permissible to achieve an effect similar to that in *Re Crown Bank* by listing every imaginable kind of business. In *Cotman v Brougham*[78] the company's memorandum had thirty sub-clauses enabling the company to carry on almost any kind of business, and the objects clause concluded with a declaration that every sub-clause should be construed as a substantive clause and not limited or restricted by reference to any other sub-clause or by the name of the company and that none of such sub-clauses or the objects specified therein should be deemed subsidiary or auxiliary merely to the objects mentioned in the first sub-clause.

The last part of this statement of objects was there to avoid a restriction that the courts had been prone to place on statements of objects. They had construed them according to a 'main objects' rule. This meant that the main object of the company could be determined either from the name of the company or from the first named object on the list of objects. All subsequent statements in the objects clause would then be considered to be powers of the company that could be validly exercised only for the purpose of furthering the 'main' object. In *Cotman v Brougham*, the draftsman had drafted the statement of objects to avoid this rule and also sought to avoid the *Re Crown Bank* restriction by the long list of thirty objects. His attempt was successful. It was held that the memorandum must be construed according to its literal meaning, although the practice of drafting memoranda in this way was criticised. As Sealy points out:

The judges saw it as their role to fight a rearguard action against these attempts to undermine the *ultra vires* doctrine. They protested frequently at the length and prolixity of the drafting – a futile gesture, and a rather unbecoming attitude for them to take, since most of them must, as counsel, have spent much professional time earlier on in their careers in drafting and settling the very terms which they now sought to condemn![79]

[77] (1890) 44 ChD 634.   [78] [1918] AC 514.
[79] Sealy, *Cases and Materials on Company Law*, 127.

However, this attitude was 'partly out of a misplaced sense of rectitude, but more justifiably because it was, after all, the strongest weapon they had to cope with cases of blatant corporate wrongdoing'.[80]

A further extension of the liberty given to companies[81] came with the acceptance of the 'subjective clause' in *Bell Houses Ltd v City Wall Properties Ltd*.[82] In that case the company's memorandum of association contained the following clause: '3(c) To carry on any other trade or business whatsoever which can, in the opinion of the board of directors, be advantageously carried on by [the plaintiff company] in connection with or as ancillary to any of the above businesses or the general business [of the company].' With reference to the subjective clause, Danckwerts LJ said in *Bell Houses:*

On the balance of the authorities it would appear that the opinion of the directors if bona fide can dispose of the matter; and why should it not decide the matter? The shareholders subscribe their money on the basis of the memorandum of association and if that confers the power on the directors to decide whether in their opinion it is proper to undertake particular business in the circumstances specified, why should not their decision be binding?[83]

Note that the protection of the public and of creditors appears to have fallen away in the minds of the judges as contractualism gains the upper hand. The problem posed by the demise of *ultra vires* and the triumph of contractualism is that the courts have lost a potent weapon of control and an excellent tool of analysis.[84] As will be argued later,[85] this loss extends not only to methods of controlling the exercise of power but to methods of determining the mode of decision-making within the company.

Where there is no question of *ultra vires*, the source of the court's interference with other corporate decision-making remains obscure. The standard statement of the contractual theory is reflected in the judgment of Jessell MR in *Pender v Lushington*:[86]

In all cases of this kind, where men exercise their rights of property, they exercise their rights from some motive adequate or inadequate, and I have always considered the law to be that those who have rights of property are entitled to exercise them, whatever their motives might be for such exercise.

Clear enough it would seem, but strangely he feels supported in this view 'by the case of *Menier v Hooper's Telegraph Works*[87] where Lord Justice Mellish observes: "I am of the opinion that, although it may be quite

---

[80] Ibid., 127.
[81] Yet another drafting device was to specify that the powers of the company were in fact objects; *Re Introductions* [1970] Ch 199, *Re Rolled Steel Products (Holdings) Ltd v British Steel Corpn* [1986] Ch 246.
[82] [1966] 2 QB 656.   [83] Ibid., 683.
[84] As pointed out by Nolan, 'Proper Purpose Doctrine and Company Directors', 17–22.
[85] See ch. 6.   [86] (1877) 6 ChD 70.   [87] (1874) LR 9 Ch 250.

true that the shareholders of a company may vote as they please, and for the purpose of their own interests, yet the majority of shareholders cannot sell the assets of the company and keep the consideration."[88]

Why support was to be had for his proposition in a statement that set limitations on the selfish exercise of rights is unclear. That the courts have imposed limitations is clear, although predicting the exercise of this power is an art not a science. Quite simply the courts appear to have reserved the right to prevent corporate decisions that in some way are unconscionable. In doing so they may either accept that there is an element of commercial morality that they feel obliged to enforce or accept that the simple contractual construct of the company is unreal: it involves the interests of others besides the shareholders; it has interests of its own. In *Standard Chartered Bank v Walker*[89] Vinelott J appealed to 'equity' in preventing shareholders from voting against resolutions proposed by banks for the restructuring of a company and the dismissal of two of its directors. The company was insolvent and the banks were not prepared to go ahead with the restructuring of the company if the resolutions were not passed. Vinelott J held that 'opposing or in any way obstructing the reconstruction proposals would be so pointlessly harmful that whatever motive inspired it would amount to the wilful dissipation of assets which the court has jurisdiction, consistently with the Mareva principles, to prevent'.

But does it? Where from? We have the imposition of 'general principles of law and equity' by Lindley MR in *Allen v Gold Reefs of West Africa*.[90] The link with judicial review is evident from a subsequent remark of Lord Lindley in *British Equitable Assurance Co v Bailey*: 'of course, the powers of altering by-laws, like other powers, must be exercised bona fide, and having regard to the purposes for which they are created.'[91]

In these instances a parallel may be drawn with wider notions of the basis of judicial review of administrative decision, in particular those that rest on the legitimacy of decision-making flowing from a process of consultation or participation; 'a sufficiently close relationship exists between the ideas underpinning claims to participation in government and the regulation of process . . . to indicate . . . [a] basis for the latter which moves beyond the mere protection of substantive interests'.[92]

This aspect of control by the courts, together with the reach of the doctrine of proper purpose, will be explored more fully in chapter 6.

---

[88] Ibid., 75.   [89] [1992] BCLC 603.
[90] [1900] 1 Ch 656; see ch. 1.   [91] [1906] AC 35.
[92] G. Richardson and H. Genn, *Administrative Law and Government Action* (Oxford University Press, Oxford, 1994), 124; and see P. McAuslan, *The Ideologies of Planning Law* (Pergamon Press, Oxford, 1980).

Justifications for types or models and methods of regulation

A number of different methods of regulation may be identified

External punitive regulation I have argued elsewhere[93] that the imposition of penal or quasi-penal rules in order to prevent a particular aspect of behaviour, used in isolation, is an ineffective way of attempting to regulate commercial behaviour because of the inherent difficulties of defining the limits of prohibited behaviour clearly enough where the underlying commercial transactions are complex. Because of the very serious results to the company of a successful prosecution of either the company or one of its senior managers, a criminal investigation is likely to be seen as a threat to be resisted. Adherence to contractualism has strengthened the view that external regulation of this type needs careful and powerful justification. The consequence is that the regulator is left outside the company trying to pierce the corporate veil in order to find out enough to prosecute.[94] Further, the speed and complexity of commercial operations make external regulation increasingly ineffective.[95] In these circumstances the corporate veil will resist penetration and the bubble will remain intact.[96] It is for this reason that prosecutors have violated the right not to self-incriminate in order to strengthen their hand.[97] Such behaviour, however, raises questions of the violation of fundamental rights. If prosecutions cannot be effective without doing so, does this not indicate that there is something amiss with the method of regulation?

However, it must be borne in mind that the existence of criminal penalties may deter some from behaving in the prohibited way. A small number of successful prosecutions may therefore not be a true reflection of the success of a measure. Nevertheless, for a number of reasons the penal approach has severe deficiencies. The problems associated with this form of regulation are greater because in many jurisdictions, including the UK, companies are primarily seen as individualistic free

---

[93] J. Dine, *Criminal Law in the Company Context* (Dartmouth, Aldershot, 1995).
[94] See Ogus, *Regulation*.
[95] Particularly but not exclusively in the financial sector. See C. Goodhart, P. Hartman, D. Llewellyn, L. Rojas-Suarez and S. Weisbrod, *Financial Regulation* (Routledge, London, 1998), 45.
[96] Ogus speaks of the company as 'a black box' resisting criminal legislation; Ogus, *Regulation*, 97–8.
[97] Gerard McCormack, 'Investigations and the Right to Silence' (1993) *Journal of Business Law* 425; Dine, *Criminal Law in the Company Context*, ch. 9.

market tools, making interference in internal affairs difficult to justify[98] and therefore it may well be resented.[99] Analysing the punitive approach to regulation, Ayres and Braithwaite[100] make a plea for a new approach to regulating companies. Based on economic analysis as well as empirical research carried out amongst pharmaceutical companies,[101] coal mining companies,[102] Australian regulatory agencies,[103] and nursing homes,[104] they observe that a highly punitive regime engenders a subculture of resistance[105] and that '[a] crucial danger of a punitive posture that projects negative expectations of the regulated actor is that it inhibits self-regulation'.[106] In essence the regulator is seen as the enemy. People will find the approach humiliating and will 'resent and resist it in ways that include abandoning self-regulation'.[107] Further, a solely punitive regime 'engenders a game of regulatory cat and mouse whereby firms defy the spirit of the law by exploiting loopholes, and the state writes more and more specific laws to cover the loopholes'.[108]

Ayres and Braithwaite argue that, added to this climate of resentment, the inefficiency, expense and uncertainty of enforcing punitive laws make it clear that a cooperative standpoint should be the starting position. A cooperative standpoint is clearly impossible when reliance is placed solely on punitive ex post facto sanctions. This viewpoint is

---

[98] R. Posner, *Economic Analysis of Law* (4th edn, Little Brown, Boston, 1992); F. Easterbrook and D. Fischel, 'Limited Liability and the Corporation' (1985) *University of Chicago Law Review* 89; Cheffins, *Company Law*, ch. 3; Ogus, *Regulation*, 29; D. Sullivan and D. Conlon, 'Crisis in Transition in Corporate Governance Paradigms: The Role of the Chancery Court of Delaware' (1997) *Law and Society Review* 713, esp. 719.

[99] Taking a lesson from the collapse of Barings, it should be noted that Barings London had considerable difficulty in penetrating the Singapore operation. The 'fortress Singapore' mentality was a significant factor in the length of time it took to uncover the Leeson losses. *Report of the Board of Banking Supervision Inquiry into the Circumstances of the Collapse of Barings* (HMSO, London, 1995) (BoBS Report), para. 2.19, setting out the clash of cultures between brokers and bankers; and see N. Leeson, *Rogue Trader* (Warner Books, London, 1996), ch. 4; S. Fay, *The Collapse of Barings* (Arrow Books, London, 1996), 102.

[100] I. Ayres and J. Braithwaite, *Responsive Regulation* (Oxford University Press, Oxford, 1992).

[101] J. Braithwaite, *Corporate Crime in the Pharmaceutical Industry* (Routledge & Kegan Paul, London, 1984).

[102] J. Braithwaite, *To Punish or Persuade: Enforcement of Coal Mine Safety* (State University of New York Press, Albany, 1985).

[103] P. Grabosky and J. Braithwaite, *Of Manners Gentle: Enforcement Strategies of Australian Business Agencies* (OUP, Melbourne, 1986).

[104] J. Braithwaite, T. Makkai, V. Braithwaite, D. Gibson and D. Ermann, *The Contribution of the Standards Monitoring Process to the Quality of Nursing Home Life: A Preliminary Report* (Department of Community Services and Health, Melbourne, 1990).

[105] Ayres and Braithwaite, *Responsive Regulation*, 19–20.

[106] Ibid., 25.   [107] Ibid.   [108] Ibid., 26.

reinforced by studies into the delivery of aid programmes in disadvantaged countries. Chambers[109] argues that an authoritarian education system followed by the delivery of aid programmes by powerful bureaucrats (whom he calls uppers) leads to the recipients (called lowers, equivalent to the regulated) being driven to three possible postures:

They can conform, and adopt and internalise the paradigms of uppers, accepting the transfer of reality. They can speak out, rebel and reject. Or they can follow a middle course of diplomacy and deceit.[110]

In particular, in this context Chambers shows how a punitive style of management leads (either alone or in combination with other factors) to deceit: 'performance tends to be exaggerated, and targets reported achieved when they have not been . . . The achievement of targets becomes a largely book-keeping affair.'[111] This deception can be compounded by self-deception by the 'uppers', and by mutual deception and further exaggerated by distance and time. These factors are by no means confined to punitive regulatory systems, but such a system seems to encourage distance between the regulator and the regulated and therefore to multiply the problems.

A regulator with both a degree of discretion and a relationship with the regulated body is necessary.

A dual-purpose regulator

Some aspect of the existence of a regulator with a dual purpose benefits the company that is regulated. The regulator both confers benefits and acts as policeman. An example is a stock exchange.[112] Anyone reading the rules of a stock exchange might be forgiven for thinking that the sole purpose of the body is to regulate the sale of shares. However, its primary purpose is to *facilitate* those sales. For that purpose it may demand information from a company and this will be freely given because the result will be the benefit of a stock exchange listing. It will therefore be at an advantage when policing issues are at stake. Because of the cosier relationship, the corporate veil is less opaque.

The problem with employing this method with commercial companies is the size of the sector. A regulator that sought to monitor the

---

[109] R. Chambers, *Whose Reality Counts* (Intermediate Technology Publications, London, 1997).
[110] Ibid., 84.
[111] Ibid., 87, giving examples of the growing of high-yield rice in India.
[112] 'The classic example of intrinsic self-regulation' – A. C. Page, 'Self Regulation: The Constitutional Dimension' (1986) *Modern Law Review* 141, 145. Note that this is industry self-regulation not individual firm self-regulation, which is increasingly being seen as a possible answer; see the arguments of Ayres and Braithwaite below.

detail of company operations would be an immense institution and the danger of suppression of variety and innovation is immediately obvious. However, the recent outbreak of Codes of Conduct overseen by the Stock Exchange have shown that using such a regulator to affect internal corporate governance mechanisms, at least for listed companies, is by no means an impossibility.

Internal controls

The third method of regulation seeks to put in place a system of internal controls that prevent aberrant behaviour. This will include all the methods of internal corporate governance. In this system the corporate veil does not obstruct because this is regulation from the inside. An example would be the systems of control in banks and insurance companies that identify transactions that are likely to be money laundering transactions.[113]

However, internal regulations may well need to have some form of external controls.

Enforced self-regulation

Ayres and Braithwaite make the strong point that the 'requirement for breaking out of the sterile contest between deregulation and stronger regulation is innovation in regulatory design'.[114] Arguing that '[t]he appropriateness of a particular strategy is contingent on the legal, constitutional, and cultural context and the history of its invocation', they put forward the strategy of enforced self-regulation. This requires an individual firm to propose its own regulatory standards. These rules would have a public enforcement mechanism. This system is distinct from co-regulation, which they take to mean industry association self-regulation. Using the Coase insight that firms are organised to produce goods cheaper than by individual contracting, the authors argue that a government should internally produce public goods, i.e. public regulation, only when this is cheaper than external contracting. They analyse enforced self-regulation as a form of subcontracting regulatory functions to private actors.[115] This form of regulation is arguably cheaper and more efficient than 'outside' regulation, in particular because it achieves greater depth within the company and engenders more cooperation. Further advantages would be the avoidance of over-strict rules for small enterprises and rules that evolve with fast-changing circumstances. 'In

---

[113] In the UK, SI 1993 No 1933.
[114] Ayres and Braithwaite, *Responsive Regulation*, 101.   [115] Ibid., 103.

too many areas, necessary regulations gather dust in the "too hard" basket because of the consensus-building demands of the command and control model.'[116] The alternative is universal legislation that is bland, such as the exhortation to produce accounts that show a 'true and fair' view of the state of a company's finances.

The authors argue also that companies would be more committed to their own rules and that the confusion of two rulebooks (state and company) would be avoided.

Public interest groups, proceduralisation and codes

Ayres and Braithwaite put forward a novel approach that, they argue, will prevent 'regulatory capture'. They believe that this problem can be minimised by 'tripartism'.[117] This involves the empowerment of public interest groups (PIGs). The strategy is to identify a PIG that is directly concerned with the enforcement of the spirit behind a particular piece of legislation (environmental agencies for environmental law, employees for Health and Safety, etc.). In order to prevent cosiness, competition between groups would be engendered. The role of these groups would then be to oversee the regulator/regulated relationship and step in where there was undue evidence of capture and corruption.

The empowerment of PIGs is argued also from the standpoint of democratic involvement: 'An opportunity for participation by stake-holders in decisions over matters that affect their lives is a democratic good independent of any improved outcomes that follow from it.'[118] The authors' thesis is that a democracy limited simply to providing a vote for citizens will be undermined by the power accrued by the corporate sector. Selective empowerment of PIGs provides some element of counterbalance to that power. Further, empowerment of PIGs will of necessity cause the building of trusting relationships since there 'is no reason for us to trust those who have no influence over our lives; but once an actor is empowered in relation to us, we are well advised to build a relationship of trust with that actor'.[119]

Similar considerations of democratic equity-building trust have led to growing interest in a movement in legal philosophy, 'la procéduralisation du droit',[120] led by the Centre de Philosophie du Droit at Université

---

[116] Ibid., 112.   [117] Ibid., ch. 3.   [118] Ibid., 82.   [119] Ibid., 84.

[120] Which may also have influenced the latest draft of the worker participation provisions of the European Company Statute. This is characterised by a framework for negotiation between the company and employees. See 'Proposal for a Compromise on the proposal for a Council Directive supplementing the European Company Statute with Regard to the Involvement of Employees' in J. Dine and P. Hughes, *EC Company Law* (Jordans, Bristol, looseleaf), A3–52. The retreat from a compulsory minimum

Catholique de Louvain. In one form this approach involves the law stepping back from creating formal substantive norms and concentrating instead in providing the framework for decision-making by ensuring that the best possible forum of interested parties can be convened to arrive at the eventual substantive norm. If applied more generally in approaches to regulation, this approach should free regulators from the impossible task of formulating the best substantive rules and allow them instead to concentrate on providing the best possible decision-making forum to achieve probity in the market place.

Both approaches have echoes in the recent outbreak of codes, including Cadbury,[121] Greenbury[122] and Hampel.[123] The two approaches have similarities in that much of the thrust of the Cadbury, Greenbury and Hampel reports was to ensure that the proper *persons* were in the right positions within the company[124] and that proper decision-making structures were in place. Thus Greenbury required the directors of a listed company to set up a remuneration committee, consisting exclusively of non-executive directors, to determine the company's policy on executive directors' pay and specific packages for each executive director. For Cadbury, the make-up and function of the board were by far the most controversial area. The committee emphasised that tests of a board's effectiveness included the way in which members as a whole work together.[125] They also felt that executive and non-executive directors are likely to contribute in different and complementary ways. Non-executive directors could make two particularly important contributions, which would not conflict with the unitary nature of the board.[126] These were the role of 'reviewing' the performance of the board and executive[127] and taking the lead 'where potential conflicts of interest arise'.[128] Further, Cadbury elicited a

standard of worker involvement together with the clear statements concerning the expected agenda and timetable for negotiations sends a clear signal that the diversity of models of companies within member states are recognised and acknowledged without a wholesale retreat from the position that the role of the employee is central to the commercial success of companies. This approach seeks to harmonise rules from a realistic understanding of diversity.

[121] *The Report on the Financial Aspects of Corporate Governance* (Gee, London, 1992).

[122] *Directors' Remuneration: Report of a Study Group chaired by Sir Richard Greenbury* (Gee, London, 1995).

[123] *Committee on Corporate Governance Final Report* (Gee, London, 1998).

[124] See the emphasis on the board's composition (separation of CEO and chairman and non-executive directors – Hampel Principles, 2.2–2.5, following Cadbury), remuneration committees (Hampel 2.11, following Cadbury and Greenbury), the role of directors and composition and appointment of directors (Hampel 3.14 and 3.19).

[125] Cadbury, *Report on Financial Aspects*, 20, para. 4.2.

[126] Ibid., 20, para. 4.5.   [127] Ibid., 20, para. 4.5.

[128] Ibid., 21, para. 4.6.

response from the Institutional Shareholders Committee, which also addresses power balance and decision-making structures, in a paper entitled 'The Responsibilities of Institutional Shareholders'.[129] This was not a specific response to the Cadbury proposals but dealt with some of the issues raised in the draft report. The Institutional Shareholders Committee acknowledge that '[b]ecause of the size of their shareholdings, institutional investors, as part proprietors of a company, are under a strong obligation to exercise their influence in a responsible manner'.[130] The paper examines ways in which this responsibility should be fulfilled including 'regular, systematic contact at senior executive level to exchange views and information on strategy, performance, Board Membership and quality of management'.[131] They also felt that

[institutional investors] should support Boards by a positive use of voting rights, unless they have good reason for doing otherwise [and] should take a positive interest in the composition of Boards of Directors with particular reference to:

(i) Concentrations of decision-making power not formally constrained by checks and balances appropriate to the particular company

(ii) The appointment of a core of non-executives of appropriate calibre, experience and independence.[132]

The Cadbury Committee clearly accepted these views and placed heavy reliance on the power of institutional shareholders within a company.

The Cadbury Committee's recommendations have drawn considerable criticism.[133] The voluntary nature of the code has been criticised,[134] and a major criticism is that the reliance on non-executive directors leads to a type of two-tier board, with different directors

---

[129] Institutional Shareholders Committee, 'The Responsibilities of Institutional Shareholders', December 1991.

[130] Ibid., 1. But Riley expresses doubts that this will happen: 'there are more good reasons for suggesting that shareholder voice . . . will encourage more "technical" than "substantive" compliance. For the more that "substantive" compliance is sought, the more time, information and expertise is required from institutions. It is surely far easier, for example, to ensure that the board has the requisite number of directors who fall within a pre-defined class of "independents" than to ensure that they are truly independent from management, highly motivated, enjoy the requisite resources and so forth'; Riley, 'Understanding and Regulating the Corporation', 595, uncannily forecasting the 'box-ticking' mentality found by the Hampel Committee. Cheffins takes a more optimistic viewpoint: 'it . . . has not because of its voluntary nature been the recipe for inactivity which some sceptics feared'; Cheffins, *Company Law*, 650.

[131] Institutional Shareholders' Committee, 'Responsibilities'.

[132] Ibid., 6.

[133] See Riley, 'Understanding and Regulating the Corporation'; V. Finch, 'Board Performance and Cadbury on Corporate Governance' [1992] *Journal of Business Law* 581.

[134] Ibid. See also Parkinson, *Corporate Power and Responsibility*, 193–4; Finch, 'Board Performance and Cadbury on Corporate Governance', 584.

fulfilling different functions.[135] This criticism must be viewed in the light of a proper understanding of the two-tier board system as it operates elsewhere in Europe.[136] It often includes provision for a supervisory board that has the power to dismiss the executive board. The Cadbury proposals do not go very far towards that system; there is no suggestion that the appointment and dismissal of all directors should be removed from shareholder control.[137]

The Hampel revisit to Cadbury and Greenbury took a less interventionist viewpoint than Greenbury and Cadbury. It started from the viewpoint that the accountability purpose of corporate governance in the UK has been emphasised in recent years over and above its 'contribution to business prosperity'. The committee 'would wish to see the balance corrected'.[138] The remit of the committee was to review Cadbury and Greenbury but also to look at corporate governance issues afresh. The committee deplored the 'box-ticking' approach to compliance with the codes and called for flexibility on the grounds that apparent compliance with the codes may conceal the fact that the substance of the recommendations is being ignored. Interestingly the aim of those who control companies is seen as 'the preservation and the greatest practicable enhancement over time of their shareholders' investment'.[139] This narrow approach permits other 'stakeholders' only a very limited role in the affairs of the company, although the committee accepted that one of the roles of management is to foster good relations with employees, customers, credit providers and others whose activities impact on the company's well-being.

The enforcement approach that requires compliance or explanation of non-compliance has the effect of permitting diversity and allowing the regulator to adopt an approach that starts from a cooperative standpoint but can be backed by escalating interference where cooperation is not forthcoming. The issue of internal controls illustrates the 'hands off' approach that makes codes a possible regulatory mechanism even for large diverse sectors of industry. The emphasis is on identifying a system

---

[135] See Cheffins, *Company Law*, 622, emphasising that if monitoring directors sit on a 'one- tier' board they 'will be in an awkward predicament. They will be compelled to act as watch-dogs at the same time as their participation in corporate decision-making leads them to identify themselves with management's decisions and to view the executive directors as colleagues.'

[136] For a detailed examination of the German system see J. J. du Plessis, 'Corporate Governance: Reflections on the German Two-Tier Board System' (1996) 1 *Journal of South African Law* 20.

[137] For a discussion of the merits (and otherwise) of the Cadbury approach, see Cheffins, *Company Law*, 642 et seq.

[138] Hampel, *Committee on Corporate Governance*, 10.   [139] Ibid., 10.

that works for individual companies, rather than imposing a standard formula of corporate governance structure externally.

When designing regulations for single companies it should be possible to build on the approaches of Ayres and Braithwaite, *procéduralisation* and codes by developing corporate governance mechanisms to represent the interest groups most closely involved in corporate governance. It may well be argued that directors are in the worst possible danger of 'capture' by their own self-interests.[140] In nearly all companies the interest groups would involve employees and probably creditors, but the thrust of the *procéduralisation* and code approach would be to expect individual companies to design the corporate governance structures, with an explanation as to how these structures best serve the aim of the corporation. The new structures would provide mechanisms to compensate for the deficiencies of reliance on shareholders as a mechanism for protecting the rights and interests of the company.

This would create a system of enforced self-regulation, with an external regulator forming a cooperative association with the regulated but with sanctions available for non-compliance. Firms would be happier to design their own rules and structures rather than have rigid formulae imposed externally, and the regulator's job, consistent with the public interest in proper corporate governance, will be to insist on a standard of equity of treatment for the constituencies most nearly connected with the commercial endeavour of the firm. The regulator should be assisted in this by an explanation by each firm of the way in which their internal mechanisms relate both to the aims of the company and to fair treatment of constituencies as well as an assessment of the firm's performance in accordance with the Royal Society of Arts suggestion[141] of assessing a firm's performance by reference to its relationship with constituents, particularly employees, rather than on the basis of profitability alone. When groups of companies are concerned, greater difficulties arise. However, the importance of internal regulation cannot be over-emphasised.

Regulation in the financial services sector

A study of the regulatory structure in the financial services sector is instructive, and a number of lessons can be drawn from it: first, that it is

---

[140] Even from the economic contractualist standpoint, directors are seen as having interests imperfectly aligned with those of the shareholders; they thus should be subject to some measures designed to align their interests more perfectly. Usually profit-related incentives are suggested.

[141] Royal Society of Arts, *Tomorrow's Company* (RSA, London, 1995).

vital to identify the aims of the regulation; secondly, the importance of internal regulation; thirdly, the consequences that can flow from restructuring finance in a group situation; and fourthly the difficulties of attempting to regulate in a world market where transactions happen at remarkable speed.

Regulation in the financial market sphere has often been divided into *prudential regulation* and *conduct of business regulation*. This division is arguably flawed in two respects: it inadequately reflects philosophical justifications for regulation, and it focuses on the type of rule imposed rather than on the type of risk that is to be addressed.

Financial markets may be said to represent a capitalist free market red in tooth and claw. Nevertheless, one aim of regulation in the financial services sphere is the protection of the individual investor.[142] This can be seen as a perfecting of markets[143] because the individual is seen as vulnerable, unable to access as much information or judge the value or comparative value of investments in comparison to other, more sophisticated investors and therefore at a disadvantage. However, regulation to achieve this end may also, and with perhaps greater justification,[144] be seen as a reflection of the state's interest in the public interest goal of protection of the financially vulnerable.[145] This aim, therefore reflects a concession approach to regulation. Attempts to explain the achievement of such public interest goals[146] in terms of perfecting the market[147] have perhaps obscured a real distinction between regulations aimed at client protection and regulations aimed at the protection of the market, i.e. systemic risk regulation.[148] It is unlikely that if Aunt Agatha loses her savings because of dishonesty in a prospectus a full-scale market collapse will ensue. It is therefore sensible to examine regulations in order to determine whether there is a risk to a victim or a risk to the market as a whole, rather than take the approach of dividing the rules into prudential and conduct of business regulations that do not reflect the true aims

---

[142] Such protection may have the side-effect of creating trusted markets that attract more volume.

[143] See page 109 above.   [144] See page 21 above.

[145] See Cheffins, *Company Law*, ch. 3, for an analysis of justifications for state intervention.

[146] G. Gemmill, 'Regulating Futures Markets: A Review in the Context of British and American Practice' in M. Streit (ed.), *Futures Markets* (Blackwell, Oxford, 1983), 295, 303 et seq, where the only 'moral hazard' identified as a reason for regulation is 'an obligation to prevent a financial collapse'.

[147] See page 109 et seq. above.

[148] The distinction is drawn in Goodhart et al., *Financial Regulation*, ch. 8, but the author argues that 'systemic and prudential considerations require similar types of regulation (e.g. capital adequacy)'. It is here argued that the difference is more fundamental than this gives credit for and extends to the type and weight of regulation.

of the regulations. This objective-based approach has led both Taylor[149] and Goodhart[150] to propose an institutional structure based on the division between systemic stability and consumer protection.[151] Systemic collapse is clearly more likely where a group of companies is at risk. The likely ramifications of a group collapse will involve all the counterparties of each member of the group.

If only a small risk of systemic collapse is involved, then the degree and nature of regulation is to be tested primarily according to the moral and financial impact on the individual, with a view to whether or not indignation at the treatment of the individual will undermine trust in the market as a whole. Regulation that seeks to prevent systemic collapse is less to be based on such moral concerns than on the highest degree of risk prevention. Reconciliation of trades is not a moral issue but a matter of minimising the risk of collapse.

Two types of regulatory rule

Prudential regulation attempts to monitor the financial soundness of a firm. This monitoring is carried out by examining solvency ratios and balance sheets, etc. It makes no distinction between monitoring for client protection purposes and monitoring to ensure that there is no danger of systemic collapse. Conduct of business regulation focuses on issues such as the truthfulness of advertising and the conduct of salespersons.

The distinction between prudential regulation and conduct of business regulation has been fundamental in UK regulation to the extent that it has been conducted in many cases by separate institutions. Thus, the Department of Trade and Industry, the Building Societies Commission and the Friendly Societies Commission had responsibility for prudential monitoring of insurance companies, building societies and friendly societies, respectively, whereas the conduct of business of these same institutions was in the hands of the self-regulating organisations, latterly the Personal Investment Authority,[152] now the Financial Ser-

---

[149] M. Taylor, *Twin Peaks: A Regulatory Structure for the New Century* (Centre for the Study of Financial Innovation, London, December 1995) and *Peak Practice: How to Reform the UK's Regulatory System* (Centre for the Study of Financial Innovation, London, October 1996).

[150] Goodhart et al., *Financial Regulation*, ch. 3.

[151] And a similar approach was recommended by the Wallis Committee of Inquiry in Australia in 1997.

[152] Mr Sharples, chairman of the Securities and Futures Authority (SFA), told the Treasury committee: 'I find that as I travel around the globe at various conferences discussing alternative systems of regulations and attending meetings, there is confusion from the outsider looking in as to who in the UK is responsible for what . . . I have

vices Authority. Quite apart from the administrative difficulties inherent in two regulators overseeing the same institution,[153] the split emphasised the focus on the nature of the rules rather than the nature of the risks. Thus, conduct of business in a way that creates a loss of £868 million[154] may well give rise to systemic danger in the market, although the majority of conduct of business rules concern client protection rather than guard against systemic risk. Thus, client protection concerns where systemic risk is small must depend on the ethical standards that society wishes to impose and it may well be that greater risks of unethical behaviour can be tolerated the smaller the risk of market collapse.

Where the focus is solely on the risk to individuals, regulation can usefully be further divided by reference to wholesale and retail markets[155] since it may well be assumed that protection of players on the wholesale markets is less justifiable. This may be justified both from an ethical standpoint, since it is to be assumed that these professionals must assume responsibility for their trading, and from the standpoint of perfecting the market, because it is likely that players on wholesale markets will have better information.

It may be argued, then, that the true division for regulators should depend on assessment of the risks to investors as opposed to whole market risks. Where systemic risks do not exist, prudential regulation as well as conduct of business regulation should reflect only the standards of protection that society considers suitable for the possible victims as an ethical and political choice. Less intrusive regulation may be considered appropriate, as contrasted with situations where regulation aims to minimise the risk of systemic collapse. The nature and weight of regulation should depend on the identification of the risks against which the regulation seeks to guard, not the type of rule that is imposed.

Identifying systemic risk

To attempt to divide regulation in this way may be laudable but is it possible? The degree to which different institutions pose systemic risks is by no means settled. Some analysts argue that banks are particularly

always been embarrassed because we sit round this table and there are two from France, there may be a couple from Germany, three from the United States and usually about ten from Britain.' Treasury Committee First Report, *Barings Bank and International Regulation* (HMSO, London, 1996), para. 83.

[153] Which includes problems such as the identification of the 'lead' regulator, and opening 'gateways' through which otherwise confidential information may flow between regulators.

[154] Estimate of loss by Barings Bank as a result of trading by Nick Leeson; BoBS Report, para. 4.11.

[155] Goodhart et al., *Financial Regulation*, n11, 7.

prone to systemic failure because of their vulnerability to runs.[156] Others, including Kaufman and Benston,[157] challenge this. Taylor proposed a system of regulation based on the insight that 'a wide range of financial institutions are systemically significant',[158] but the proposed wide-ranging systemic regulator was rejected by the Deputy Governor[159] of the Bank of England, who reiterated the view that banks pose unique systemic risks and therefore preferred an institutional approach to regulation.[160] There may be distinctions between undeveloped markets, where traditional hazards consisting of undue credit risks of various descriptions are still the major problem and should be controlled by traditional methods of requiring capital adequacy and improved auditing procedures, and developed markets, where such procedures are well established but no longer adequate.[161] This is because the speed of transactions, the globalisation of markets and the complexity of transactions have undermined the adequacy of external regulation in the traditional mould. This transformation has been particularly acute in the banking sector:

First, the dividing line between commercial banks and investment banks has become increasingly blurred and now hardly exists . . . Second, the complexity[162] of banks' business has increased, and the legal, operational and geographic structures of banks has also become more complicated. Third, the greater use of derivatives[163] and off-balance sheet positions has made the occasional, e.g. monthly, balance sheet data less reliable as a guide to the bank's state of health . . . For all these reasons, external regulation, both in its regulatory mode of seeking to lay down *ex cathedra*, common rules and ratios that all banks should follow, and in its supervisory/monitoring mode of checking whether banks are complying with the rules is becoming less effective and less feasible.[164]

One controversy is whether the use of derivatives themselves enhances

---

[156] Ibid., 9, and see ch. 8 of the same work arguing for a systemic regulator to regulate banks only.

[157] G. Kaufman and G. Benston, 'The Appropriate Role of Bank Regulation' (1996) *Economic Journal* 106.

[158] Taylor, *Twin Peaks.*   [159] Speaking in 1996.

[160] Goodhart et al., *Financial Regulation*, 158.   [161] Ibid., ch. 6.

[162] BoBS Report, para. 55: 'as markets have liberalised and traditional banking business has become less profitable, the demarcation between banking and other financial services is becoming less and less distinct.'

[163] Here it must be emphasised that the temptation to 'demonise' derivatives trading must be resisted. 'There is nothing inherent in a derivative which will cause losses. It is the choice of derivatives, the manner in which those derivatives are used and above all the controls which are applied to a derivatives portfolio which will determine the outcome of derivatives trading.' E. Bettelheim, H. Parry and W. Rees (eds.), *Swaps and Off-Exchange Derivatives Trading: Law and Regulation* (Financial Times Law and Tax, London, 1996), xxxvi.

[164] Goodhart et al., *Financial Regulation*, 39.

the possibility of systemic risk; 'The derivatives markets constitute not only a possible means of reducing risk, but also a composite $7 trillion risk to the financial systems themselves.'[165] Although risks are lessened by netting,[166] marking to market and standardisation of products,[167] the speed and complexity of the transactions together with the web of financial relationships involved make systemic collapse caused by non-hedged transactions a real danger. Dr Al Wojnilower, economics adviser at CS First Boston, warned: 'I don't think in human history there's been an instance of gambling ever failing to grow or addictions ever failing to capture more addicts, except after what everybody recognises to be a very bad trip. So it seems to me that this will grow until such time as there is a crisis which is enough to really frighten a lot of people and the politicians for whom they vote.'[168] It is perhaps indicative of this danger that Nick Leeson's losses over two months from 1 January 1995 to 27 February 1995 amounted to £473 million.[169] 'This included a . . . £278 million deterioration between 23rd February 1995 and 27th February 1995.'[170] That there was a systemic risk from the Barings collapse was admitted by the BoBS Report,[171] although it was described as 'minimal'.[172] It might therefore be argued that where derivatives trading of any substantial proportions is taking place there should be a presumption that the institution involved poses a systemic risk to the markets and, unless that presumption can be convincingly displaced, the weight of regulation imposed should reflect this risk. However, the BoBS Report on the collapse of Barings found that: 'While the use of

[165] A. Hudson, The Law on Financial Derivatives (Sweet & Maxwell, London, 1996), 215.
[166] See now EC Directive 89/647/EEC as amended; A. Hudson, 'Financial Derivatives and European Company Law' in B. Rider and M. Andenas (eds.), Developments in European Community Law Vol 1 (Kluwer, London, 1996).
[167] Hudson, The Law on Financial Derivatives, ch. 6, analysing the effectiveness of these measures.
[168] Speaking to Australian Broadcasting Corporation's Four Corners programme, cited together with other warnings in L. Hunt and K. Heinrich, Barings Lost (Reed Academic Publishing Asia, Singapore, 1996), 18 et seq.
[169] And see Leeson's account of the loss of £3 million while he ate breakfast (Leeson, Rogue Trader, 147–8), £50 million over a weekend (180), £50 million on 23 January 1995 (223).
[170] BoBS Report, 57, and see graphs at 58, 63, 66 and 74.
[171] BoBS Report, para. 14.7.
[172] Owing to the fact that 'all of the positions on the Far Eastern exchanges in which Barings executed trades, were either liquidated (proprietary positions) or transferred to other clearing members (client positions) at, we understand, no loss to the exchanges, members of the exchanges or their clients, following the collapse of Barings'. Which partially misses the point that the collapse of Barings could have caused a general run on banks, leading to the feared systemic collapse. As it happened, the speedy sale of Barings may have been the key to averting any such effect. However, the collapse did have serious global consequences; see Hunt and Heinrich, Barings Lost, ch. 10.

futures and options contracts did enable Leeson to take much greater levels of risk (through their leverage) than might have been the case in some other markets, it was his ability to act without authority and without detection that brought Barings down.'[173] This led the Treasury Committee to conclude: '**it is not the case that the demise of Barings illustrates an inherent riskiness of derivative trading**',[174] pointing out that the 'main economic function of derivatives is to allow the trading of risks arising from changing economic variables such as interest rates, foreign exchange rates, equity and commodity prices'.[175]

With great respect to the two august report writers, a degree of confusion has arisen in their thinking. The main *economic function* of derivatives may be as stated. This does not prevent the creation of high risk as a result. Further, both the Bank of England and the Treasury Committee seem unable to grasp the concept of concurrent causes.[176] The issue is not whether Leeson's ability to escape detection was the cause of Barings' collapse or whether trading in derivatives poses high risks. The two factors are not either/or. Almost certainly both contributed. It is therefore strange to find the flat denial by the Bank that the admittedly greater risks of trading in derivatives made no contribution to the downfall.[177] It would seem prudent for any regulator to operate a presumption that trading in derivatives poses a risk to the whole market that requires a high level of supervision.

Model of regulator

It follows from the discussion earlier in this chapter that, rather than a model of regulator relying on simple external prescriptive rules, a regulatory organisation that provides a service for the regulated organisation will stand the best chance of performing regulatory functions, especially if its rule-making, policing function is not too distant from the benefits provided. Only this model of regulator can adopt a cooperative

---

[173] BoBS Report, para. 14.3.
[174] Treasury Committee First Report, *Barings Bank*, para. 8; the bold font is in the original.
[175] Ibid.
[176] *R v Benge* (1865) 4 F & F 504. See also M. Allen, *Textbook on Criminal Law* (4th edn, Blackstone, London, 1997), 35: 'the act of the accused need be neither the sole cause nor the main cause of the prohibited consequence.'
[177] And has an echo of Peter Baring's statement: 'The recovery in profitability has been amazing . . . leaving Barings to conclude that it was not actually terribly difficult to make money in the securities business.' BoBS Report, para. 12.32; Leeson, *Rogue Trader*; Fay, *Collapse of Barings*, 109; extract of minutes with Bank of England director of supervision, 13 September 1993.

approach such as that described by Ayres and Braithwaite,[178] who put forward the idea of 'a benign big gun'.

Their vision of a benign big gun is a regulator that has at its command a pyramid of sanctions. The pyramid is used by deploying a 'tit for tat' approach to regulation. This involves encouraging cooperation, but if it is not forthcoming using a lower-level sanction. If cooperation is then forthcoming, a full cooperative mode is re-established. If no cooperation is forthcoming, the regulator moves up the pyramid to a heavier penalty. It is necessary that the regulator should have at its command a regulatory pyramid enabling it to choose a gradation of stances from persuasion to licence revocation. Regulatory agencies have a maximum capacity to lever cooperation when they can escalate deterrence in a way that is 'responsive to the degree of uncooperativeness of the firm, and to the moral and political acceptability of the response'.[179] The agency with only cooperation or a nuclear-style penalty will be less able to negotiate cooperation because the regulated will know that the mega penalty will not be used except in very extreme cases. The SFA has operated this system to the extent that it will visit firms perceived to be high risk more often that those that have built a reputation of cooperation and low risk.[180]

An important point in urging a cooperation model is that the regulator can choose which level of management to cooperate with. It can use negotiation at lower levels while maintaining a hard-line stance in relation to top management.[181]

A different but similar approach is mooted by Goodhart et al.[182] Arguing that regulation is similar to contract, they seek incentive structures to encourage cooperation. Their approach would require significant interference in the internal autonomy of institutions since one factor in reducing incentives to risk-loving behaviour is seen as dismantling the heavy reliance on bonus payments that was a feature of the Barings culture, yet which does not appear in the Bank of England Report or the Treasury report as having any significance. The essence of the approach adopted bears considerable similarities with the Ayres and Braithwaite approach, using as incentives for cooperation a more liberal

---

[178] Ayres and Braithwaite, *Responsive Regulation*, esp. 35 et seq.
[179] Ibid., 36.
[180] US bank regulators have adopted similar risk-related schedules. K. K. King and J. M. O'Brien, 'Market Based Risk-Adjusted Examination Schedules for Depository Institutions' (1991) 15 *Journal of Banking and Finance* 955. See also Goodhart et al., *Financial Regulation*, ch. 3.
[181] Ayres and Braithwaite, *Responsive Regulation*, 79.
[182] Goodhart et al., *Financial Regulation*, ch. 3, 'Incentive Structures for Financial Regulation'.

approach by the regulator with fewer visits. Both schemes suggest a considerable degree of self-regulation by individual firms, the Ayres and Braithwaite enforced self-regulation being similar to the 'menu' approach of Goodhart et al. whereby a firm will put in place its individual risk control mechanisms, which will then be evaluated by the regulator to determine the degree of risk generated.[183]

It must be emphasised that establishment of the model of regulator is only the first modest step in determining a model of regulation. The next important enquiry is to determine what methods the regulator will use. Of course, it is quite possible to distort the model of regulator from a dual-purpose regulator to a mere prescriptive rule-maker, thus losing any advantages otherwise associated with the model. In determining methods of regulation it is instructive to examine in some detail one of the most infamous regulatory failures[184] of modern times, the collapse of Barings Bank.

Are lessons available from that débâcle?

The collapse of Barings Bank

Barings Bank sustained losses estimated at £868 million as a result of the actions of Nick Leeson trading options and derivatives on the relatively young SIMEX, the Singapore futures and options exchange. Although the story reveals cumulative failures, a number of significant reasons for the disaster have emerged, quite apart from Leeson's actual misconduct. It is interesting in that respect to note that there is no evidence that he gained financially from his misconduct other than in retaining his employment and falsely representing his activities profiting from the substantial bonus[185] system operating at Barings.

Significant regulatory failures included:

- Nick Leeson was in charge both of trading and of auditing his own trades.[186]
- There was an undocumented and vague command structure within Barings both in Singapore and between Singapore and London.[187]

---

[183] Ibid., esp. 51 et seq.
[184] Regulatory failure is used here in the sense of failure of both internal and external regulatory controls. The Chairman of the SFA giving evidence to the Treasury Committee remarked that 'it takes two to make the disasters . . . the rogue and the management failure . . . We have got to address management and we have got to make management pay attention to their responsibilities.' Treasury Committee First Report, *Barings Bank*, para. 12.
[185] £130,000 in 1993 and proposed £450,000 for 1974; BoBS Report, para. 13.79.
[186] BoBS Report, ch. 7, esp. para. 7.14; Treasury Committee First Report, *Barings Bank*, paras. 9 et seq.
[187] BoBS Report.

- The Bank of England gave unofficial and undocumented permission for capital transfers in excess of its own rules.[188]
- Barings management were more concerned with profit than with control systems.[189]
- The 'solo-consolidation' of the group was badly handled.
- There was a lack of expertise amongst regulators at all levels. Barings' higher management did not understand the market in which they were now playing, Nick Leeson was able to throw investigators off the scent with explanations that were at best thin, at worst nonsense, but were technical and complex and therefore appeared convincing to the uninitiated.[190]
- There was hostility between various factions within Barings, causing resistance to external interference and audit.[191]

Two principal lessons need to be drawn from these factors:

1. Regulators (either within or outside companies) must not permit growth in markets with which they are unfamiliar,[192] or permit methods of settlement to be out of control.
2. Internal controls are vital.

Although the dual role of Nick Leeson was noted several times, the regulators (particularly the Bank of England) were much more concerned with capital margin issues.

It seems clear from the reports both that managers were concerned with creating a financially consolidated structure for the group[193] and that this 'solo-consolidation' caused considerable difficulties for the regulators.[194] Thus,

if the linkage between an authorised institution and one of its subsidiaries is sufficiently strong . . . the Bank may permit the subsidiary to be treated as effectively a division of the institution and included in the institution's unconsolidated prudential returns filed with the Bank. This is known as 'solo-

---

188 BoBS Report, para. 11.
189 Ibid., para. 7.12; Fay, *Collapse of Barings*, 27–35.
190 BoBS Report, paras. 5.53–5.62, 7.54–7.99. It is significant that in ch. 14, 'Lessons Arising . . .', the first 'lesson' is that management teams have a duty to understand fully the businesses they manage.
191 BoBS Report, para. 13.20, identifying personality clashes and concluding: 'a matrix structure . . . can only work effectively especially in a global operation, with tight controls, with a clear understanding of individual responsibilities and with managers at the "hubs" communicating effectively. This did not happen in the case of BFS.'
192 BoBS Report, para. 11.22: 'The Bank [Barings] did not, at their own admission, really understand BSL's [Barings' Singapore subsidiary] business.'
193 Ibid., ch. 2.
194 Difficulties with international cooperation of regulators is detailed at paras. 12.14 et seq.

consolidation' . . . the requirements . . . include requirements that management of the solo-consolidated subsidiary must be under the 'effective direction' of the parent bank and that there should be no obstacle to the payment of surplus capital up to the parent bank.[195]

The emphasis on the need for internal controls may be the central lesson for modern systems of regulation. The emphasis probably needs to be on monitoring internal systems of control rather than collecting 'objective factors' such as capital adequacy. Clearly no collection of objective financial data can ensure that 'effective' control of a parent by a subsidiary exists. Nor can they iron out the hostility between personalities that caused the failure of systems of reporting and control in the Barings group. Although few would deny that collection of data plays a part in indicating to institutions what is the acceptable risk–capital ratio, the speed with which such indicators can be undermined where there are no adequate internal monitors is frightening and adequately illustrated by the Leeson saga. The implications of this central lesson will be considered further in the context of methods of regulation.

Methods of regulation

External prescriptive rules

The consideration above of the prescriptive model of regulator shows that prescriptive rules alone cannot supply a satisfactory solution. It is partly for this reason that the apparently simple option of merely banning certain forms of trading, such as derivative trading, does not merit wide coverage here. As noted above,[196] it is probably a mistake to demonise derivatives trading. The impossibility of uninventing something that has been invented and the unlikely scenario of all jurisdictions cooperating in a global market mean that unilateral action even by large trading blocs such as the EU would be ineffective and competitively damaging, and it would beg the big question of the exact utility of these trades.[197] Nor does it seem feasible to separate hedging from speculation and ban the latter.[198]

---

[195] BoBs Report, para. 12.9.   [196] note 163.

[197] On which see Hudson, *The Law on Financial Derivatives*, esp. 6.3.1; F. Edwards and C. Ma, *Futures and Options* (McGraw-Hill, New York, 1992), esp. ch. 7, 'Social Benefits of Futures Markets and the Role of Speculation'; M. Streit, *Futures Markets* (Blackwell, Oxford, 1983), esp. chs 3 (J. Burns) and 9 (D. Newbery).

[198] In any case it may be argued that speculation makes hedging cheaper. See Edwards and Ma, *Futures and Options*, ch. 7. On the impossibility of identification see Hudson, *The Law on Financial Derivatives*, Part 6; Streit, *Futures Markets*, ch. 1.

Tit for tat

Ayres and Braithwaite use Scholz[199] game theory models to argue for a tit for tat approach to regulation. This approach 'means that the regulator refrains from a deterrent response as long as the firm is co-operating: but when the firm yields to the temptation to exploit the co-operative posture of the regulator and cheats on compliance, then the regulator shifts from a co-operative stance to a deterrent response'.[200] Ayres and Braithwaite also point out that one of the motivations of the regulated is often altruistic, a belief that the standards that are sought to be enforced are right. From the point of view of understanding this motivation in terms of rational self-interest they point out that, 'if we expand backward with self-interest as an explanation until it absorbs everything, including altruism, then it signifies nothing – it lacks explanatory specificity or power'.[201] In *To Punish or Persuade*, Braithwaite concludes that it is not possible to develop a sound regulatory enforcement policy 'unless you understood the fact that sometimes business actors were powerfully motivated by making money and sometimes they were powerfully motivated by a sense of social responsibility'.[202]

Enforced self-regulation

What appears to be the ideal is an external regulator forming a cooperative association with the regulated in a relationship that ultimately has coercive power. We have seen above that there is much to be said for a system of 'enforced self-regulation', to be understood as a vision of self-regulation relating to a method of self-regulation by firms, not a model of *industry* self-regulation such as was alleged to exist in the UK financial markets following the 1986 Financial Services Act.

How can enforced self-regulation be adapted to reflect the differing aims of financial services regulation that are identified above? It has been argued that regulation that aims to protect the consumer, with its public interest focus, may require less weight of regulation and less intrusiveness, while still needing flexibility not to be found in detailed rule making, particularly of the penal kind. Here it is instructive to return to recent developments considered earlier. One is the proliferation of codes, including Cadbury,[203] Greenbury[204] and Hampel.[205] The

---

[199] F. Scholz and C. Wei, 'Regulatory Enforcement in a Federalist System' (1984) 80 *American Political Science Review* 1249.

[200] Ayres and Braithwaite, *Responsive Regulation*, 21.   [201] Ibid., 23.

[202] Braithwaite, *To Punish or Persuade*, 32.

[203] *Report on the Financial Aspects of Corporate Governance.*

[204] *Directors' Remuneration.*

[205] *Committee on Corporate Governance Final Report.*

other is the growing interest in a movement in legal philosophy, '*la procéduralisation du droit*',[206] led by the Centre de Philosophie du Droit at Université Catholique de Louvain. It will be remembered that the two approaches have similarities in that much of the thrust of the Cadbury, Greenbury and Hampel reports was to ensure that the proper *persons* were in the right positions within the company.[207] The enforcement approach, which requires compliance or explanation of non-compliance, has the effect of permitting diversity and allowing the regulator to adopt an approach that starts from a cooperative standpoint but can be backed by escalating interference where cooperation is not forthcoming.

The issue of internal controls illustrates the 'hands-off' approach that makes codes a good regulatory mechanism for the protection of individuals where systemic risk is not an issue. Cadbury[208] recommended that 'the directors should report on the effectiveness of the company's system of internal control' and that this report should be reviewed by auditors. Hampel accepted that the issue of 'effectiveness' could not be addressed by this mechanism, partly because of the possibility of legal action against auditors. Hampel therefore requires only that directors should report on the systems of internal control and that auditors should report privately to directors on their effectiveness. This mechanism may well be sufficient for the protection of market players. It replicates the system operated by Barings and is therefore arguably wholly insufficient for situations where systemic risk is a danger.

The approach adopted by the Financial Services Authority's Code of Market Conduct appears to go against this reasoning since it seeks to lay down prescriptive rules concerning abusive market behaviour. The emphasis is on the definition and prohibition of certain types of behaviour, such as improper manipulation of markets and misuse of privileged information, rather than seeking to place responsibility for the monitoring of possible abuses by the trading institutions as principal trader or employer. It can be argued that the code approach should seek to encourage institutions to set up mechanisms to create control systems to ensure proper use of information and to detect movements in the market that might indicate improper trades or improper misuse of information. These mechanisms should then be the subject of report to regulators. In a case when external monitoring shows that these controls do not operate effectively the regulator's cooperative stance would then be modified in respect of the relevant institution. The code as presently drafted looks far more like a more user-friendly repetition of complex legislation such as the insider dealing legislation in the Criminal Justice Act 1993, Part V.

---

[206] See note 120 above.   [207] See note 124 above.   [208] Code 4.5.

However, where market collapse is an issue there seems to be a growing consensus that the regulators need to assure themselves of the adequacy of internal controls so that more intrusive regulation is called for. External regulation that does not penetrate the firm is now ineffective, as was convincingly demonstrated by the Barings collapse. The regulators did not know and had no way of knowing what was going on inside Barings. In these circumstances a far preferable route is that indicated by the Bank of England in its paper on RATE (Risk Assessment, Tools of Supervision and Evaluation).[209] This approach 'involves undertaking an initial risk assessment of a bank or banking group, including through on-site visits and liaison with other regulators where appropriate, in order to identify areas of concern or remedial action, and to draw up a programme of supervisory work for the coming period'.[210] The risk assessment scheme seeks to merge quantitative measures such as capital ratios, qualitative measures such as organisation and management culture, and indicators of risk control into a single risk rating in order to determine the relative need for site visits. This has the desired effects of permitting diversity in institutions and allowing loyalty to internal culture and rules, but combines this with a real internal penetration by the regulator. It is easy to see the application of the sanctions pyramid approach in relation to RATE, which while permitting the individual design of internal controls by individual institutions nevertheless requires a report to the regulators of the way in which such controls work and the individuals working them together with an assessment of the quality of communication achieved by those individuals.[211]

Conclusion

This study shows how important regulation by internal rules is. Once self-regulation by firms is seen as a goal, a major benefit and burden is the variety of forms that will suit different organisations. This is a benefit because it is the flip side of all the criticisms of outside, prescriptive rules. It will not cause resentment by seeking to force all regulated organisations into one mould, the focus will be on the individual risks not the rules, there would no longer be any confusion between the regulator's rules and internal rules, satisfying one of the problems identified by Ayres and Braithwaite. Simple external regulation is no longer effective. As Goodhart et al. argue:

---

[209] 1997, now adopted by the FSA; see *FSA Plan and Budget*, 1998–9, para. 3.
[210] *FSA Plan and Budget*, 1998–9, para. 3.
[211] See also 'The New Techniques for Risk Management' in Goodhart et al., *Financial Regulation*, 73.

Until recently, financial regulation was primarily *externally imposed* upon the regulated . . . While much external regulation will remain, the increasing complexity of operation and speed of portfolio adjustment among financial institutions make it less satisfactory. This raises the question of how a shift from external regulation to internal self-regulation, reinforced by appropriate incentive structures, is to be managed.[212]

Consistently with identified aims of regulation there is room for a more hands-off Code approach, where no systemic risk is identified, and a more intrusive risk assessment approach, where there is that risk. In both cases the regulator should seek to operate a pyramid of sanctions, escalating the sanctions only where cooperation is not forthcoming.

Applying these lessons to the regulation of corporate groups generally, it is instructive to realise that the free market contractualist approach has been a significant factor in formulating external prescriptive rules. Marginalising state regulation and excluding the regulators from the heart of corporate decision-making has created a tendency to retreat to the margins and to regulate by the imposition of penal or quasi-penal sanctions. That any kind of external approach such as this cannot work is shown by the Barings collapse. There is an absolute necessity for internal controls, backed by some form of Ayres and Braithwaite enforcement mechanisms. The way in which regulators seek to control the financial services markets cannot be duplicated for all companies and certainly not for all groups of companies, or the market for regulators would be a very large one. Some method of control using guideline codes, internal regulations and an outside authority must be found. It must also be borne in mind that we are assuming that both the state and society in the shape of affected individuals have the right to enforce adherence to the dual concessions that have permitted the company to continue their operations. Thus, the state has conceded limited liability, and the individuals who formed the company have permitted it to operate as a separate unit, provided it operates within society's norms.[213] Further, as we shall see in chapter 5, it is arguable that the world economy has reached a crisis point that may be equivalent to the way in which financial markets view systemic collapse. The increasing polarisation of wealth in the richest nations of the world, the ecological crisis and the problem of non-sustainable growth all lead to the conclusion that groups of companies can no longer be left to self-regulate without a legal mechanism for challenging their decisions or there will be consequences as catastrophic as the envisaged systemic collapse of financial markets. The regulatory possibilities will be examined in chapter 6.

---

[212] Goodhart et al., *Financial Regulation*, 45.   [213] See ch. 1.

5   Transnational corporations out of control

Many studies have highlighted a growing polarisation of world resources,[1] with wealth increasingly concentrated in the hands of the few
in terms of disparities both among nations and within nations,[2] and a
simultaneous and linked environmental crisis.[3] Few studies doubt that
the giant transnational corporate enterprises have played their part in
creating both strands of this 'globalisation of poverty',[4] more particularly because of their embrace of the free market classical economic
theories, which, as we have seen, underpin so much of corporate activity.
The immense power of corporations is indicated by a comparison
between the economic wealth generated by corporations, measured by
sales, compared with a country's gross domestic product (GDP). On
this basis 'the combined revenues of just General Motors and Ford . . .
exceed the combined GDP for all of sub-Saharan Africa',[5] and fifty-one

[1] More than 1.3 billion people live in absolute poverty. See UN Development Programme,
  Human Development Report 1998/9 (Oxford University Press, New York, 1999); Third
  World Network, 'A World in Social Crisis: Basic Facts on Poverty, Unemployment and
  Social Disintegration', *Third World Resurgence* No. 52 (1994).
[2] The United Nations' *Human Development Report 1992* (Oxford University Press, New
  York, 1992) found that the 20 per cent of the people who live in the world's wealthiest
  countries receive 82.7 per cent of the world's income; only 1.4 per cent of the world's
  income goes to the 20 per cent who live in the world's poorest countries. See D. Korten,
  When Corporations Rule the World (Kumarian Press, Connecticut, 1995); M. Chossudovsky, *The Globalisation of Poverty* (Pluto Press, Halifax, Nova Scotia, 1998);
  P. Harrison, *Inside the Third World* (3rd edn, Penguin, Harmondsworth, 1993);
  R. Chambers, *Whose Reality Counts* (Intermediate Technology, London, 1997).
[3] M. Hertsgaard, *Earth Odyssey* (Abacus, London, 1999); H. Heerings and I. Zeldenrust,
  Elusive Saviours (International Books, Utrecht, 1995); J. Karliner, *The Corporate Planet*
  (Sierra Club, San Francisco, 1997).
[4] In 1990 there were at least 212 million people without income or assets to guarantee the
  necessities for a basic existence. See UN Development Programme, *Human Development
  Report 1992* (Oxford University Press, New York, 1992); United Nations Population
  Fund, *The State of World Population 1992* (New York, 1992).
[5] Karliner, *The Corporate Planet*, 5; 'Global 500: The World's Largest Corporations',
  Fortune, 7 August 1995; World Bank, *World Development Report 1996* (Oxford University
  Press, New York, 1997).

of the largest one hundred economies are corporations.[6] Further, the number of transnational corporations jumped from 7,000 in 1970 to 40,000 in 1995, and they account for most of the world's trade:

These corporations and their 250,000 foreign affiliates account for most of the world's industrial capacity, technological knowledge and international financial transactions. They mine, refine and distribute most of the world's oil, gasoline, diesel and jet fuel. They build most of the world's oil, coal, gas, hydroelectric and nuclear power plants. They extract most of the world's minerals from the ground. They manufacture and sell most of the world's automobiles, airplanes, communications satellites, computers, home electronics, chemicals, medicines and biotechnology products. They harvest much of the world's wood and make most of its paper. They grow many of the world's agricultural crops, while processing and distributing much of its food. All told, the transnationals hold 90 per cent of all technology and product patents worldwide and are involved in 70 per cent of world trade.[7]

However the phenomenon of globalisation of the world economy is a complex one and this chapter looks briefly at some of the themes that have been the subject of recent studies. Some attention will be paid to the role of institutions that have a regulatory capacity, such as the World Trade Organisation and the International Monetary Fund. Other regulatory influences, such as the role of economic, social and cultural human rights, are considered later in the chapter.

In order to cover the multitude of issues with some coherence they are considered under the following headings:

• the effect of TNCs on development;
• the displacement of domestic production;
• the effects of the banking and international money systems;
• the undermining of political systems and the absence of control of transnationals;
• environmental issues;
• labour issues.

Each of these issues has given rise to lengthy, scholarly and hot disputes. It will be appreciated that because of the length of the list they can be dealt with only here in outline, serving as a background to the main theme of the role of transnational groups and their possible governance.

---

[6] S. Anderson and J Cavanaugh, *The Rise of Global Corporate Power* (Institute for Policy Studies, Washington DC, 1996).
[7] Karliner, *The Corporate Planet*, 5; see also UNCTAD, *World Investment Report 1995: Transnational Corporations and Competitiveness* (United Nations Conference on Trade and Development, Division on Transnational Corporations and Investment, New York, 1995), xix–xx.

Development issues

The foundation of the debate about the effect of transnational corporations (TNCs) on development is the hypothesis that 'the advantages of transnational direct investments are unequally distributed between TNCs and host countries, because TNCs have the ability to absorb gains that could otherwise be reinvested'.[8] Empirical studies examined by Bornschier and Stamm[9] appear to show that penetration by TNCs adds to overall economic growth in the short term but reduces growth performance in the long term. This conclusion was based on studies in 1985 and also on examination of GNP per capita, a method that has, however, attracted some criticism. 'There is little basis for assuming that economic growth, as we currently define and measure it, results in automatic increases in human welfare.'[10] Paul Ekins[11] argues that growth can be demonstrated to be beneficial only when growth has taken place through the production of goods and services that are inherently valuable and beneficial, when these goods and services have been distributed widely throughout society, and when the benefits outweigh any detrimental effects.[12]

As Korten points out, measurements of GNP ignore those calculations and 'the results are sometimes ludicrous. For example, the costs of cleaning up the *Exon Valdez* oil spill on the Alaska coast and the costs of repairing the damage from the terrorist bombing of the World Trade Center in New York both counted as net contributions to economic output.'[13] The transnationals have been successful in diverting attention from their *production* of environmentally damaging wastes to 'end of pipeline' clean-up solutions, as a result of which a study prepared for the Organisation for Economic Cooperation and Development (OECD) forecast an 'environmental industry' of $300 billion by 2000.[14]

However, it is clear that for developing countries the arrival of a powerful international company 'offers considerable attractions . . . The

---

[8] V. Bornschier and H. Stamm, 'Transnational Corporations' in S. Wheeler (ed.), *The Law of the Business Enterprise* (Oxford University Press, Oxford, 1994), 333 at 336.
[9] Ibid.
[10] Korten *When Corporations Rule the World*, ch. 3, 'The Growth Illusion', 39.
[11] P. Ekins, *The Living Economy* (Routledge, London, 1986).
[12] This debate reflects the general criticism of the free market economists discussed in ch. 2, in particular Dworkin's question 'Is wealth a value?'
[13] Korten, *When Corporations Rule the World*, 40.
[14] The OECD characterises the environmental industry as 'including firms which produce pollution equipment and a range of goods and services for environmental protection and management'; OECD, *The OECD Environment Industry: Situation, Prospects and Government Policies* (OECD, Paris, 1992); and see J. Karliner, 'The Environmental Industry: Profiting from Pollution' 24 *The Ecologist* 59.

prime advantage is that they help the balance of payments with an immediate inflow of capital.'[15] But the disadvantage of welcoming TNCs is the fact that 'their purpose is to maximise profits for western owners, not to promote the welfare of their host nations'.[16] Thus TNCs 'make money and send it back home, for that, after all, is their *raison d'etre*'.[17]

The movement of corporations into a global situation means that national interests, whether of home or host state, are irrelevant to their operations. 'Because they span national borders, many MNEs [multi-national enterprises] are less concerned with advancing national goals than with pursuing objectives internal to the firm – principally growth, profits, proprietary technology, strategic alliances, return on investment, and market power.'[18] Further, 'despite numerous attempts by local and national governments, spurred by citizens' movements, to limit corporations' power and increase their accountability to the public, today these economic powerhouses maintain a firm grip on many key aspects of political life in their home countries, corrupting the democratic process',[19] and TNCs 'are also using the accelerating process of globalisation to gain an increasing degree of independence from governments'.[20] Indeed, as we have seen from earlier chapters, it is their duty to be focused on these concerns and not national or local interests should their foundations be in free market economist theory.

The assessment of TNCs' contribution to development therefore depends on a more fundamental debate about whether growth of wealth is equivalent to development and can be measured in simple terms such as an increase in GNP. In order to take this assessment further it is necessary to examine the impact of TNCs on other areas of concern to host countries.

The displacement of domestic production

Harrison observes that '[m]ultinationals . . . can come to dominate the commanding heights of local industry, as their immense advantages of

---

[15] Harrison, *Inside the Third World*, 356.
[16] Ibid., 358.   [17] Ibid.
[18] Office of Technology Assessment, US Congress, *Multinationals and the National Interest: Playing by Different Rules* (US Government Printing Office, Washington DC, 1993), 1–4, 10.
[19] Karliner, *The Corporate Planet*, 7, tracing the 'capture' of the US government.
[20] Ibid., 9, quoting Takuya Negami, a senior executive at the Kobe Steel Corporation and chair of the Environmental Cooperation Task Force of Keidanran: 'the nation state is not really dead, but it's being quickly retired.'

resources and knowhow give them a massive start on local firms'.[21] There are countless stories of the displacement of indigenous peoples by the exploitation of natural resources by large corporations. This is perhaps the simplest mechanism by which local industries are displaced. However, the drive for ever increased profitability (here again the echo of our free market economists) creates other mechanisms that displace local industries and create unemployment.

The arrival of a powerful corporation with modern technology displaces traditional manufacturing and agriculture, driving those ousted from the land into cities. 'Most [governments] have worked on the theory that the traditional sector will wither away naturally and its workers get absorbed into the modern sector. They are certainly right on the first count, but dangerously wrong on the second.'[22] An example of the mechanisms involved is given by Karliner:

In the 1980s, US free market farm policies lowered price supports for the small farmer. As a result, a large number of family farms went into bankruptcy, while major food corporations enjoyed record profits. At the same time, Mexico, in preparation for NAFTA [the North American Free Trade Agreement], wiped out important protections for its small, food producing farmers. Consequently US agribusiness transnationals moved into the lucrative Mexican market. They effectively took over land dedicated to subsistence agriculture there, converting it to pesticide-intensive crops such as strawberries, broccoli, cauliflower and canteloupes for export to the world market. They then turned round and began selling Mexican farmers corn and beans grown in the Midwest. In theory this is a more 'efficient' system, with large corporations growing the most productive crops on both sides of the border and distributing them in a businesslike way. However, such efficiency not only undermines Mexico's food security, increases the use of pesticides and threatens the viability of organic agriculture, but it has also caused thousands of farm families in both the United States and Mexico to lose their land.'[23]

The effects of the international money and banking systems

The IMF-World Bank reforms brutally dismantle the social sectors of developing countries, undoing the efforts and struggles of the post-colonial period and reversing 'with the stroke of the pen' the fulfilment of past progress.

---

[21] Harrison, *Inside the Third World*, 357, with figures; for example, in 1976 foreign investors controlled 33 per cent of Brazil's electrical machinery industry, 44 per cent of rubber, 51 per cent of chemicals, 55 per cent of non-electrical machinery, 61 per cent of iron and steel and 100 per cent of automobiles.

[22] Ibid., 198.

[23] Karliner, *The Corporate Planet*, 20–1; for many other examples see Harrison, *Inside the Third World*; Karliner, *The Corporate Planet*; and Hertsgaard, *Earth Odyssey*.

Throughout the world, there is a consistent and coherent pattern: the IMF-
World Bank reform package constitutes a coherent programme of economic and
social collapse.[24]

Even on the free market economic model criteria adhered to by these
institutions, any success is elusive:

On the basis of existing studies, one certainly cannot say whether the adoption
of programs supported by the Fund led to an improvement in inflation and
growth performance. In fact it is often found that programs are associated with a
rise in inflation and a fall in the growth rate.[25]

It is not possible here to analyse in depth the complex interlocking
factors that have led to these claims of serious failure, but a pattern can
be discerned. The fundamental starting point is the adherence of the
most powerful institutions (including transnationals) to the creed of
growth:

Perhaps no single idea is more deeply embedded in modern political culture
than the belief that economic growth is the key to meeting most important
human needs, including alleviating poverty and protecting the environment.[26]

The second step is the consequent call for global free markets in
which the huge transnationals are able to dominate small producers.
The establishment of the World Trade Organisation (WTO) in 1995
with a mandate to regulate freedom of trade marked a turning point in
this process. Thus, even without the assistance of the IMF/World Bank
packages, transnationals were on a winning ticket because their vertical
integration and relatively small overhead costs, as well as global mobility
and huge reserves, enable them to cushion any sudden market movement. However the IMF/World Bank packages for developing nations
assist transnationals in a number of ways. The sequence works like this:

Large amounts of corporate debt in developed countries have been
transferred to the state because countries were lent money to reimburse
the private sector banks.[27] In more than 100 debtor nations[28] the IMF
and World Bank work together to impose 'structural adjustment programmes', which appear to benefit transnationals directly. Korten
quotes a Philippine government advertisement (1995): 'To attract
companies like yours . . . we have felled mountains, razed jungles, filled
swamps, moved rivers, relocated towns . . . all to make it easier for you
and your business here.'[29] How does it work? Following the oil price

[24] Chossudovsky, *Globalisation of Poverty*, 68–9.
[25] M. Khan, 'The Macroeconomic Effects of Fund Supported Adjustment Programs'
(1990) 37 *IMF Staff Papers* 196–222.
[26] Korten, *When Corporations Rule the World*, 37.
[27] Chossudovsky, *Globalisation of Poverty*, 22.
[28] World Bank, *World Debt Tables 1994–5* (World Bank, Washington DC, 1994).
[29] Korten, *When Corporations Rule the World*, 159.

rises imposed by the OPEC countries in the mid 1970s, the foreign debts of developing countries increased enormously. From 1970 to 1980 the long-term external debt of low-income countries increased from $21 billion to $110 billion and that of middle-income countries rose from $40 billion to $317 billion.[30] With default on these loans an inevitability, the IMF and World Bank were put into a position to impose structural adjustment packages to ensure that payments were made. 'Each structural adjustment package called for sweeping economic policy reforms intended to channel more of the adjusted country's resources and productive activity toward debt repayment and to further open national economies to the global economy. Restrictions and tariffs on both imports and exports were reduced, and incentives were provided to attract foreign investors.'[31] Cahn argues that the World Bank is a governance institution:

[it is exercising its power] through its financial leverage to legislate entire legal regimens and even . . . [altering] the constitutional structure of borrowing nations. Bank-approved consultants often rewrite a country's trade policy, fiscal policies, civil service requirements, labor laws, health care arrangements, environmental regulations, energy policy, resettlement requirements, procurement rules, and budgetary policy.[32]

It is well documented that the consequent 'austerities' cause cuts in all social and in particular health programmes, a move of the population away from rural areas into cities, the vicious-circle effects of poor health and lack of proper food and education, and a consequent willingness of a population to work at any task however ill paid and poorly regulated.[33] This is a situation tailor-made for a transnational corporation seeking to locate its plant at the least expensive site globally. Negative externalities in the form of health, safety and environmental regulations either will be minimal or can be negotiated in that direction with a government that needs the transnational investment in order to be able to repay its debts. At the end of the day, however, the result is a huge disparity in income within the developing countries between those who are 'in on the act' of development and associated with the incoming transnationals, and the majority whose conditions worsen. Further, the export of profits to the developed world and the repayment of debt amount to a huge subsidy

[30] World Bank, *World Debt Tables 1992–3: External Finance for Developing Countries* (World Bank, Washington DC, 1992), 212. See also *The Economist* Nov 27 1999.

[31] Korten, *When Corporations Rule the World*, 184.

[32] J. Cahn, 'Challenging the New Imperial Authority: The World Bank and the Democratization of Development' (1993) 6 *Harvard Human Rights Journal* 160.

[33] Korten, *When Corporations Rule the World*; Chossudovsky, *Globalisation of Poverty*; Harrison, *Inside the Third World*; I. Wilder, 'Local Futures: From Denunciation to Revalorisation of the Indigenous Other' in G. Teubner (ed.), *Global Law without a State* (Dartmouth, Aldershot, 1997); Heerings and Zeldenrust, *Elusive Saviours*. However new IMF Rules include social indicators.

by the poor nations of the rich ones,[34] and lead to the growing disparity
of incomes and living conditions between nations. While transnationals
base their *raison d'être* on profit maximisation they will remain an
integral part of this process, unless it can in some way be regulated.

The undermining of political systems and the absence of control of transnationals

A starting point for this section is to remember how tenuous are the
controls over companies operating in a single country. To a considerable
extent the Sullivan and Conlon vision of a crisis in corporate governance
is a reality.[35] Shareholders and governments are unable or unwilling to
exert much control. Add to this the study of the Barings collapse –
which showed how tenuous a hold even internal company controls can
have over speedy operations involving transactions comprising large
sums of money, and how poorly regulators in different jurisdictions can
communicate – and multiply the problems many times over, because the
Barings group was tiny in comparison with the largest transglobal
corporations. Add to this the emphasis in managerial training on global
rather than national or regional issues and we begin to get a picture of
absence of control. If we then add in the temptation to export dirty or
labour-intensive work to avoid stringent environmental controls[36] or
labour standards,[37] and remember that fifty-one of the largest economic
units are corporate groups rather than nation states and that the
exporting will be done to the poorest of the nation states, the power
picture is almost complete – save for the intervention of the international
money system, which obligingly pressurises countries into playing host
to the global corporations in order to attempt to pay off debts owed to
the rich nations of the world.

The imposition of conditions attached to loans that require 'good
governance' and the holding of multi-party elections are seen by many
as a sham.[38] The very nature of the economic reforms imposed causes
such poverty, illness and despair that the mass of the people are likely to
cause unrest so that a 'civilian government takes more and more powers

---

[34] Estimated variously but probably in the region of $200 billion. See Hertsgaard, *Earth Odyssey*, 307.
[35] S. Sullivan and D. Conlon, 'Crisis and Transition in Corporate Governance Paradigms: The Role of the Chancery Court of Delaware' (1997) *Law and Society Review* 713. See ch. 1 above.
[36] See Karliner, *The Corporate Planet*, 150.
[37] Ibid., 155.
[38] Korten, *When Corporations Rule the World*; Chossudovsky, *Globalisation of Poverty*; Harrison, *Inside the Third World*.

to cope with civil strife'.[39] Thus 'the poorer a nation is the more likely it is to suffer from deprivation of political and civil rights'.[40]

Further, the poorest are likely to be under-educated and more concerned with finding the next meal than with a discussion of politics and exercising an informed right to vote. The path to democracy is undermined by global economics, ably assisted by the global groups. Even the recent adoption of the so-called 'sustainable development' model by corporations[41] creating 'stakeholder' constituencies may be seen as anti-democratic because 'it redefines citizens and their communities as constituencies of transnational corporations in the world economy',[42] rather than encouraging the pursuit of democracy through the ballot box. Further, the 'needs' of transnationals for stable political conditions in host countries may well persuade governments to repress protest at the behest of corporations,[43] whether the protest has legitimate roots or not.[44] Karliner quotes the general manager of Shell Nigeria as saying in 1995: 'for a commercial company trying to make investments, you need a stable environment . . . Dictatorships can give you that.'[45]

If we turn, then, to the other side of the coin, which is to see whether or not controls can be placed on global corporate operations, we can see immediately how poor a position nation states are in. Even the wealthy nations have considerable difficulty in collecting taxes from global companies.[46] Poor host countries are in a very difficult position indeed. So much so that some scholars argue that corporations themselves are creating a global law that transcends national law altogether,[47] and many scholars are attempting to redefine the role of nation states.[48] The possibilities for regulation and the call by TNCs for self-regulation are discussed in chapter 6. International law offers no solutions; see **Barcelona Traction Light and Power Co** [1970] ICJ 3.

---

[39] Harrison, *Inside the Third World*, 400 et seq.
[40] Ibid., 410, with figures.
[41] Seen by some commentators as an attempt to 'capture' the environmental movement and press for de-regulation; see Karliner, *The Corporate Planet*, 41.
[42] Ibid., 42.
[43] 'Extreme inequality can be maintained only by armed force'; Hertsgaard, *Earth Odyssey*, 262.
[44] For an example of such intervention in Mexico prompted by Chase Manhattan Bank, see Karliner, *The Corporate Planet*, 210.
[45] Ibid., 86.
[46] See the discussion of transfer pricing in ch. 2 above.
[47] See chapters by G. Teubner, Hans-Joachim Mertens, Jean-Phillippe Robe and Peter Mulchlinski in Teubner (ed.), *Global Law without a State*.
[48] J. Dunning (ed.), *Governments, Globalisation and International Business* (Oxford University Press, Oxford, 1997).

Environmental issues

Here we can start with an insight of Kenneth Boulding. In 'The Economics of the Coming Spaceship Earth'[49] he suggests that many problems are rooted in the fact that we are acting like cowboys on an open frontier when in fact we are inhabiting a living spaceship with a finely balanced life support system:[50]

Astronauts live on spaceships hurtling through space with a human crew and a precious and limited supply of resources. Everything must be maintained in balance, recycled; nothing can be wasted. The measure of well-being is not how fast the crew is able to consume its limited stores but rather how effective the crew members are in maintaining their physical and mental health, their shared resource stocks and the life support system on which they all depend. What is thrown away is forever inaccessible. What is accumulated without recycling fouls the living space. Crew members function as a team in the interests of the whole. No-one would think of engaging in non-essential consumption unless the basic needs of all were met and there was ample provision for the future.[51]

Korten explains how this translates into the concept of a 'full world'. In the past, 'cowboy' behaviour has permitted countries that exceeded their national resource limits to obtain what was necessary for expansion by 'reaching out to obtain what was needed from beyond their own borders, generally by colonising the resources of non-industrial people.[52] Although the consequences were sometimes devastating for the colonised people, the added impact on the planetary ecosystem was scarcely noticed by the colonisers.'[53]

Korten believes that the world is now full so that continuing such behaviour will impoverish everyone. Cowboy behaviour has two basic effects. It acts as colonialism did to 'transfer income from the middle to the upper classes',[54] increasing the disparity of income within and between nations, and it means that absolute environmental limits have been reached as the world has become full. On the latter front, acid rain and global warming present two examples and, of course, transglobal

---

[49] K. Boulding, 'The Economics of the Coming Spaceship Earth' in Henry Jarrett (ed.), *Environmental Quality in a Growing Economy* (Johns Hopkins University Press, Baltimore, MD,1968).

[50] See also Korten, *When Corporations Rule the World*, ch. 2, 'End of the Open Frontier'.

[51] Ibid., 26, summarising Boulding's vision.

[52] See also Hertsgaard's account of 'mining ecological capital' in China; *Earth Odyssey*, 248.

[53] Korten, *When Corporations Rule the World*, 27.

[54] L. Davis and R. Huttenback, *Mammon and the Pursuit of Empire* (Cambridge University Press, New York, 1986), 16; and see R. Douthwaite, *The Growth Illusion* (Council Oak Books, Tulsa, OK, 1993).

companies play their part in exacerbating these problems.[55] However, the most relevant issue to the present enquiry is the perception that 'economic globalisation has greatly expanded opportunities for the rich to pass their environmental burdens to the poor by exporting both wastes and polluting factories'.[56] It is the failure to regulate companies, which continue to operate on a 'cowboy' basis, exporting their negative externalities to countries that have no power to regulate them, because they fear losing inward investment or are unable to pay back debts due to the world financial system, that has exacerbated the disparity between rich and poor nations. The exact extent of this effect is a matter of debate, but a few instances can be given:

One of the keys to understanding the global problem of waste and pollution, however, is that much of its incidence in the developing world is due to developed nations' illegal shipment of their own waste to these regions. . . [T]rucks entering Eastern Europe [from Germany] export hundreds of thousands of tons of waste that Westerners find too expensive or too inconvenient to dispose of themselves. The pressure is mostly financial. Under US and European environmental laws today, the cost of disposing of hazardous industrial and mining waste can be as high as several thousand dollars per ton . . . Shipping such materials abroad is often much cheaper.[57]

The exporting nations can pose as environmentally aware:

Japan has reduced its aluminium smelting capacity from 1.2 million tons to 149,000 tons and now imports 90% of its aluminium. What this involves in human terms is suggested by a case study of the Philippine Associated Smelting and Refining Corporation (PASAR). PASAR operates a Japanese-financed and constructed copper smelting plant in the Philippine province of Leyte to produce high grade copper cathodes for shipment to Japan. The plant occupies 400 acres of land expropriated by the Philippine Government from local residents at give-away prices. Gas and waste water emissions from the plant contain high concentrations of boron, arsenic, heavy metals, and sulfur compounds that have contaminated local water supplies, reduced fishing and rice yields, damaged the forests, and increased the occurrence of upper respiratory diseases among local residents. Local people whose homes, livelihoods and health have been sacrificed to PASAR are now largely dependent on the occasional part-time or contractual employment they are offered to do the plant's most dangerous and dirtiest jobs.[58]

Karliner chronicles the migration of the chlorine industry from developed nations to Brazil, Mexico, Saudi Arabia, Egypt, Thailand, India,

---

[55] Heering and Zeldenrust, *Elusive Saviours*; Chossudovsky, *Globalisation of Poverty*; Karliner, *The Corporate Planet*.
[56] Korten, *When Corporations Rule the World*, 31.
[57] M. Czinkota, I. Ronkainen and M. Moffett, *International Business* (4th edn, Harcourt Brace, New York, 1996), 8.
[58] Korten, *When Corporations Rule the World*, 31–2.

Taiwan and China, and similar strategies being followed by the nuclear power industry, the automobile industry and tobacco marketing.[59] Mark Hertsgaard gives graphic accounts of industrial conditions in developing nations that would not be tolerated in developed nations, including the chlorine discharged from the Chongquing paper factory:

> a vast roaring torrent of white, easily thirty yards wide, splashing down the hillside from the rear of the factory like a waterfall of boiling milk . . . Decades of unhindered discharge had left the rocks coated with a creamlike residue, creating a perversely beautiful white-on-white effect. Above us, the waterfall had bent trees sideways; below, it split into five channels before pouring into the unfortunate Jialing.[60]

These are just a few instances of the many horrific accounts to be found in environmental studies.

There is no doubt that increased awareness of environmental issues, international conferences,[61] international accords and codes of conduct, the rise of corporate environmentalism (if it is not all 'greenwash',[62]) and the concept of sustainable development have created a debate that will not go away. However, the issue for this work is whether or not some legal mechanism affecting the governance of groups is likely to be effective in lessening the frightening ability of transnationals to act without constraint.

Labour law issues

The impact on employees of the push for ever greater efficiency is a repetition of the effects on the environment and is part of the picture creating ever-increasing globalisation of poverty.[63] An added issue is the apparent failure of initiatives on human rights to protect this constituency. Since labour law issues are an important element of economic, social and cultural human rights (and possibly of political human rights), why is it that they appear toothless?

---

[59] Karliner, *The Corporate Planet*, 81–2.
[60] Hertsgaard, *Earth Odyssey*, 3.
[61] Such as the United Nations Conference on Environment and Development 'Earth Summit' in 1992. For a good description, see Hertsgaard, *Earth Odyssey*, 262 et seq.
[62] As Karliner suspects. See Karliner, *The Corporate Planet*, ch. 6, 'The Emerald City', an account of the PR activities of some TNCs, such as the protection of a rare butterfly by Chevron at an annual cost of $5,000, which is widely publicised in advertisements costing $200,000 per 30 seconds.
[63] See Harrison, *Inside the Third World*, esp. at 186 et seq; Karliner, *The Corporate Planet*, 155; Hertsgaard, *Earth Odyssey*, esp. 17.

Human rights: economic and social rights as 'second class' issues

Economic, social and cultural rights are indisputably the 'junior branch' of human rights law.[64] The disparity was made clear by the UN Committee on Economic, Social and Cultural Rights in its statement to the Vienna World Conference of 1993:

> The shocking reality . . . is that states and the international community as a whole continue to tolerate all too often breaches of economic, social and cultural rights which, if they occurred in relation to civil and political rights, would provoke expressions of horror and outrage and would lead to concerted calls for immediate remedial action. In effect, despite the rhetoric, violations of civil and political rights continue to be treated as though they were far more serious, and more patently intolerable, than massive and direct denials of economic, social and cultural rights.[65]

Alston has shown that the rejection by the US Reagan administration of the concept of social, economic and cultural rights as having the status of rights at all was influenced by a number of factors.[66] One was the influential arguments of Secretary of State Abrams,[67] invoking the distinction between public rights (i.e. civil and political rights) and social, economic and cultural rights, which, he argued, were 'left in the private sphere'. This public/private dichotomy has a significant impact on thinking about the nature and place of companies and is closely linked to the individualism that Alston identifies as part of the American psyche: 'This country has chosen individualism as a central value. It has sustained its complex multicultural and multireligious diversity, and avoided confrontations by separating church from state and keeping national government out of the family.'[68] As we shall see, adherence to this concept of private individualism has heavily influenced company law jurisprudence, giving great credence to legal and economic contractualists.

---

[64] See A. Eide, C. Krause and A. Rosas (eds.), *Economic, Social and Cultural Rights: A Textbook* (Martin Nijhoff, Dordrecht, 1995), 15.

[65] UN Doc E/C.12/1992/2,82. See D. Beetham, 'What Future for Economic and Social Rights?' (1995) *Political Studies Association* 43.

[66] P. Alston, 'US Ratification of the Covenant on Economic Social and Cultural Rights: The Need for an Entirely New Strategy' (1990) 84 *American Journal of International Law* 365.

[67] *Review of State Department Country Reports on Human Rights Practices for 1981*, Hearing before the Subcommittee on Human Rights and International Organisations of the House Committee on Foreign Affairs, 97th Congress, 2d Sess 7 (1982).

[68] E. Erikson and K. Fritzell, 'The Effects of the Social Welfare System on the Well-being of Children and the Elderly' in A. Palmer, T. Smeeding and E. Torrey (eds.), *The Vulnerable* (University of Chicago Press, Chicago, 1988), cited in Alston, 'US Ratification', 384.

The political divide

Partly because of the perception of economic, social and cultural rights as impinging on private freedoms, they became pilloried in the USA as an attempt to introduce 'uneconomic, socialist and collective rights',[69] which in turn led to the introduction of such rights being perceived as part of a 'hidden agenda' to destroy capitalism: 'To put it bluntly: the effect of the hidden agenda was to help delegitimise the market economy (capitalism) that is an indispensable precondition of a traditional liberal (bourgeois) society.'[70]

Thus grew a perception of Western thought prioritising political rights set against Soviet/third world thought prioritising social, economic and cultural rights. That this was a false perception is explained by Alston, citing the adherence of Western governments to the Covenant on Economic, Social and Cultural Rights, and identifying the problem as American rather than Western.[71]

The original division between civil and political rights on the one hand and economic, social and cultural rights on the other stemmed from 'a controversial and contested'[72] decision of the UN General Assembly in 1951, which was based on the underlying assumption that civil and political rights were absolute, immediate and justiciable, whereas economic, social and cultural rights were programmatic and would be costly to implement. Even where the rights are formulated as creating legally binding obligations on contracting states, individuals have no right of enforcement: 'traditionally, whereas civil and political rights were seen as justiciable, i.e. rights which could be invoked by the individual against the public authorities, economic and social rights were generally regarded as "programmatic".'[73] Although one must accept[74] that this 'neat distinction' is now too simplistic,[75] it is nevertheless true that the rights built into economic, social and cultural treaties are less well known generally and less easy to enforce. For

---

[69] Alston, 'US Ratification', 366.
[70] Irving Kristol, 'Human Rights: the Hidden Agenda', *National Interest* (winter 1986/7) 3; and Alston, 'US Ratification', 391.
[71] Alston, 'US Ratification', 387.
[72] Eide, Krause and Rosas (eds.), *Economic, Social and Cultural Rights*, 22.
[73] L. Betten and N. Grief, *EU Law and Human Rights* (Longman, London, 1998), 10.
[74] As do Betten and Grief, ibid.
[75] See, for example, Michael K. Addo, 'Justiciability Re-examined' in R. Beddard and D. Hill (eds.), *Economic, Social and Cultural Rights: Progress and Achievements* (Macmillan, London, 1992), pointing out that justiciability may be achieved through 'inquisitorial justiciability' using the investigative processes built into many of these provisions; and see Eide, Krause and Rosas (eds.), *Economic, Social and Cultural Rights*, chs 1, 2 and 3.

example, labour rights are 'quite far from reaching a reasonable degree of their juridization'.[76]

From the perspective of the detractors of economic, social and cultural rights, their nature has provided two apparently contradictory arguments. On the one hand, the rights would be too costly and burdensome to implement; on the other, their vague nature and lack of exact standards mean they are not rights at all, mere ephemera. Thus Alston cites J. P. Anderegg[77] as on the one hand arguing that acceptance of the Covenant on Economic, Social and Cultural Rights would 'bring with it an enormous and incalculable commitment to an expanding, centralised welfare state with reduced liberties for the individual', and on the other hand exhorting those seeking to persuade the US administration towards ratification not to pursue the line that 'the Covenant could convincingly be portrayed as being devoid of any substantive practical or legal significance. Metaphorically speaking, it could be characterized as being the ultimate toothless tiger.'[78]

Positive and negative enforcement

The distinction between civil and political rights on the one hand and economic, social and cultural rights on the other has often been seen to lie in the distinction between positive and negative categories of rights. This distinction has again led to two arguments against the adoption of the economic, social and cultural category. Enforcement of positive obligations to create a programme of reform is much more difficult than enforcement of an individual right to non-interference.[79] This difficulty has fuelled concerns that acknowledging the existence of social, cultural and economic rights will in some way dilute civil and political rights. Secretary of State Abrams used the distinction between positive and negative categories of rights, without so labelling them, and concluded that 'the rights that no government can violate [i.e. civil and political rights] should not be watered down to the status of rights that governments should do their best to secure [i.e. economic, social and cultural rights]'.[80] Arguing that these assumptions are simplistic and have now been shown to be ill founded, Eide points out that:

---

[76] K. Drzewicki, 'The Right to Work and Rights in Work' in Eide, Krause and Rosas (eds.), *Economic, Social and Cultural Rights*, 172.
[77] Adjunct Professor, Columbia Law School, in hearings before the Senate Committee on Foreign Relations 1979.
[78] Alston, 'US Ratification', 366.
[79] For a consideration of this issue in the field of criminal sanctions, see J. Dine, *Criminal Law in the Company Context* (Dartmouth, Aldershot, 1995).
[80] Alston, 'US Ratification', 373.

Some civil rights require state obligations at all levels – also the obligation to provide direct assistance, when there is a need for it. Economic and social rights, on the other hand, can in many cases best be safeguarded through non-interference by the State with the freedom and use of resources possessed by the individuals.[81]

Consequences

Although many of the concerns voiced by opponents to social, cultural and economic rights are gradually losing favour, there are nevertheless significant consequences of their second-class status. Many of these are reflected in the sources of labour rights that currently influence the EU and the UK. In particular, the dual division between the economic thrust of the EU[82] and the decision to leave human rights issues to the Council of Europe,[83] and the division at Council of Europe between civil and political rights and economic, social and cultural rights, have left labour rights in a doubly disadvantaged situation.

The following section takes one element of the economic, social and cultural rights debate to examine it in more detail. It is the consideration of workers' rights, particularly of rights to participate in corporate decision-making. Not only are employees normally viewed as the group (after shareholders) most affected by company decisions, the way in which their input is treated and policed can be seen as a template for other input[84] and for providing means of controlling corporate decision-making.[85]

Labour law and human rights

Valticos puts forward three purposes for international labour law: as an aid to fair competition, as furthering the cause of peace, but, overwhelmingly, as 'the concept of social justice' for its own sake.[86]

---

81 Eide et al., *Economic, Social and Cultural Rights*, 38–9.
82 In the preamble to the Treaty of Rome the 'constant improvement of the living and working conditions of the peoples of the Community' was stated to be its 'essential objective'. However, it was envisaged that this aim would be achieved 'principally through the liberalisation of trade and economic mobility . . . and not through the harmonisation of social legislation'; S. Deakin and G. Morris, *Labour Law* (Butterworth, London, 1995), 99.
83 See Betten and Grief, *EU Law*, 53.
84 See C. Villiers, *European Company Law – Towards Democracy* (Ashgate, Aldershot, 1998).
85 See ch. 6.
86 N. Valticos, 'International Labour Law' in R. Blanpain and C. Engels (eds.), *Comparative Labour Law and Industrial Relations in Industrialised Market Economies* (Kluwer, London, 1993), 49.

Drzewicki agrees that 'whatever the historical motives at the outset were, the philosophy of social justice has remained the prime objective of the International Labour Organisation'.[87] The Constitution of the ILO (revised 1946) states that 'labour is not a commodity' and that 'all human beings, irrespective of race, creed or sex, have the right to pursue both their material well-being and their spiritual development in conditions of freedom and dignity, of economic security and equal opportunity'.[88] The reasons for concluding international treaties on labour rights may thus be seen as primarily protective of employees, redressing the imbalance of their otherwise enfeebled status.

However, this leaves worker participation in a 'no-win' situation. Implementation by way of human rights routes is difficult, and at the same time the insistence on a 'rights' basis has the effect of alienating cultures with a strong belief in market forces. The weaker position of economic, social and cultural rights has strengthened the hand of the legal and economic contractualists in two ways. First, the perception that they are not strong or fundamental rights has left the loophole that other political theories are of equal validity; and secondly the emphasis on the bestowing of rights on workers fosters the perception that employees are alien to central decision-making, thus playing into the hands of those who see companies as solely the property of their shareholders. It is this alienation of workers that has been one of the causes of the rise in legal and economic contractualism as foundation theories for company law with the consequent view of the worker as an 'outsider'.

The destructive role that market economics plays in the advancement of workers' interests is detailed by Paul O'Higgins in his analysis of the ILO's rejection of the doctrine by their adoption of the principle that 'labour is not a commodity'.[89] O'Higgins draws attention to the judgment of Higgins J in *Ex parte H v McKay*[90] in which the issue was whether 'fair and reasonable wages' were paid by an employer. He said:

If Parliament meant that the conditions shall be such as they can get by individual bargaining – if it meant that those conditions are to be fair and

---

[87] Drzewicki, 'The Right to Work', 169. Peace and social justice were seen as indivisible in the Preamble to the Constitution of the International Labour Organisation of 1919: 'universal and lasting peace can be established only if it is based upon social justice' (para. 1). But see *Democratisation and the ILO – Report of the Director General (Part I)*, International Labour Conference 79th session, 1992, 23.

[88] See K. Ewing, *Britain and the ILO* (2nd edn, Institute of Employment Rights, London), 1992); and K. Ewing, 'The Bill of Rights Debate: Democracy or Juristocracy in Britain?' in K. Ewing, C. Gearty and W. Hepple (eds.), *Human Rights and Labour Law: Essays for Paul O'Higgins* (Mansell, London, 1994).

[89] Paul O'Higgins, 'Labour Is Not a Commodity – An Irish Contribution to International Labour Law' (1977) *Industrial Law Journal* 225.

[90] (1907) 2 CAR 2–18.

reasonable, which employees will accept and employers will give, in contracts of service – there would have been no need for this provision. The remuneration could safely have been left to the usual, but unequal, contest, the 'higgling of the market' for labour, with a pressure for bread on one side, and the pressure for profits on the other. The standard of 'fair and reasonable' must, therefore, be something else; and I cannot think of any other standard appropriate than the normal needs of the average employee, regarded as a human being living in a civilised community.

As we shall see, the market economists have sought to factor out this approach.

Constitution of the International Labour Organisation

The ILO operates on a tripartite structure of representatives of governments, employers and employees. The constitution of the ILO contains a number of principles, such as freedom of association and non-discrimination, but less general standards are enshrined in conventions and recommendations. By the ILO constitution, Article 19(5)(d), a state ratifying a convention must take 'such action as may be necessary to make effective its provisions'. Recommendations provide soft law guidance on the detailed implementation of conventions or exhort the adoption of higher standards.[91] Adoption of a new recommendation or convention occurs by a two-thirds majority vote in the International Labour Conference. This consists of delegations from member states, each comprising two government representatives, one employers' delegate and one employees' delegate, the latter nominated in agreement with the most representative organisations within the relevant member state. The ILO constitution provides for jurisdiction over disputes relating to the interpretation of the constitution or a convention to belong to the International Court of Justice. However only one dispute has followed this course. It is more common for the standing secretariat of the ILO, the International Labour Office, to be consulted on the meaning of the conventions.[92] There is no possibility of enforcement of standards by individuals, but states must submit reports at regular intervals (two or four years). The reports are examined by a Committee of Experts and submitted to the Committee on the Application of Conventions and Recommendations. Although these procedures bear some similarity to those under the European Social Charter, the tripartite nature of all the bodies of the ILO makes it a more credible operation. Further, there is a system of complaints, which may be

---

[91] See Ewing, *Britain and the ILO*; Deakin and Morris, *Labour Law*, 115.
[92] Opinions are communicated to the third body of the ILO, the Governing Body, and published in the Official Bulletin.

instigated by member states against each other, by the Governing Body or by employers' or employees' organisations.

The European Social Charter

The European Social Charter (ESC) was signed in 1961 by eleven Council of Europe members. Amending Protocols were adopted in 1988 (First Additional Protocol), 1991 (Amending Protocol) and 1995 (Second Additional Protocol). In 1996 a revised Charter was adopted. The First Additional Protocol contained the right of workers to information and consultation and to take part in the determination and improvement of working conditions;[93] and these provisions are now contained in the 1996 consolidation. By November 1997, twenty-one Council of Europe member states had ratified the original Charter, and thirteen States had signed the revised Charter.

Because the rights enshrined in the Charter cannot be invoked by individuals in either national and international courts, and owing to the perception of economic, social and cultural rights as second-class rights, the European Social Charter has a much lower profile than the parallel European Convention on Human Rights. Only in exceptional cases can it be invoked by individuals, either in national courts or before an international body.[94]

The enforcement mechanism is a rather elaborate reporting procedure set out in Articles 21–29. Reports are submitted by contracting parties on a regular basis, examined by the Committee of Independent Experts, and subsequently by the Committee of Governmental Representatives and the Parliamentary Assembly. The reports and comments of all these bodies come together before the Committee of Ministers, which issues recommendations to contracting parties that fail to comply with the Charter's requirements. Significant weaknesses in the procedure include the reluctance of the Committee of Ministers to issue recommendations.[95] New procedures were identified by the 1991 Protocol, which is not yet formally in force, but they have been operating at the request of the Committee of Ministers. States that have not ratified the Charter no longer have a vote on the issue of recommendations, and these must now be approved by a two-thirds vote of contracting states.

---

[93] Articles 1–4.

[94] Grief and Betten, *EU Law*, 47, cite the right to strike in the Netherlands as a possible exception.

[95] None were issued until 1993. According to Grief and Betten this is partly because of a reluctance by politicians to criticise each other and partly because of the composition of the Committee of Ministers, which contained representatives from states that had not ratified the Charter. Understandably they were reluctant to criticise those who were at least on paper committed to the Charter. See *EU Law*, 48.

There are also procedural streamlines such as the ability of the Committee of Experts to seek clarification and additional information from contracting states.[96] A second Additional Protocol was adopted in 1995 which provided for a system of complaints submitted by recognised bodies, including recognised national bodies of employers and workers,[97] concerning the 'unsatisfactory application' of the Charter. This procedure will come into force when five member states of the Council of Europe have expressed consent to be bound by it. Nevertheless, the ESC remains a poor shadow of the European Convention, and this has prompted suggestions that individual enforcement rights should be given in some instances, such as participation rights.[98]

The Charter of the Fundamental Social Rights of Workers[99]

This comprised a non-binding political declaration by eleven of the heads of state of the European Union in 1989.[100] It was always without legal effect, providing for a reporting procedure whereby the European Commission publishes an annual report on the implementation of the Charter.[101] Betten and Grief argue that the reporting procedure is weakened by the three principles on the basis of which it operates: respect for the principle of subsidiarity, respect for the diversity of national systems and preservation of business competitiveness ('having regard to the need to reconcile economic and social considerations').[102] They argue that the third principle, in particular, is inconsistent with the fundamental character of human rights. Deakin and Morris note that 'in some respects it is significantly weaker than the parallel instruments of the ILO and the Council of Europe'.[103]

The objective is to require functional development.[104] Articles 17 and 18 of the European Works Council Directive concern information, consultation and participation for workers. The original draft required account to be taken of 'present norms'. The reference to present norms was deleted from the final draft, leaving reference to 'practices in force

[96] Article 2 of the Protocol, amending Article 24 ESC.
[97] Including UNICE (European Confederation of Employers) and ETUC (European Trade Union Congress).
[98] Grief and Betten, *EU Law*, 52.
[99] Commission of the European Communities, *Charter of the Fundamental Rights of Social Workers* (Office of Official Publications of the European Communities, Luxembourg, 1990).
[100] For a detailed discussion see B. Bercusson, *European Labour Law* (Butterworth, London, 1996), 575 et seq. See also C. Barnard, *EC Employment Law* (rev. edn, Wiley, Chichester, 1996), 59 et seq; Deakin and Morris, *Labour Law*, 102 et seq.
[101] Charter of the Fundamental Social Rights of Workers, 1989, para. 29.
[102] Betten and Grief, *EU Law*, 71.
[103] Deakin and Morris, *Labour Law*, 103.
[104] Bercusson, *European Labour Law*, 595.

in the various member states'. Bercusson questions whether this implies less respect for each state's autonomy, pointing out the shift from a reference to norms in force in each member state to 'practices' in various member states; this implies a standard to be distilled from a variety of practices.[105] This is an interesting suggestion, given the path taken by the Davignon Group of Experts, who sought to find a way of respecting national differences in participation practices by providing an agenda for negotiation rather than substantive norms (see chapter 6).

The Articles impose a requirement for information, consultation and participation,

particularly in the following cases:

(i)   when technological changes which, from the point of view of working conditions and work organisation, have major implications for the workforce, are introduced into undertakings;
(ii) in connection with restructuring operations in undertakings or in cases of mergers having an impact on the employment of workers;
(iii) in cases of collective redundancy procedures;
(iv) when transfrontier workers in particular are affected by employment policies pursued by the undertaking where they are employed.[106]

The Protocol on Social Policy

At the Maastricht summit in 1991 a Social Chapter was proposed that would have comprised a number of Treaty amendments to Articles 117–120, the only Treaty Articles containing significant social policy objectives.[107] This move was blocked by the UK, which nevertheless agreed that the other fourteen member states of the EU could proceed with a separate Protocol and Agreement on Social Policy aiming to 'implement the 1989 Social Chapter'. Article 2(1) and (2) provides for qualified majority voting on matters of health and safety, working conditions and information and consultation of workers, but these matters are said not to include co-determination (Article 2(3)). The legal status and effect of these instruments were unclear,[108] although the status of the UK in relation to the instrument caused much of the discussion. This difficulty has now been resolved and the unanimity among the

---

[105] Ibid.
[106] Directive 94/45/EC (OJ L254/64 of 30 September 1994).
[107] Now Articles 136–143. Article 117 contained the agreement of the member states on the need to improve working conditions and an improved standard of living for workers. Article 118 promoted cooperation between member states on matters relating to social policy. Only Article 119 (equal pay for equal work) and Article 120 (requiring member states to 'endeavour to maintain the existing equivalence between paid holiday schemes') laid substantive obligations on the member states. Article 120 proved to be of little significance and was repealed by the Treaty of European Union negotiated at Maastricht in 1992.
[108] Deakin and Morris, *Labour Law*, 105; Barnard, *EC Employment Law*.

members of the EU has been restored by incorporation of the Chapter into the Treaty of Amsterdam.[109]

The European 'labour law' Directives: Collective Redundancies, Acquired Rights, European Works Councils

With this general background a number of Directives containing rights to consultation, information and protection were enacted.

Council Directive 75/129/EEC[110] relates to collective redundancies. Article 2 provides:

1. Where an employer is contemplating collective redundancies, he shall begin consultations with the workers' representatives in good time with a view to reaching an agreement.
2. These consultations shall, at least, cover ways and means of avoiding collective redundancies or reducing the number of workers affected.

In order to achieve this object the workers must be supplied with proper information.[111]

Similar rights appear in the Acquired Rights Directive,[112] which provides for the transfer of an employment contract in the event of a transfer of undertakings. The new undertaking must afford the same conditions of employment as the transferor.[113] Article 6(1) requires both transferor and transferee to give the information to the employees' representative in 'good time'.[114]

Council Directive 94/45/EC on the establishment of European Works Councils (EWCs) was approved on 22 December 1994. It was a measure approved under the Protocol and Agreement on Social Policy and so originally did not apply to UK firms. It requires the establishment of an EWC in EU-scale undertakings with at least 1,000 employees in the member states and at least 150 employees in each of at least two member states.[115] That this will have immense significance in shaping the future of company structures cannot be doubted,[116] and current proposals for a European Company are based on it.

---

[109] See C. Barnard, 'The UK, the Social Chapter and the Amsterdam Treaty' (1997) *Industrial Law Journal* 275.
[110] 17 February 1975 (OJ L48/29 of 22.2.1975), as amended by Directive 92/56/EEC of 24 June 1992 (OJ L245/3 of 26.8.92).
[111] Article 3(2).
[112] 77/187/EEC of 14 February 1977 (OJ 1977 L61/126).
[113] Article 3(1).
[114] And see Barnard, *EC Employment Law*, 7.76 et seq.
[115] Articles 2(1)(a) and (c). And see J. Dine and P. Hughes, *EC Company Law* (Jordans, Bristol, 1991, looseleaf); Bercusson, *European Labour Law*, ch. 19.
[116] For an assessment of the economic significance see Bercusson, *European Labour Law*, ch. 19.

The structural proposals: Societas Europa and Fifth Directive

The proposals for a Fifth Company Law Directive and the proposed European Company Statute[117] have been under discussion for many years.[118] Both contain a variety of models of company structure and worker participation. Their long and inglorious history has almost certainly been influenced by the same fears that have hampered the introduction of social, economic and cultural rights. Companies are seen as in the private sphere and worker participation is simultaneously seen as too burdensome and too vague and collective rights are seen as a 'hidden agenda' for destroying capitalism. It is perhaps at this level of the failure to incorporate substantive rights into the corporate structure that the phobia against economic, social and cultural rights is most clearly seen in its corporate context. Its expression has robbed corporate law of a vital element of control over management which has systematically been destroyed by the adherence to contractualist theory.

Striking the balance

There is a tendency to portray [labour] legislation as conferring 'rights' upon workers . . . It is probably more accurate to view labour legislation as a form of legal regulation of business activity which . . . explicitly or implicitly strikes a balance between the interests of management autonomy and the interests of workers' protection.[119]

The culmination of the failure of the economic, social and cultural rights approach to labour rights and the consequent rise of individualist philosophies has left companies with an imbalance. The absence of shareholder control of management and the absence of employees from the decision-making structure of the company leaves us with management power but an absence of responsibility. How has this happened? The free market individualist theories have been given too much credence – enough to prevent the introduction of widespread high standards in the workplace and the harmonisation of company law because of a fear of 'outsiders' such as employees gaining access to corporate strategy – leading to the downgrading of economic, social and cultural rights, including labour rights.

Thus, the widely differing models of worker participation that exist in EU member states have for many years been the subject of attempts at

---

[117] See also ch. 3.
[118] See Dine and Hughes, *EC Company Law.*
[119] Steven D. Anderman, *Management Decisions and Workers' Rights* (3rd edn, Butterworth, London. 1998), 1.

European level to harmonise this situation,[120] with strenuous efforts being made to introduce worker representation at board level. The United Kingdom opposed these moves vigorously for reasons associated with the adoption of an economic contractualist perspective. First, workers were clearly seen as outsiders, to the extent that fears were voiced that breaches of confidentiality were inevitable if workers were permitted to sit at board level.[121] UK lawyers consistently wished to separate 'labour law' (which was any matter concerning employees) from 'company law' (which, *inter alia*, they saw as concerning the decision-making structure within companies). Further, as negotiations progressed it became clear that the structures envisaged would create a 'barrier to takeovers'. The takeover mechanism is regarded by economic theorists as an emanation of free markets, a market in corporate control that acts as a policing mechanism to ensure efficient management.[122] In structures where workers occupied places in the boardroom it was no longer possible to gain control of management simply by purchase of shares because the shareholders no longer had the sovereign right to dismiss all members of the board. Such takeovers became very much more difficult and less attractive. The UK government relaxed its usual stance towards European legislation in order to urge legislation to get rid of barriers to takeovers.[123] However, no such legislation has been forthcoming; on the contrary, there is still strong pressure to improve worker representation in all companies. It may be seen that worker representation may have a valuable role to play because insertion of this mechanism into the decision-making procedures of companies prevents sudden takeovers and potential asset stripping, inserts local issues into decision-making, and thus potentially stabilises corporate culture. This may be part of the antidote to transnational colonialism.

Conclusion

Transnational companies are out of control. Although critics of this assumption will point to the programme of 'sustainable development' referred to in many corporate codes of conduct and individual good

---

120 See Dine and Hughes, *EC Company Law*; Bercusson, *European Labour Law*; J. Dine, 'Why Not Employee Participation in the European Community Context?' (1995) 16 *Company Lawyer* 44.

121 F. Kubler, 'Dual Loyalty of Labour Representatives' in K. Hopt and G. Teubner (eds.), *Corporate Governance and Directors' Liabilities: Legal, Economic and Sociological Analyses on Corporate Social Responsibility* (Walter de Gruyter, Berlin, 1985).

122 B. Cheffins, *Company Law* (Clarendon, Oxford, 1997), 119, although it is far from clear that it works. See J. Charkham, *Keeping Good Company: A Study of Corporate Governance in Five Countries* (Clarendon Press, Oxford, 1994), 309.

123 Dine and Hughes, *EC Company Law*, ch. 8.

practice,[124] together with environmental auditing,[125] and international codes of conduct such as the OECD Guidelines on Multinational Enterprises (OECD, 1992) there is nevertheless a significant problem that will inevitably be compounded by the addiction to 'growth'. The political and economic power of many transnationals dwarfs the traditional regulator, the nation state, makes the idea of shareholder control laughable, and leaves us groping for alternative control mechanisms. One that is often suggested is the combination of pressure groups and consumers, fuelled by the power of international communications such as the worldwide web and the press generally.[126] The following chapter takes this idea forward and seeks to bolster it with a legal framework based on consideration of a possible structure to support participation by employees.

The combined effects of the subsidiary role afforded to economic, social and cultural rights and the exaggerated reliance on individualist philosophies have left Europe with widely differing models of worker participation. International obligations and the social aspirations of the EU will be achieved only if participation becomes commonplace. However, the variety of models of participation has made this extremely difficult. Hepple suggests,[127] as alternatives to regulation by Directives, cross-border monitoring to ensure that countries enforce their own labour laws, application of domestic legislation extraterritorially, codes of conduct, and the mobilisation of consumer power. These ideas also form the basis of the approach suggested in the final chapter of this work.

---

[124] Many are detailed in M. McIntosh, D. Leipziger, K. Jones and G. Coleman, *Corporate Citizenship* (Pitman, London, 1998).

[125] Although financial auditing gets a bad press in F. Clarke, G. Dean and K. Oliver (eds.), *Corporate Collapse* (Cambridge University Press, Cambridge, 1997).

[126] Karliner, *The Corporate Planet*; McIntosh et al., *Corporate Citizenship*.

[127] W. Hepple, 'New Approaches to International Labour Regulation' (1997) *Industrial Law Journal* 353.

6   A way forward?

It remains to pull together the threads of the discussion so far and to suggest a legal framework that may be of some assistance in reversing the trend towards ever greater polarisation of world resources. Any changes to legal structure can only be based on political will and, as we have seen, the enormous power and influence of the global corporations makes changes that will be seen as detrimental to their immediate interests extremely hard to negotiate. Nevertheless, a suggested legal framework may be worth promoting, if only to spur companies to greater efforts to prove that controls are not necessary.

It will be no surprise to the reader of this work that the suggested first step towards formulating a legal framework will be to reject the underpinning of free market economics and the consequent demand of corporations to be permitted to self-regulate. As we have seen in chapter 5, global companies are potentially damaging to democracy by creating a climate for dictatorship that is then welcomed as a stable regime. Even the creation of consultation regimes may be seen as undemocratic because it 'redefines citizens and their communities as constituencies of transnational corporations in the world economy'.[1]

The world economy may be viewed as in a position where 'systemic collapse' is a real risk as natural resources are increasingly destroyed or polluted and the only hope of millions is to increase their standard of living to match those of Western countries. In the absence of a redistribution of resources, this development can occur only at the expense of further destruction of ecosystems.

The role of the transglobal corporations has been to export pollution from developed countries, to exploit poverty in order to produce cheap goods, and to promote an extravagant and wasteful lifestyle in developed countries at the expense of the poor of other nations. This systemic collapse is not susceptible of simple solutions, or any one approach, but

---

[1] P. Harrison, *Inside the Third World* (3rd edn, Penguin, Harmondsworth, 1993), 400 et seq.

it is necessary first to acknowledge the gravity of the situation and to accept that growth of economies cannot provide the answer since a levelling up of lifestyles will inevitably bring more environmental destruction with it.

The gravity of the situation means that strong regulation is justified. However, the difficulty is to find a regulator. The financial world authorities are the subject of regulatory capture by free market economics. Can there be a replacement?

We saw in chapter 4 that codes and proceduralisation have gained ground in recent years in the regulatory debate and it would seem that there clearly is a place for the multitude of codes of practice that have grown up to regulate corporate governance, labour law and environmental issues.[2] The task is to create a legal framework that can go some way to enforcing internal self-regulation put in place in response to codes or standards of practice. Here there are considerable difficulties since the power of the global companies has caused the invisibility of the UN draft code on corporate governance and has been used to downgrade many other initiatives.[3] Nevertheless, it should be possible to harness the desire of companies to create goodwill and build on the best practice that they widely advertise to breathe new life into a Code of Practice. The aim of such a code would be to require companies to formulate internal rules providing consultation rights for the communities where the operation of the company has most impact.

The next step needs to be an acceptance of the dual concession theory.[4] This means accepting that the legitimation of corporate activity lies with the communities where corporations operate, not merely with the state that has 'delegated' powers to them. We have seen in chapter 1 that shareholders may be viewed as having a derivative right to see that the company is properly run as a product of their property in the share. However, although the overwhelming adherence is to the profit maximisation creed, the shareholders' ability and willingness to control the excesses of groups of corporations are in grave doubt. It is therefore important to understand that legitimacy of control lies with the state delegation of the power to operate with limited liability and the devolution of powers by the founders on condition the norms of the local community are adhered to.

Many have argued that one factor in preventing further polarisation of resources and degradation of the environment is the communities that

---

[2] For international initiatives see M. McIntosh, D. Leipziger, K. Jones and G. Coleman, *Corporate Citizenship* (Pitman, London, 1998).
[3] For examples see J. Karliner, *The Corporate Planet* (Sierra, San Francisco, 1998), ch. 6.
[4] See ch. 1.

feel the impact of the operation of companies. Thus: 'Every local community equipped with rights and obligations constitutes a new global order for environmental care.'[5]

The problem is to craft a system in which the communities that feel the impact are equipped to challenge the global companies. It is a more unequal battle than that between David and Goliath. Thus, solutions such as wider ownership participation in companies[6] are of limited value in areas of the world that are exploited because of extreme poverty. Further, as Karliner explains, any progress must depend on 'developing ways of thinking and acting both locally and globally at the same time'.[7] It may be optimistic but it is surely heading in the right direction:

> The unregulated internationalization of capital is now being followed by the internationalization of peoples' movements and organisations. Building peoples' international organizations and solidarity will be our revolution from within: a civil society without borders. This internationalization or 'globalization from below' will be the foundation for a participatory and sustainable global village.[8]

It does seem that local organisations, backed by international groups that can mobilise press coverage and organise consumer boycotts, probably represent the only significant voice that poor local communities have.[9] In response to such pressures:

> Corporations operating in various communities around the world have halted or significantly reduced their pollution of local water, land and air resources . . . Some campaigns have succeeded in convincing transnationals, on a local and sometimes on a national or company wide basis to provide their workers not only with better wages, but also with improved health and safety conditions inside factories.[10]

It seems, then, that to create a legal framework to assist this initiative it is necessary to think both locally and globally. Thinking locally will require the consultation of public interest groups (PIGs) in the community.[11] This is a requirement of the dual concession theory because the operation of corporations within that community is invalid unless

---

[5] Vandans Shiva, Indian environmentalist, from Karliner, *The Corporate Planet*, 197. See also Harrison, *Inside the Third World*; D. Korten, *When Corporations Rule the World* (Kumarian Press, Connecticut, 1995).

[6] Jeff Gates, *The Ownership Solution* (Penguin, Harmondsworth, 1998).

[7] Karliner, *The Corporate Planet*, 199.

[8] *From Global Pillage to Global Village*, Declaration following a meeting of organisations following the NAFTA agreement; see Karliner, *The Corporate Planet*, 200.

[9] For instances of success see McIntosh et al., *Corporate Citizenship*; H. Heerings and I. Zeldenrust, *Elusive Saviours* (International Books, Utrecht, 1995); Karliner, *The Corporate Planet*.

[10] Karliner, *The Corporate Planet*, 201.

[11] See ch. 4 and I. Ayres and J. Braithwaite, *Responsive Regulation* (Oxford University Press, Oxford, 1992), 82 et seq.

those on whom a significant impact is made have an input into the decision-making process. While promoting this consultation it is important to remember that the consultees are citizens not merely of the global company but of their nation state, and the restoration of democratic input into decisions made within that state is important. It is therefore incumbent on the local state to provide rights to challenge the validity of decisions made in contravention of consultation procedures. Although there is much debate on the proper role of nation states in the globalisation process,[12] they are still the principal participants in international law and only the reach of international law is likely to affect global companies. However, as we have seen in chapter 4, requiring and enforcing absolute standards on a national scale let alone an international scale may be extremely difficult.

Consultation is, of course, not a cure-all solution since the consultees may well be ignored. However, where a legitimate concern can be raised at a local level and transmitted to well-funded Western pressure groups, that is a recipe for the application of pressure via publicity.

The proposal works like this. An international treaty creating a Code of Conduct for companies will require nation states to require companies operating on their territory to formulate internal rules providing for consultation rights for local communities that are to be affected by significant operations of corporations. As explained later, it is envisaged that these rights would be structured in a way similar to those in works councils. Inevitably, difficulties in defining such groups will arise and can be dealt with in a way analogous to the bidding procedure for PIGs suggested by Ayres and Braithwaite; those seeking to be consulted would make a bid containing reasons for their concern and need to be involved. The validity of this bid could be evaluated in one of two ways: either it could be judicially pronounced upon at that stage or it could be left to the company's discretion to accept or reject the bid. If the bid is rejected by the company, that rejection would put it at risk of a subsequent challenge to the decision. In bidding in this way many local groups would need assistance from Western-based and Western-funded pressure groups. Here the improvement in international communications, particularly the internet, will greatly assist.

What is the result of a failure to consult?

Here we need to consider two factors: one is the need for increasing democratisation of decision-making within the nation state and the

---

[12] J. Dunning (ed.), *Governments, Globalisation and International Business* (Oxford University Press, Oxford, 1997).

other is the underpinning of this proposal by the dual concession theory. It is therefore proposed that nation states should use their international treaty-making power to put in place a mechanism for judicial review that would be extended to corporate decisions. If decisions were made by corporations in breach of the Code and/or of their internal rules made to comply with the Code, those decisions would be regarded as invalid in the state where the impact of the decision was to be felt.

This use of the judicial review mechanism has, as we have seen in chapter 4, two possible foundations. One is the traditional state concession/delegation theory,[13] but some have argued that there is a more 'bottom–up' aspect, in particular those who argue that judicial review rests on the legitimacy of decision-making flowing from a process of consultation or participation; 'a sufficiently close relationship exists between the ideas underpinning claims to participation in government and the regulation of process . . . to indicate . . . [a] basis for the latter which moves beyond the mere protection of substantive interests'.[14]

These debates about judicial review of *ultra vires* decisions have, as we have seen in chapter 4, a close parallel with judicial pronouncements about the validity of corporate decision-making, especially in the UK. It would therefore not be extraordinary to argue that empowering local groups to take part in consultations would enhance their democratic rights, since the decisions taken by those corporations are often made with the agreement of local governments.

So far, we have both a local and a global strategy but it has a fundamental flaw in that, even if local groups in a poor country could mobilise support to help to make their bid for consultation, if they were denied consultation rights or if the consultation were carried out in bad faith it is likely that the institutions of that country would look unfavourably on an attempt to prevent the consequent decision being implemented. Here again we must think globally, remembering that it is the group structure that makes the global entity so strong. Here we need to look to the conflict of laws, to abandon the free market based concept of place of incorporation,[15] and to espouse an amended 'real seat' concept that would permit challenge to the decision of a corporation if it contravened the laws of the place where significant impact would be felt.

---

[13] See C. Forsyth, 'Of Fig Leaves and Fairy Tales: The Ultra Vires Doctrine, The Sovereignty of Parliament and Judicial Review' [1996] *Cambridge Law Journal* 122; D. Oliver, 'Is the Ultra Vires Rule the Basis of Judicial Review?' [1987] *Public Law* 543; P. Craig, *Administrative Law* (3rd edn, Sweet & Maxwell, London, 1994).

[14] G. Richardson and H. Genn, *Administrative Law and Government Action* (Oxford University Press, Oxford, 1994), 124; and see P. McAuslan, *The Ideologies of Planning Law* (Pergamon Press, Oxford, 1980).

[15] See ch. 3.

Further, and this would probably need to form part of the international treaty, the wrongful decision should be challengeable in any country where the group had significant operations. This, of course, would need some definition of group structure. As we have seen in chapter 2, one of the most intractable problems in the regulation of groups is trying to define the parameters of a group. However, if we accept that one of the most important factors defining the existence of a significant relationship between companies is the flow of money[16] rather than the share structure, thus avoiding the pitfalls of the formal *Konzernrecht*,[17] it would be possible to formulate a test based on the dominance concept to be found in the Fourth and Seventh EC Directives.[18]

At present the concept of dominance is not a free-standing test of a parent–subsidiary relationship; proof of significant ownership and voting powers in the allegedly related companies is required. However, if these latter requirements were dropped and the sole test one of economic and/or dominance in decision-making, this could include relationships such as franchising and outsourcing. This arrangement could then allow the testing of the consultation process in Western countries where many of the global companies' customers reside. It is suggested that such actions would be a real inroad into the ability of global companies to conceal their more dubious operations from the eyes of their ultimate consumers. Of course, the challenge to the decision made in the host country might well be ineffective in terms of stopping or reversing what is actually going on there but a combination of money penalties and poor publicity could be a very effective weapon.

This scheme follows closely the Ayres and Braithwaite vision of cooperation with a regulator followed by penalties of increasing severity should the cooperation not be forthcoming.

Two things remain. One is to hope that this structure may one day be considered; another is to explain in more detail the way in which it could work. This follows in the form of a study explaining how lack of compliance with the required consultations with works councils in accordance with the European Works Council Directive[19] could invalidate a decision made by that company. It explains how a system based on the contractarian vision of the company operating solely for the benefit of its shareholders, and the directors therefore being responsible for running the company in the interests of those shareholders, can be

---

[16] *DHN Food Distributors and Tower Hamlets LBC* [1976] 1 WLR 852.
[17] See ch. 2. See now the *OECD* Principles of Corporate Conduct 1999.
[18] Fourth Council Directive of 25 July 1987, 78/660/EEC (OJ 1978 L222); Seventh Council Directive of 13 June 1983, 83/349/EEC (OJ 1983 L193).
[19] Directive 94/95/EC of 22 September 1994 (OJ 254/64).

realigned to comply with rules requiring consultation of employees. This realignment utilises the concept of 'constitutional disability' which is at the heart of the proposals outlined in this chapter.

Constitutional disability: the impact of the European Works Council Directive

Much thought has been applied to the structure of fiduciary duties, which seek to realign the directors' duties with their interests to the company and to prevent them taking personal advantage of their powerful position. The role of the 'ownership' part of the equation, however, has met with less careful analysis. If the shareholders are also in a position where their personal interests conflict with those of the company, traditional contractarian-based company law has held that this does not matter because the shareholders are exercising property rights and should have no restrictions placed upon that exercise. As we have seen, this doctrine puts shareholders in a position to push the company to short-term profit maximisation so that, even if they were effective controllers, their control might well be exercised in a way that would increase the polarisation of resources.

The consequence of this emphasis on the dominance of shareholders is that, if directors act in breach of their fiduciary duties, their breach may be forgiven by the shareholders. This doctrine over-simplifies the conception of the company as a separate and distinct person.

In the UK, mechanisms to limit this extreme view include the limitation of ratification where the majority of shareholders are practising a fraud on the company,[20] the inability to change Articles of Association where this is not for the benefit of the company,[21] a recognition that in insolvency the shareholders cannot trump the creditors,[22] and *obiter* statements that the company amounts to more than

---

[20] *Atwool v Merryweather* (1867) LR 5 EQ 464n; *Estmanco (Kilner House) Ltd v Greater London Council* [1982] 1 WLR 2; *Smith v Croft (No 2)* [1988] Ch 114. 'The shareholder's right to waive a breach of duty derived from the traditionally exclusive association of the company with its shareholders. The new conception however, reflecting a community of interests, will in some circumstances displace the shareholders as "owners" and thus render it inappropriate, in those circumstances, for shareholders to forgive the breach,' Ross Grantham, 'The Judicial Extension of Directors' Duties to Creditors' [1991] *Journal of Business Law* 1.

[21] *Allen v Gold Reefs of West Africa* [1900] 1 Ch 656; *Dafen Tinplate v Llanelly Steel* [1920] 2 Ch 124; *Greenhalgh v Arderne Cinemas* [1951] Ch 286.

[22] *Liquidator of West Mercia Safetywear v Dodd* [1988] 4 BBC 30; *Kinsella v Russell Kinsella Pty Ltd* (1986) 10 ACLR 395; *Winkworth v Edward Baron Development Co* [1987] 1 All ER 114; *Standard Chartered Bank v Walker* [1992] 1 WLR 561; Grantham, 'The Judicial Extension of Directors' Duties'; L. Sealy, 'Liquidator of West Mercia Safetywear v Dodd' [1988] *Cambridge Law Journal* 175.

just the sum of its shareholders.[23] Other jurisdictions have been more robust, removing certain decisions from the ambit of the usual decision-making bodies where a conflict of interest occurs and requiring that a proper system of decision-making should so far as possible prevent such conflicts.[24] There are echoes of this approach in the UK, with the increased emphasis on the involvement of non-executive directors and such mechanisms as the remuneration committee. It is notable that *Guinness v Saunders*[25] turned on the constitutional inability of a committee to take decisions that rightly belong to the board.

Two distinct but overlapping legal movements can be discerned. These are the move away from contractarian notions of the company and the classification of a failure to construct proper systems of control as a breach of fiduciary duty. In moving in these directions, the UK may be laying the foundation for coping with the impact of European legislation, which takes the more radical approach of designating particular decision-making structures as apt in the determination of particular corporate decisions. The law relating to the fiduciary duties of directors needs to undergo significant change in order properly to implement existing European measures, in particular the European Works Council Directive.[26] Article 11(3) of the European Works Council Directive imposes on member states the obligation 'to provide for appropriate measures in the event of failure to comply with the Directive, in particular to ensure that adequate administrative or judicial procedures are available to enable the obligations deriving from the Directive to be enforced'.[27]

This obligation probably goes beyond the requirement for implementing legislation and includes reviewing fundamental concepts to

[23] For example, in *Fulham Football Club v Cabra Estates* [1994] 1 BCLC 363, in which the Court of Appeal accepted that 'the duties owed by directors are to their company and the company is more than the sum of its members'. Cited in S. Deakin and A. Hughes, Chapter 3 in *Company Directors: Regulating Conflicts of Interest and Formulating a Statement of Duties*, Law Commission Consultation Paper No. 153 (Law Commission, London, 1999).

[24] An example is the Dutch law examined by the European Court of Justice (ECJ) in *Co-operative Rabobank 'Vecht en Plassengebied' B.A. v Minderhoud* [1998] 1WLR 1025. See also the report prepared by Ernst and Young, 'The Simplification of the Operating Regulations for Public Limited companies in the European Union' (European Commission, 1995) and Nils Clausen, 'The Monitoring Duty of the Danish Board of Directors' (1991) 12 *Company Lawyer* 68.

[25] *Guinness v Saunders* [1990] 2 AC 663.

[26] European Works Council Directive 94/95/EC of 22 September 1994 (OJ 254/64 of 30.9.94). It is likely that similar arguments would be relevant to the Operating Collective Dismissals Directive (Directive 75/129, OJ L48/29 of 22.2.1975) and the Transfer of Undertakings Directive (Directive 77/187/EEC, OJ L61/26 of 5.4.77)

[27] See also Cases C-382/92 and C-383/92, *EC Commission v UK* [1994] ECR 1–2435; B. Bercusson, *European Labour Law* (Butterworth, London, 1996), 269–71.

ensure sympathetic embedding of the legislation in UK law. Wedderburn noticed a mismatch between concepts in a different situation, but
the concept of sympathetic implementation translates to this issue.
Wedderburn sees the European employment initiatives as having the
dual aim of both protecting workers and controlling anti-competitive
strategies,[28] but argues that, because of the individualist contractual
nature of labour relations, 'collective agreements negotiated at European level are in the UK translated into national law via individual
contracts of employment'.[29] Thus the common law doctrine of freedom
of contract gets in the way of full recognition of the status of employees
because they can individually agree to derogate from the terms of the
collective agreement. The inadequacies of the doctrine of freedom of
contract are mirrored by the inadequacies of the narrow notions of
fiduciary duties owed to the company (meaning solely shareholders) and
the exclusion from fiduciary duties of a standard of care and skill in
carrying them out.[30] This narrow conception of fiduciary duties also
creates a hostile implementation environment for European legislation.

Increasingly, companies will be seen as a community of interests and
the current overlap between fiduciary duties and duties of skill and care
may provide us with the tool to manage this change as the duty of loyalty
to the company is increasingly reflected in a duty to ensure that proper
systems for decision-making are set up. Real oversight of managerial
decision-making by employees may come to replace the contemporary
vacuum of control.

Worker participation: the Davignon Report

In 1996 a legal expert group working party was established under the
chairmanship of Viscount Davignon to attempt to find a solution to the
disagreements on the worker participation proposals for the European

---

28 '[C]ommentators have argued that such community legislation on labour law as we
have is not merely for the protection of workers but is part of the arrangements for an
integrated economic free market. It has been persuasively argued, for example, that the
1975 Directive requiring consultation about proposed redundancies with worker's
representatives . . . is enacted not merely for production [sic] of the workers but for –
perhaps primarily for – the safeguarding of undistorted competition.' K. W. Wedderburn cited in Paul Davies, 'The Emergence of European Labour Law' in W. McCarthy,
Legal Intervention in Industrial Relations (Blackwell Business, Oxford, 1992), 54.
29 Ibid., 54.
30 A further difficulty may lie in the personification of the employer from labour law
perspectives. This fails to take account of the institutional structure of companies:
'Many systems of law personify the "employer"; in the private sector "he" is normally a
company . . . it is arguable that employment law should jettison the concept of
"employer" and seek, not veils of personality, but centres of decision-making in the
company or (more realistically) group of companies.' Wedderburn, cited in ibid., 54.

Company (Societas Europa). Its report was published in May 1997. The group took as a starting point the importance of the involvement of the workforce in company decision-making:

Globalisation of the economy and the special place of European industry raises fundamental questions regarding the power of social partners within the company. The type of labour needed by European companies – skilled, mobile, committed, responsible and capable of using technical innovations and of identifying with the objective of increasing competitiveness and quality – cannot be expected simply to obey the employer's instructions. Workers must be closely and permanently involved in decision-making at all levels of the company.[31]

Further, the group accepted that a concerted approach to work organisation within the company 'will improve industrial relations, increase worker participation in decisions, and is likely to lead to an improvement in product quality'.[32] In this chapter it is suggested that the involvement of employees at the heart of corporate governance will improve not only 'product quality' but the quality of decision-making and could go some way to replace a system deficient in ensuring that decision-making in companies corresponds to the fiduciary ideal, i.e. it is for the benefit of the company.

The challenges

One important thrust behind the European Initiatives is the desire to build a real partnership between capital and labour, and to replace the outdated fiction of shareholder control with the 'community of interests' identified by the Davignon group.[33] When established, a European Works Council is 'to be informed and consulted . . . on the progress of the business . . . and its prospects. . . in particular . . . the structure, economic and financial situation, the probable development of the business and of production and sales, the situation and probable trend of employment, investments, and substantial changes concerning orga-nisation, introduction of new working methods or production processes, transfers of production, mergers, cut-backs or closures of undertakings, establishments or important parts thereof, and collective redundan-cies'.[34] The 'definitions' provide that 'consultation' means the exchange of views and the establishment of dialogue between employees' repre-sentatives and central management or any more appropriate level of

---

[31] Report of the Davignon Group of Experts (European Commission, May 1997), para. 19.
[32] Ibid., para. 20.
[33] See S. Wheeler, 'Works Councils: Towards Stakeholding' (1997) *Journal of Law and Society* 44.
[34] European Works Council Directive, Annex, para. 2.

management.[35] This is a minimum requirement. Thus, the requirements go some way to meet the call for 'a framework of labour law
which circumscribes and limits management's control of the enterprise'.[36] Thus also, despite the provision that asserts, in relation to ad
hoc meetings where exceptional circumstances 'affecting the employees'
interests to a considerable extent', that this information or consultation
meeting 'shall not affect the prerogatives of the central management',[37]
it seems clear that these prerogatives no longer extend to the ability to
take unilateral action in the absence of consultation with a European
Works Council.[38]

What tools have we at our disposal in order to ensure the comfortable
implementation of such a restraint on managerial power? It is arguable
that the development of fiduciary duties can be a central plank in
meeting these challenges, moving the law away from its contractual
emphasis in this regard and putting employees in a central corporate
governance position.

Fiduciary duties: acting in the 'interests of the company'

The imposition of fiduciary duties on directors of companies has long
been considered by academics.[39] It has a long history; indeed, in the
UK, an unbroken history.[40] Generally 'the law has refused to review the
board's business discretion but has stood against the tide of human

---

[35] Ibid., Article 2(1)(f).

[36] B. Bercusson 'Workers, Corporate Enterprise and the Law' in R. Lewis (ed.), *Labour
Law in Britain* (Oxford University Press, Oxford, 1986), 153. 'Can company law be
integrated into labour law so that employees become a central concern of the law
governing the enterprise? Could the functioning of enterprises become dependent on
compliance with standards and procedures laid down by labour law? So long as the two
spheres of company and labour law are kept distinct, "one is necessarily led" in the
words of an eminent French labour lawyer [B. Goldman and A. Lyon-Caen, *Droit
commercial européen*, Daloz, Paris, 1983, pp. 301–2] "to the conclusion that non-
compliance with a labour law obligation [will] not affect the validity of a transaction in
commercial law".' Ibid., 154.

[37] European Works Council Directive, Annex, para. 3, subparas. 3 & 4.

[38] Bercusson, *European Labour Law*, 299–300.

[39] L. Sealy, 'Fiduciary Relationships' [1962] *Cambridge Law Journal* 69; A. Boyle, '*A-G v
Reid:* The Company Law Implications' 16 *Company Lawyer* (5), 131; L. Sealy, 'The
Director as Trustee' [1967] *Cambridge Law Journal* 83; L. Sealy, 'The Director as
Trustee' in E. McKendrick (ed.), *Commercial Aspects of Trusts and Fiduciary Obligations*
(Oxford University Press, Oxford, 1992). Lindley LJ in *Re Lands Allotment* [1894] 1
Ch 616, said, 'although directors are not properly speaking trustees, yet they have
always been considered and treated as trustees on money which comes into their hands
or is actually under their control'. R. C. Nolan, 'The Proper Purpose Doctrine and
Company Directors' in B. Rider (ed.), *The Realm of Company Law* (Kluwer, London,
1998).

[40] Unlike Italy and Germany there have been no upheavals in corporate doctrine.

nature and required company directors to act not in self interest but in the interests of the company'.[41]

This insistence[42] fits well with the individualist thrust of neo-classical market economist theories.[43] It does mean that 'the interests of the company' must be given some content if they are to be used as a yardstick. As we have seen in chapter 4, the issue was considered at length by Berle, who expressed the fear that any departure from the view that the board should use its powers solely for the maximisation of profits was to abdicate responsibility over the board. The interests of the company must therefore be seen as co-extensive with the interests of the shareholders, or measurement of the directors' performance becomes impossible.

In the UK a similar debate continues, principally considering whether and the extent to which duties are owed to creditors.[44] So far as employees are concerned, this leaves them as described by Bercusson:

In company law the employee is an outsider – a contract worker – in contrast to the shareholder who is an insider member. The worker's only legal relation to the company is through a contract of employment whereby he provides labour for a wage. He is just another and, individually, a very minor creditor. In short, company law regards as an outsider someone who may have worked a lifetime for a company and is an integral part of its activities, while it regards as an insider with the rights and powers of a member someone who has perhaps picked up a few shares without any other involvement.[45]

---

[41] R. Grantham, 'The Content of the Director's Duty of Loyalty' [1991] *Journal of Business Law* 1.

[42] *Regal Hastings Ltd v Gulliver* [1967] 2 AC 134n (HL); *Scottish Co-operative Wholesale Society Ltd v Meyer* [1959] AC 324.

[43] A. Byre, *EC Social Policy and 1992* (Kluwer, Deventer, 1992), 119, argues that 'the nexus of contracts theory [means that] shareholders are simply one of the inputs in the nexus, ownership is not a meaningful concept. Someone owns each input but no-one owns the totality . . . if nexus theory is to be accepted then room is created for social responsibilities of a company.'

[44] L. Sealy, 'Casenotes' [1988] *Cambridge Law Journal* 175, commenting on *Liquidator of West Mercia Safetywear v Dodd* (1988) 4 BBC 30, said 'well meant but ill focused dicta about directors' "duties" to creditors can be seen as both unnecessary and potentially pernicious'. Whereas Grantham, 'The Content of the Director's Duty of Loyalty' 1, stated of the idea that company interests equal shareholder interests: 'This intuitively attractive though antiquated notion of the company has now begun to give way in the face of obligations being imposed upon the directors to consider groups other than shareholders.' Sealy ('Casenotes', 175) points out the dangers: 'So long as the acts under challenge could be defended as being consistent with the interests of any other group, there would be no basis to interfere. The concept of "the enterprise" can, in consequence, come into reckoning only in a negative sense, as part of the director's or controller's defence: that they were justified in disregarding the traditionally exclusive claim of the membership out of regard for other interests in the composite enterprise.' See also L. Sealy, ' "Bona Fides" and "Proper Purpose" in Corporate Decisions' (1987) 15 *Monash University Law Review* 265.

[45] Bercusson, 'Workers, Corporate Enterprise and the Law', 139.

If employees are to take the place envisaged by the Davignon group, and other 'outsiders' are to be drawn into consultation rights, company lawyers must throw off the shackles left by the echoes of the Berle viewpoint and acknowledge that the 'interests of the company' do indeed mean more than the interests of the shareholders. This will bring the law into line with the reality that directors do in fact consider the interests of many interested groups.[46] This entails a move from the simple contract model of a company to a stakeholder or constituency model.[47]

What can replace the simple shareholder yardstick?

As we have seen, the major problem of opening up to any form of stakeholder model is the issue of balancing the interests of the constituencies. As we saw in chapter 1, Sullivan and Conlon have argued[48] that the move from contract to constituency models has created a crisis in corporate governance. Shareholders, directors and the courts have lost the convenient yardstick of the majority decision of the shareholders.

Solutions include that of Leader,[49] who argues that the directors are obliged to decide issues by identifying the personal and derivative rights of corporate stakeholders, giving paramountcy to the derivative rights that equate to the ongoing health of the company as a viable concern.[50] Xuereb has argued for a similar balancing act, involving the long- and short-term interests of employees and shareholders.[51] That these analyses reflect the complexity of the task facing managers cannot be doubted, or that the presentation of the company as an ongoing concern is an accurate picture when the interests of the company fall to be identified. However, what they fail to address is the importance of the

---

[46] As noted in the Hampel Report (*Committee on Corporate Governance Final Report*, Gee, London, 1997) and in Royal Society of Arts, *Tomorrow's Company* (RSA, London, 1997).

[47] Such as that in Germany where it is accepted that directors must consider the interests of employees. See J. J. du Plessis, 'Corporate Governance: Some Reflections on the South African Law and the German Two-tier Board System' in F. Patfield (ed.), *Perspectives on Company Law II* (Kluwer, London, 1997). See also G. Proctor and L. Miles, 'Cutting the Mustard: Stakeholders in the Boardroom' [1988] *Business Law Review* 169.

[48] D. Sullivan and D. Conlon, 'Crisis and Transition in Corporate Governance Paradigms: The Role of the Chancery Court of Delaware' (1977) *Law and Society Review* 713.

[49] S. Leader, 'Private Property and Corporate Governance, Part I: Defining the Interests', in F. Patfield (ed.), *Perspectives on Company Law I* (Kluwer, London, 1995).

[50] See ch. 1.

[51] P. Xuereb, 'The Juridification of Industrial Relations through Company Law Reform' [1988] *Modern Law Review* 156.

systems of internal regulation of decision-making.[52] The discussion of the process of decision-making if more than one set of interests is to be considered has traditionally seen it as a balancing act between opposing interests to the extent that the one great obstacle to worker directors was seen to be the likelihood that they would leak information to their fellow employees[53] despite the fact that they would be subject to the same fiduciary duty of loyalty as other directors and therefore in precisely the same situation as a nominee director.[54]

The tone of the debate is captured by the opposing views of Grantham and of Sealy. Grantham calls for creditors' interests to be taken into account as an element in the interests of the company, particularly when insolvency looms,[55] whereas Sealy counters with the comment that it would be ridiculous if directors were permitted to undertake one course of action at one time while a similar action could be found to be a breach of duty at another time.[56] The point here is not the opposing views on the interests of creditors, but the underlying assumption that there must be a conflictual opposition of views. The alternative possibility – that matters could be resolved by exchange of information and discussion – seems to be ignored.[57]

If the balance is present in the system of decision-making, it should encourage the common interests identified by Davignon and Bercusson and create the possibility of decisions made in the light of the best possible input of information. As with current boards, the input of information creates an atmosphere in which a consensus can often be reached despite the fact that in a single-tier system the executive members may have to put aside their duties to their individual departments in order to address the issue of duty to the company. It is in the provision of systems to achieve this that the European initiatives are of

---

[52] See the case study on Barings in ch. 4.

[53] See the discussion of the Bullock Report (1977) in Bercusson, 'Workers, Corporate Enterprise and the Law', showing that workers on the board were considered as likely to take part in collective bargaining.

[54] See E. Boros, 'The Duties of Nominee and Multiple Directors' (1989) 10 *Company Lawyer* 211. Lord Denning in *Boulting v Association of Cinematograph, Television and Allied Technicians* [1963] 2 QB 606 said: 'so, also if a director of a company becomes a member of a trade union on the terms that he is to act in the company's affairs on the instructions of the trade union, or in accordance with the policy of the trade union (rather than according to what he thinks best in the interests of the company), such an agreement of membership is unlawful.' Denning's judgment was a dissent, but he dealt only with the director's duties issue.

[55] Grantham, 'The Content of the Director's Duty of Loyalty'.

[56] Sealy, 'Casenotes'. Although this argument may have lost force following the introduction of section 214 of the Insolvency Act 1986.

[57] Perhaps as part of the thrust of reorganisations under sections 425–7 of the Companies Act 1985.

particular value but, as Wedderburn has pointed out, systems are of little value unless the implementing law can receive them gracefully.[58]

Are UK fiduciary duties European friendly?

The answer is probably not. The key statements in the Law Commission's Consultation Paper No. 153[59] appear in footnote 89 and paragraph 2.21. Footnote 89 consigns the 'stakeholder' debate to near oblivion and assumes that it is possible to formulate a coherent statement of directors' duties without first settling the fundamental question of to whom those duties are owed. Paragraph 2.12 states clearly: 'Shareholders are owners of the enterprise.'

The question then becomes whether contractual notions of fiduciary duties can be adapted to create an atmosphere in which the challenges of the European initiatives can work well. Is there already a duty for managers to ensure that systems of corporate governance are in place within the company in order to assist them with the complex balancing act they must perform? To an extent the issues have been obscured by labelling certain matters 'company law' and others 'labour law', with the consequent polarisation of workforce and company management[60] and misapprehensions concerning the scope and content of fiduciary duties.

The interaction between fiduciary duties and the duties of skill and care

The fiduciary's duty is described as follows: 'A fiduciary is someone who has undertaken to act for or on behalf of another in a particular matter in circumstances which give rise to a relationship of trust and confidence.[61] The distinguishing obligation of a fiduciary is the obligation of loyalty. The principal is entitled to the single-minded loyalty of his fiduciary.'[62] But, as Grantham points out, there are two formulations of

---

[58] Bercusson, 'Workers, Corporate Enterprise and the Law', quoting Wedderburn.
[59] See now Law Commission Report No. 261, September 1999.
[60] This appears to have led to the co-determination structures in Germany being seen as collective bargaining at board level rather than cooperative decision-making. On the former see Bercusson, 'Workers, Corporate Enterprise and the Law', 146. Discussing the Bullock Report (1977), Bercusson said 'the report saw worker directors on the board as the catalyst or stimulus for collective bargaining at company level'.
[61] In Australia the prevailing wisdom is that 'the fiduciary undertakes or agrees to act for or on behalf of or in the interests of another person in the exercise of a power or discretion which will affect the interests of that other person in a legal or practical sense'. See *Hospital Products Ltd v United States Surgical Corporation* (1984) 156 CLR 41.
[62] See Deakin and Hughes in *Company Directors*, 236–7.

the fiduciary rule: one to act in the interests of the company, the other to act in the *best* interests of the company. The former gives discretion once loyalty is established, the latter requires a review of business judgement.

The movement toward the use of objective consequences does in some respects blur the distinction, so apparent in the wholly subjective formulation, between the honesty of the belief and the care and skill taken in its formulation. The reasonable board as well as being disinterested, and thus presumably loyal, will also be one that displays an adequate level of care and skill. For the board to reach the standard of the reasonable board with respect to honesty therefore, it will be necessary also to display a certain degree of care and skill.[63]

If the 'best interests' test is adopted, then, the overlap between the duty of skill and care and the fiduciary duty of loyalty is almost complete. Why should this matter? It matters because, as well as creating a possible cure for the perceived low standard of skill and care,[64] it might well explain the extension of fiduciary duties to cover the absence of proper control systems within the company.

Is there a fiduciary duty to ensure proper structures?

As decision-making becomes more complex and because the focus of management is on the company as a going commercial concern, it is arguable that the duty of loyalty to the company has as an essential component the construction of proper systems of governance.[65] That this may properly be regarded as fiduciary in nature stems from the purpose of the systems being to safeguard the alignment between the interests of the company and the behaviour of the decision makers, i.e. it is an underpinning of the essence of loyalty to the company, which is the whole focus of fiduciary duties.[66]

In *Selangor United Rubber Estates v Craddock (No 3)*[67] Ungoed-Thomas said: 'However much the company's purposes and the directors' duties, powers and functions may differ from the purposes of a strict settlement and the duties, powers and functions of its trustees, the directors and such trustees have this indisputably in common – that the

---

[63] Grantham, 'The Content of the Director's Duty of Loyalty', 6.

[64] V. Finch, 'Company Directors: Who Cares About Skill and Care?' [1992] *Modern Law Review* 179.

[65] It is notable that the absence of proper controls led to the downfall of Barings. See *Report of the Board of Banking Supervision Inquiry into the Circumstances of the Collapse of Barings* (HMSO, London, 1995).

[66] In this respect it must be noted that the duty may be explicable in *economic* terms as imposed in order to align the interests of the managers with those of the institution but not in *economic contractualist* terms because the contractualist element relates solely to the foundational contractors.

[67] [1968] 1 WLR 1555 at 1575.

property in their hands or under their control must be applied for the specified purposes of the company or the settlement.'

Thus, as well as the 'primary'[68] or overarching[69] duty of good faith to the company, directors are required to exercise their powers for a proper purpose. The way in which fiduciary duties are currently viewed leaves open two routes that will create an implementation-friendly atmosphere for the adoption of the European initiatives that will include employees in decision-making. One is to view the 'proper purpose' doctrine in the light of the constitutional reality of decision-making within the company; the other is to accept that there is a fiduciary duty to ensure good systems of management.

Constitutional issues and the proper purpose doctrine

One of the manifestations of the fiduciary duties of directors is their obligation to use powers 'for a proper purpose'.[70] A recent debate concerns the issue of whether the proper purpose doctrine defines only the scope of directors' powers or whether there is a separate category controlling powers by reference to the purpose for which the powers are exercised.[71] Nolan argues convincingly for the existence of the second category of control.[72] However, this does not negate the existence and utility of control exercised by the court by reference to the scope of powers granted by and defined by the constitution. Here it is argued that the constitutional grant of powers should be examined in more detail to determine which organ of the company is able to make particular decisions or disabled from doing so. In a situation where power has not been bestowed on a particular decision-making forum, it is argued that purported exercise of such a power is use of power for an improper purpose. This has variously been held to mean for a purpose imposed by the court, but perhaps more convincingly it has been held to mean in the interests of the company as discerned by scrutiny of its constitution.

In *Howard Smith v Ampol Ltd*[73] it was confirmed that benefit to the company or the proper purpose for which powers are conferred are not

---

[68] Xuereb, 'The Juridification of Industrial Relations' 156; A. Boyle and R. Sykes, *Gore-Brown on Companies* (44th edn, Jordans, Bristol, looseleaf), 27–4.

[69] See J. Dine, 'Private Property and Corporate Governance Part II: Content of Directors' Duties and Remedies' in Patfield (ed.), *Perspectives on Company Law I*.

[70] For a full discussion see Nolan, 'Proper Purpose Doctrine and Company Directors'.

[71] See Nolan, ibid., and R. Grantham, 'The Powers of Company Directors and the Proper Purpose Doctrine' (1994–5) *King's College Law Journal* 16.

[72] Nolan, 'Proper Purpose Doctrine and Company Directors'.

[73] *Howard Smith v Ampol Petroleum Ltd* [1974] AC 821.

to be established by an investigation of the honesty of the director's beliefs or the calculation of an objective benefit to the company, but may be established by an investigation into the proper constitutional working of the company. The powers exercised by the management must reflect the constitutional balance within the company:

> The constitution of a limited company normally provides for directors, with powers of management, and shareholders, with defined voting powers having to appoint the directors, and to take, in general meeting, by majority vote, decisions on matters not reserved for management. Just as it is established that directors, within their management powers, may take decisions against the wishes of majority shareholders, and indeed that the majority of shareholders cannot control them in the exercise of those powers while they remain in office . . . so it must be unconstitutional for directors to use their fiduciary powers over the shares in the company purely for the purpose of destroying an existing majority, or creating a new majority which did not previously exist.[74]

Thus, directors acting outside the powers given to them by the essence of the corporate constitution are held to have used them for an improper purpose and to be in breach of their fiduciary duties to the company. Sealy has argued that the issue of constitutional propriety rather than the scope of the given power in particular cases is the essence of the proper purpose cases:

> it is submitted that [the] take over cases miss the real issue by focusing on the scope of the power exercised by the directors on the particular occasion. It would be more satisfactory to build on the basis of such cases as *John Shaw & Sons (Salford) Ltd v Shaw*,[75] where the separate roles of the different constitutional organs are recognised, and to say that the question: Which shareholders should have control? is, at least prima facie, no more the business of the directors in constitutional terms than management is the concern of shareholders.[76]

The result of a separation of powers is to create the possibility of constitutional disability, which may afflict one of the decision-making organs of the company when it acts outside its constitutional role. This will extend to situations where it acts in conflict of interest and duty.

Constitutional divisions and ultra vires
So far we have been considering misuse of directors' powers leading to a finding of breach of duty. However, it is possible for directors to cause the company to act outside its capacity. Under UK common law such

---

[74] Ibid., 837. See also *Lee Panavision Ltd v Lee Lighting Ltd* [1992] BCLC 22.
[75] [1935] 2 KB 113.
[76] L. Sealy, *Cases and Materials on Company Law* (6th edn, Butterworth, London, 1996), 291.

actions would be *ultra vires*, unratifiable and void.[77] Now statutes enable such actions to be ratified by special resolution.[78] It is well settled that abuse of *directors'* powers can be ratified by a majority vote of shareholders,[79] but Sealy identifies a new category of abuse of the *company's* powers:

> if we read carefully the judgments in some cases, and particularly that of Browne-Wilkinson LJ in *Rolled Steel*,[80] we find references to acts which are an *abuse* of the company's powers, and not just in excess of those powers. This may be a different concept . . . [W]here [directors] *abuse* [the company's] powers (of which a good example might be using its money to pay a shareholder's debt, as in *International Sales and Agencies Ltd v Marcus*[81]), it would surely be just as much an abuse for the shareholders to purport to ratify the act as for the directors to commit it in the first place.[82]

Non-ratifiable abuse of powers: the company as greater than its shareholders

It may thus be argued that, where the constitutional arrangements within a company are ignored, decisions taken are certainly a breach of directors' duties and may be an abuse of the company's powers. In the latter instance the company is recognisably a greater entity than simply its shareholders and they would have no standing to forgive the actions by ratification.[83] Bennett puts the issue well in his consideration of the proper purpose doctrine:

> [T]he words 'the company' do not mean the entity itself divorced from its members nor do they mean the members divorced from others who may have an interest. If the former were the case, it would always be a breach of director's duty for directors to vote to declare a dividend since a dividend enriches the members at the expense of the company with no corresponding benefit to the company. Similarly if the second were the case it would be open to two people who were the sole directors and shareholders of a company to appropriate its assets or to make contracts grossly disadvantageous to the company.[84]

How would this new understanding apply to a company with obligations to inform and consult a European Works Council? In those

---

[77] *Ashbury Railway Carriage and Iron Co Ltd v Riche* (1875) LR 7 HL 653.
[78] Companies Act 1985, section 35.
[79] *Hogg v Cramphorn Ltd* [1967] Ch 254; *Bamford v Bamford* [1970] Ch 212.
[80] *Rolled Steel Products (Holdings) Ltd v British Steel Corporation* [1986] Ch 246.
[81] [1982] 3 All ER 551.
[82] Sealy, *Cases and Materials*, 156. For examples of possible abuses of the power of the company, see *Att-Gen's Reference (No 2 of 1982)* [1984] QB 624; *R v Phillipou* (1989) 89 CrAppR 290; *R v Rozeik* [1996] BBC 271.
[83] D. Bennett, 'The Ascertainment of Purpose When Bona Fides Are in Issue – Some Logical Problems' (1989) *Sydney Law Review* 5.
[84] Ibid., 6. See also cases in ibid.

circumstances, failure to consult may be seen as a failure to operate the proper constitutional structure of the company and any action under-taken absent the use of the proper procedures may be use of powers for an improper purpose and therefore in breach of fiduciary duties. That such an action should be ratifiable by shareholders (other than employee shareholders) would seem to be an abuse of their position and a defeat of the entire legislative thrust of the European Works Council Directive. It may well be, then, that such a decision should be classified as an abuse of the company's powers and therefore unratifiable. In order fully to implement the spirit of the Directive it may well be that *locus standi* to challenge such actions would need to be given to employees to avoid replicating the section 309 nonsense.[85]

This is not to say that the act would be invalid vis-à-vis a third party. In *Rolled Steel* it was accepted that even at common law an act in excess or abuse of the powers of a company could confer rights on third parties.[86] The issue is whether acts in abuse of the company's powers could be ratified by shareholders so as to relieve the directors of their liability. Sealy adds, 'it would surely be better to say that the share-holders, even if they act unanimously, are no more competent to act in abuse of its company's powers than the directors'.[87] The issue has been canvassed more with regard to possible creditor rights than in the context of employee rights. The premise then is that an abuse of powers, i.e. a decision taken with unconstitutional disregard for consti-tuency interests or by operating incorrect constitutional systems, cannot be forgiven by the shareholders. Sealy tentatively cites a judg-ment of the Australian court in *Kinsella v Russell Kinsella Pty Ltd*[88] in favour of the proposition, noting however that it is 'coloured' by the fact that the company was on the verge of insolvent liquidation at the time when the relevant action was taken. In that case, Street CJ said: 'where directors are involved in a breach of their duty to the company affecting the interests of shareholders, then shareholders can either authorise that breach in prospect or ratify it in retrospect. Where, however the interests at risk are those of creditors I can see no reason in law or in logic to recognise that the shareholders can authorise the breach.' Similarly, in *Winkworth v Edward Baron Development Co Ltd,*

---

[85] Section 309 of the Companies Act 1985 requires the directors of a company to take account of the interests of employees, but the remedy for failure is an action by the company, i.e. the shareholders.

[86] See Nolan, 'The Proper Purpose Doctrine and Company Directors', 5–7; section 35 of the Companies Act 1985; *Freeman and Lockyer v Buckhurst Park Properties (Magnal) Ltd* [1964] 2 QB 480; *Hely Hutchison v Brayhead Ltd* [1968] 1 QB 549.

[87] Sealy, *Cases and Materials*, 156.

[88] (1986) 10 ACLR 395.

Lord Templeman said: 'A duty is owed by the directors to the company and to the creditors of the company to ensure that the affairs of the company are properly administered and that its property is not dissipated or exploited.'[89]

These cases (and others) have often been cited to show that in certain circumstances, particularly when the company is on the brink of insolvency, directors must take account of interests other than those of the shareholders. Although that is undoubtedly so, the cases coupled with the notion of abuse of the powers of the company conceal a further requirement that directors should act in a constitutionally correct way; in other words, the requirement that they should use powers for their proper purpose in fulfilling their duty of loyalty to the company ensures adherence to proper constitutional boundaries. Only in this way can the directors be confident that the affairs of the company are properly run. Where the shareholders and directors are separately or together constitutionally incapable of making a particular decision because they are in a position of conflict of interest in the sense described above, purporting to do so abuses the powers not only of those directors but of the company and may thus be incapable of shareholder ratification. The situation is one where the interests of the governing bodies are in conflict with the interests of the company. This occurs where the interests of the company are seen as adding up to more than the combined interests of the shareholders and directors together, thus inevitably putting the decision-making organs into a conflict of interest.

New light has been thrown on this concept of constitutional disability by the decision of the ECJ in *Cooperative Rabobank 'Vecht en Plassengebied' B.A. v Minderhoud*.[90] The case concerned a holding company of a group of companies and a subsidiary, of which the holding company was the sole director. Both companies were party to an agreement with a bank by which credit and debit balances held for any members of the group could be set off against each other. On the insolvency of the subsidiary the receiver sought payment of the amount standing to the credit of the subsidiary, but the bank offered a smaller amount, having set off various debits standing to other members of the group. The receiver argued that the agreement with the bank was invalid because it was contrary to a provision of the Netherlands Civil Code. This stated that, where there was a conflict of interest between a director and the company, a legal instrument could be concluded only by the company's commissioners. The question arose as to whether this law was contrary to Article 9(1) of the First Directive on company law.

---

[89] [1987] 1 All ER 114, at 118.   [90] [1998] 1 WLR 1025.

Article 9(1) provides:

In favour of a person dealing with a company in good faith, any transaction decided on by the directors shall be deemed to be one which is within the capacity of the company to enter into, and the power of the directors to bind the company shall be deemed to be free of any limitation under the memorandum or articles of association; and a party to a transaction so decided on shall not be bound to enquire as to the capacity of the company to enter into it or as to any such limitation on the powers of directors, and shall be presumed to have acted in good faith unless the contrary is proved.

Despite accepting that the purpose of the First Directive is, *inter alia*, the protection of third parties,[91] the ECJ held that a national law disabling an organ where a conflict of interest arose was valid, even if third parties were adversely affected.[92] This conclusion was supported by reference to the draft Fifth Directive,[93] which requires authorisation of transactions by the supervisory organ where conflicts of interest arise.[94] At first sight this is a strange decision because it reduces the possible scope and reach of the First Directive on company law dramatically. If the intention is truly to protect third parties then this decision is a poor one. The First Directive now protects third parties against restrictions on decision-making organs that are contained in the constitutional documents of the company (about which it is possible the third party could have known, but they remain protected unless bad faith is proved) and they are not protected where a conflict of interest within a company organ arises (a matter that it would be extremely difficult for a third party to find out about). From the current perspective, however, the important issue is the external Dutch law that removed decision-making from an organ where conflict of interest arises. The ECJ has settled that, where an external rule disables a decision-making organ on this basis, even third party rights may be affected.

The question arises as to the applicability of this decision in current UK law. It may well be that a law designating a particular decision-making body as the relevant one for the purpose of particular decisions would disable the usual organs and mean that purported decisions by those organs would be invalid. This appears to be the rationale behind *Guinness v Saunders*.[95] As matters stand it is suggested that such

[91] Directive 68/151/EEC, 1968 OJ Spec ED 41, para. 19.
[92] Ibid., para. 24.
[93] It may therefore have attained a 'soft law' status. See also A. Boyle, 'Draft Fifth Directive;: Implications for Directors' Duties, Board Structure and Employee Participation' (1992) 13 *Company Lawyer* 6.
[94] Article 10(1) of the draft Fifth Directive. See J. Dine and P. Hughes, *EC Company Law* (Jordans, Bristol, 1991, looseleaf).
[95] [1990] 2 AC 663.

decisions in abuse of company powers, which are decisions taken where there is a conflict of interest, would normally be considered not to affect any third parties because the decisions would be regarded as within the capacity of the company, although by reason of the conflicts of loyalty involved they might well be in breach of fiduciary duties.

As UK law stands, the decision taken by the directors in the situation in *Cooperative Rabobank 'Vecht en Plassengebied' B.A. v Minderhoud* might well be in breach of duty. It would not be *ultra vires* because there is no national law removing the decision-making powers from directors where there is a conflict of interest and duty. Further, it is unlikely to be seen as an abuse of the powers of the company because the interests of the creditors could be seen as important in this context and were served by the agreement. The agreement did breach the duty to shareholders, who could therefore ratify the breach. However, where there is a rule that changes the corporate governance structure of a corporation by adding decision-making structures, the ECJ may well follow the same reasoning as in *Cooperative Rabobank*. This may particularly be the case where the requirement for the change in structure comes from a European initiative.

The effect of the European Works Council (EWOC) Directive may be seen as precisely in point. By external decree (equivalent to the Dutch law) it adds decision-making structures to the corporate governance system of a company in certain circumstances and determines that particular decisions must be arrived at by using the relevant procedure (as the Dutch law decreed particular procedures where there was a conflict of interest). From the perspective of UK law alone it might well be considered, in the specified decisions, either that employee interests have become part of company interests or that the constitutional structure of the company has been violated by the directors if they fail to follow the correct procedure. Thus, a decision taken by directors without using the correct consultation procedures may not be considered *ultra vires* on a reference to the ECJ to determine the effect of violating the procedural requirements of the EWOC Directive, but must surely be regarded as either an abuse of the powers of the company or at the very least a breach of the directors' fiduciary duties.

A route to adopting European-friendly fiduciary duties would therefore be an acceptance that constitutional disability in the organs of a company will mean that acts taken in ignorance or in contravention of the disability are an abuse of the powers of the company and, as such, a breach of fiduciary duties not susceptible to ratification by shareholders. This is the first step to reformulating the company as an inclusive enterprise and has the advantage that the emphasis is on the procedures for decision-making[96] rather than on the situation where a single decision-making organ attempts a confrontational balancing operation. Enforcement issues are outside the scope of this chapter but a partial answer may lie in increased employee/shareholder action.[97]

The fiduciary duty to adopt proper systems of decision-making

An alternative route to creating implementation-friendly fiduciary duties is to focus on the necessity for proper systems of decision-making rather than the bigger issues of constitutional balance.

The introduction of non-executive directors and committees to determine management pay formed part of the outcome of the Cadbury, Greenbury and Hampel reports.[98] The recommendations did not make it clear whether the failure to act in compliance with those recommendations would constitute a breach of fiduciary duties. However, there seems to be a growing body of law that points to the conclusion that decisions made other than in accordance with proper procedures are invalid and may amount to a breach of fiduciary duties. In *Guinness v Saunders*,[99] the payment to Mr Ward of £5.2 million was invalid because it was made in breach of the Articles. The court did not determine whether those making the decision were in breach of their fiduciary duties to the company, but it seems likely that this was in fact the case. Gower is unclear as to whether or not there is a difference between following the express terms of the Articles, which 'may not' be a breach of fiduciary duty, and exercising a power for an improper purpose, which clearly is.[100] In any event the line is difficult to draw and may be further complicated by the calculation as to whether the 'proper purpose' is objectively based or constitutionally based.

It is at this point that the argument that no valid decision can properly be taken without consideration of the company as a holistic going concern, inclusive of the interests of stakeholders other than shareholders, overlaps with the argument that directors may breach their duties of loyalty by a failure to put in place proper systems of management that are capable of protecting the company. This second argument

[96] It owes much to '*la procéduralisation du droit*', a philosophy propounded by the Catholic University of Louvain, in particular by Professor Jacques Lenoble.
[97] S. Schwab and R. Thomas, 'Realigning Corporate Governance: Shareholder Activism by Labor Unions' [1998] *Michigan Law Review* 1018.
[98] See now the combined Code, para. 12.43A, *Listing Rules*, in force 11 January 1999 (Stock Exchange, London).
[99] [1990] 2 AC 663.
[100] L. Gower, *Gower's Principles of Modern Company Law* (6th edn, ed. Paul Davies, Sweet & Maxwell, London, 1997), 605.

relies not on the vision of the company as greater than the shareholders, but on the fact that if proper systems of management are not in place the company – *whatever stakeholders are involved* – will be damaged. Normally, as in the *Guinness* case, the systems will be there to protect shareholders, but where duties are imposed by non-company law regulations, such as health and safety regulation, it is arguable that failure to provide proper systems of management for these other duties will be a breach of the fiduciary duty to the company because the direct beneficiary of the provision of these legal systems is the company even though the indirect beneficiaries are other stakeholders.

An interesting development in this context is *Bishopgate Investment Management Ltd (in liquidation) v Maxwell (No 2)*[101] where failure to follow the correct stock transfer procedures led to a finding that the director was in breach of fiduciary duties. In that case the defendant, Ian Maxwell, signed share transfer documents that caused shares held by the company of which he was a director as trustee of a number of pension funds to be transferred for no consideration to another company. The defendant had signed the share transfers without enquiry as to the purpose of the transfer, signing merely because his brother and co-director had done so.

It was argued on the basis of *McWilliams v Sir William Arroll & Co Ltd*[102] that, where the alleged breach of duty was an omission, the plaintiff must prove that compliance would have prevented the damage. Thus, in cases where the lack of provision of safety equipment was the issue, '[h]e or his personal representative must show that the omission to provide the safety equipment caused the accident. He or his personal representative must therefore prove that he would have used the equipment and that it would have been effective.'[103] Although the *McWilliams* case was a claim by an employee against his employers and the occupiers of the site for failure to provide safety equipment, it was used by the Court of Appeal to illustrate the parameters of a fiduciary duty to create and follow proper systems of decision-making.

In *Bishopsgate*, Hoffman LJ rejected the notion of requiring a causal connection between an omission to act and the loss caused by concentrating on the positive act of signing the transfer, which he designated a positive breach of fiduciary duty and the use of powers for an improper

---

[101] [1994] 1 All ER 261, where failure to follow procedures for stock transfers set out in accordance with the procedures in the company's Articles was held to be a breach of fiduciary duty, either because of the failure to follow the correct procedure or because that failure was evidence of a failure to act for the benefit of the company.

[102] [1962] 1 WLR 295.

[103] Hoffman LJ in *Bishopsgate*.

purpose.[104] It is notable that the transfers were signed by two directors in accordance with the Articles. Thus the breach was a failure to give proper consideration to the consequences of the transfer and its impact on the company. This decision creates a strong possibility that any exercise of powers that fails to follow proper decision-making mechanisms, imposed either by the constitution or by outside constraints, may be regarded as a breach of a positive fiduciary duty rather than as an omission and makes a considerable dent in the causation argument. Thus, in the safety situation, a positive decision to divert resources away from purchasing or servicing essential safety equipment would become the breach of a fiduciary duty rather than an omission to provide such equipment.

Conclusion

This chapter has first set out a legal structure that is intended as support for the notion of preventing further polarisation of wealth on a global scale. The fundamental issue is the free market economic contractualism on which many of the global corporations and the world system of banking and loans are based. Secondly, at the micro-level, in the study on the implementation of the European Works Council Directive, we can see that the difficulties of implementing such a system, even on the minor scale of consulting employees, are manifold and the complications of dovetailing regulations are formidable. The inclusion of this detailed study is intended to indicate that the hurdles ahead have been neither misunderstood nor underestimated, but it is incumbent on those of us who have the resources to think and write about these questions. I hope that the concept of constitutional disability – in the form of a challenge to a corporation's decisions where there has been lack of proper consultation – can make a contribution – to the debate, and that the possibility of utilising private law remedies rather than looking for a global external regulator provides a tool for those seeking equity in economic affairs.

---

[104] Ralph Gibson LJ decided that the breach was a misapplication of the funds of the company and Leggatt LJ delivered an enigmatic concurrence (*Bishopsgate*).

Index